The Women's Rights Era

THE WOMEN'S RIGHTS ERA

50 Years of Gender Equality Advocacy and Reform Across the Globe

Jennifer M. Piscopo

polity

First published by Polity Press in 2027.

Polity Press
65 Bridge Street
Cambridge CB2 1UR, UK

Polity Press
111 River Street
Hoboken, NJ 07030, USA

ISBN-13: 978-1-5095-6674-7 – hardback
ISBN-13: 978-1-5095-6675-4 – paperback

A note on the cover illustration

Coco Masuda created the illustration for the poster for the historic 1995 Fourth World Conference on Women in Beijing. Ten years later, the United Nations held the Beijing At Ten conference in New York City, examining progress on the Beijing Platform for Action, and again commissioned Masuda to create an artwork for its poster. After various ideas were presented, it was agreed that the new illustration, which is used on the cover of this book, should feature the same beloved figure, but with a different background to reflect the changes in the environments in which women lived.

A catalogue record for this book is available from the British Library.

Library of Congress Control Number: 2026933285

Typeset in 11.5 on 14pt Adobe Garamond
by Cheshire Typesetting Ltd, Cuddington, Cheshire
Printed and bound by Ashford Colour Ltd.

For further information on Polity, visit our website:
politybooks.com

For all the women who fought, in ways large and small,
for women's rights.
And for all the women who will fight for a feminist future.

Contents

1 The Women's Rights Era 1
2 International Advocacy for Women's Rights 32
3 Political Regimes and Constitutional Rights 61
4 Elections and Government 88
5 Education and Workforce Participation 110
6 Family Law and Care Work 141
7 Reproductive Rights 166
8 Violence Against Women 189
9 After the Women's Rights Era? 214

Acknowledgements 236
Notes 238
Index 268

ONE

The Women's Rights Era

In 1995, Hillary Clinton was not yet a former US presidential candidate, the first woman nominated by a major political party. She was not yet a US senator or secretary of state. She was the 'first lady' – wife of then US president Bill Clinton – and the chair of the United States' delegation to the Fourth World Conference on Women. Held in Beijing, China, the conference was one of the largest international events ever convened: 189 countries sent 6,000 official delegates, who deliberated alongside more than 4,000 accredited representatives from non-governmental organizations (NGOs), while more than 30,000 activists met at the parallel forum for civil society organizations.[1] At the Beijing conference, Hillary Clinton was scheduled for a keynote address, a speech that would go ahead despite political pressure from domestic forces that did not want her to attend, let alone speak. Critics on the right denounced Clinton's support for the United Nations' 'radical' agenda for gender equality. Critics on the left argued that Clinton's presence would legitimize China's communist government. Resisting pressure from all sides, Clinton and her team – most notably, then US Ambassador-at-Large for Women's Issues Melanne Verveer – made and executed a plan that would have decades-long consequences for global understandings of gender equality.[2] When Clinton took the stage, she helped immortalize the refrain: 'human rights are women's rights and women's rights are human rights'.

Linking women's rights to human rights had enormous rhetorical and conceptual power. The connection did not originate with Clinton and her team, though Clinton's speech catapulted the human rights frame into the public imagination.[3] The idea that women's rights are human rights had entered international policy discussions two years earlier, in 1993, at the second United Nations World Conference on Human Rights in Vienna. Here, activists presented countries' delegations with a petition demanding recognition of women's rights as human rights. Signed by 500,000 people from 24 different countries, the petition worked.[4] The resultant Vienna Declaration affirmed that 'the human rights of women and of the girl-child are an inalienable, integral and indivisible part of universal human rights'.[5] The petition itself reflected the achievement of a globally connected movement for women's rights, wherein activists from Latin America to Africa had questioned the implicit male bias that placed harms such as wartime rape and sex trafficking outside of international human rights law. This movement itself had anchors in an even earlier moment: the United Nations' declaration of 1975 as International Women's Year and of 1975–1985 as the UN Decade for Women, both launched by the First World Conference on Women in Mexico City in 1975.

International Women's Year inaugurated what this book calls 'the women's rights era': five decades of significant and consequential global organizing for women's rights, from 1975 to 2025. The 1975 Mexico City conference was followed by the Second World Conference on Women in Copenhagen in 1980 and the Third World Conference on Women in Nairobi in 1985. The 1990s subsequently marked a high point for international organizing, as policymakers and activists met at the 1993 Vienna conference, the 1994 Cairo conference (formally, the International Conference on Population and Development, a focal point for reproductive rights advocates), and the 1995 Beijing conference. In subsequent years, 'Beijing+ events' – such as the Generation Equality forums held in Paris and Mexico City in the early 2020s – have continued to bring women's rights advocates together.

Prior to 1975, the United Nations had not addressed women and women's rights through separate convenings. The Mexico City conference marked a turning point, producing a combined Declaration and Plan of Action that, at 203 pages, was the world's first international document tackling the challenges women faced in 'all aspects of their lives'.[6] The document used rights-based language, talking throughout about the 'rights of women' across policy areas and calling for 'equal rights between men and women'.[7] Similar language appeared in the Copenhagen and Nairobi conference reports. But it was at Beijing, at the World Conference on Women's largest stage to date, that the connection between women's rights and human rights crystallized. The resultant Beijing Platform for Action (PfA) laid out a comprehensive blueprint for the policies that would achieve women's human rights in 12 areas:

poverty, education, health, violence against women, armed conflict, the economy, power and decision-making, institutions for women's advancement, human rights, the media, the environment, and girls. The 132-page document became – and still is – one of the primary reference points used by international organizations, national governments, policymakers, advocates and activists at all levels.

The launching, planning, and convening of these hallmark international conferences and their plans of action are not symbolic gestures. At the United Nations, the women's rights era unfolded thanks to the tireless work of women diplomats, women UN staffers, and women NGO leaders. Thousands of women from all walks of life, from grassroots women to diplomatic elites, poured time, emotion, and energy first into convincing the United Nations to hold the events and then into planning and executing them. Before each world conference, women activists organized and attended regional and national preparatory meetings at which they networked, shared research, and established common policy objectives. Lasting alliances, collaborations, and organizations formed among and across women working in diverse sectors and across diverse countries.

The four world conferences on women and their related events became focal points for negotiating and establishing the global women's rights agenda. They did not operate alone: other international organizations, from the World Bank to the Organization for Economic Cooperation and Development (OECD) also held their own women-focused global meetings and summits during the women's rights era. Regional governmental organizations such as the Organization of American States (OAS), the European Union, and the African Union (AU) did the same. Regional feminist networks such as Latin America's Encuentros Feministas (Feminist Encounters) also organized convenings, and activists used these gatherings to prepare for attending and lobbying at the international conferences and to strategize for how to translate the conferences' agendas into domestic policy and practice. Together, all these events created a platform for women's voices, legitimized women's policy perspectives, and produced documents stating their demands in plain language.

These documents became the *feminist blueprints* of the women's rights era. The era itself boosted women's activism in tangible ways.[8] In 1975, women's movements were found in 73 per cent of countries – though only 37 per cent of countries had movements *not* organized by governments. Scholars call these 'autonomous women's movements', meaning that the movements can independently articulate and lobby for their preferred agendas. By 2015, 98 per cent of countries had women's movements and 96 per cent of countries had *autonomous* women's movements. The most significant increases in women's movement development occurred in regions that hosted UN world conferences on women. In Latin America, the largest jump occurred from 1975 to 1985, the decade following the Mexico City conference (the Encuentros Feministas, for instance, began in 1981). In sub-Saharan Africa, the biggest boost occurred from 1985 to 1995, the decade following the Nairobi conference.

The policy demands emerging from this global movement also produced real change. Take women's access to political decision-making power, a common objective expressed by women across the globe. Researchers show that countries with more internationally connected women's groups (formally called women's international NGOs or WINGOs) elect their first woman to parliament earlier than countries without WINGOs. Countries with greater proportions of WINGOs also more rapidly cross key thresholds related to 10, 20, and 30 per cent women parliamentarians. Using data on women's legislative representation in 150 countries, Pamela Paxton, Melanie Hughes, and Jennifer Green generated the following prediction: 'if a country were to increase its number of WINGOs by 10, we would expect the probability of attaining 10 per cent women in politics to increase by 9 percent'.[9] The rate at which women gain access to parliament matters not just for advancing women's political equality, but for accelerating other aspects of gender equality. As decades of gender and politics research has shown, women's presence in parliament shapes policies that enhance reproductive rights, combat violence against women, reduce maternal mortality, expand maternity and parental leave, and increase social welfare spending, among other outcomes.

An era of progress

This book surveys these and other accomplishments of the women's rights era, from 1975 to 2025. This 50-year period begins with the Mexico

City conference, passes through the landmark Beijing conference, and continues into the first quarter of the new century. These five decades coincide with waves of democratization, in which many Global South countries transitioned away from different combinations of colonialism, armed conflict, and authoritarian regimes. Democracy's promise of equal political and civil rights dovetailed with women's claims for women's rights, and especially with women's demands for the legal and political changes that would advance gender equality. In this way, democracy and gender equality became inextricably linked in the global imagination.

The women's rights era thus marked a period of great optimism about transformation and progress. Feminist blueprints such as the Beijing PfA led countries to rewrite their constitutions and statutes, a process of statutory change that granted women more rights, protections, and opportunities. Across the globe, discriminatory measures fell. Nearly every country created some kind of ministry or agency to address women's issues and adopted some kind of bureaucracy to mainstream gender into policy and practice. Over 100 countries adopted gender quotas for women candidates or reserved seats in their parliaments for women legislators. More and more women were elected to national parliaments, chosen to lead political parties, and appointed to cabinet. Women became presidents and prime ministers of the world's economic and political powerhouses, including the United Kingdom, Germany, Brazil, and Mexico.

Yet by 2025 the protagonists of this era – the multiple generations of activists, practitioners, policymakers, and scholars who had fought for women's rights – seemed decidedly less ebullient. International organizing for women's rights continued, but in a period where enthusiasm for democracy has waned. Since 2009, the proportion of people living in non-democracies has been higher than the proportion of people living in democracies.[10] Regime type is not solely to blame for the pessimistic turn, however. Democratic and non-democratic governments alike are rolling back some of the women's rights era's earlier gains, especially in areas related to sexual and reproductive rights. Observers point to new global movements that are anti-rights – alliances of conservatives and reactionaries that oppose the global, multilateral vision of human rights that had previously helped advance equality not just for women but for racial, ethnic, and religious minorities, LGBTQIA+ people, migrants, people with disabilities, and other marginalized groups.

Still, progress has never been completely linear. Global efforts to secure women's rights – such as the international and national woman suffrage movements of the early twentieth century – predate the women's rights era. Significant conservative turns also predate the women's rights era. Take the post–Second World War era in the West. While men fought overseas, women went to work in factories. When the returning servicemen needed their jobs back, public discourses began idealizing motherhood, leveraging traditional gender roles to push women out of the workforce and back into the domestic sphere. This cycle of progress and resistance continued throughout the women's rights era, as conservative forces never disappeared. They even scored important victories, such as keeping women's access to abortion out of the Cairo declaration and thwarting lesbian activists' efforts to have sexual orientation mentioned in the Beijing PfA. Though struggles between progressive and conservative forces have been ever present, what makes the 1975–2025 period distinctive is the balance between these forces. The era is characterized by a combination of international activity, women's organizing, and policy advances related to women's rights, including concrete changes to constitutions, laws, and policies. These reforms occurred across the globe despite concerted opposition. On balance, reforms during the women's rights era moved the needle towards rather than away from women's rights, and thus towards rather than away from gender equality.

To be sure, these changes were and are not magical. They do not produce gender-equal utopias. Like all policy objectives, gender equality objectives are contested: even women's rights proponents might disagree on which policies generate more equality. The exact policy changes might reflect the victory of certain groups of women over others, perhaps prioritizing the interests of women from dominant social groups. The messiness of the policy process means that women's rights gains are not uniform, neither across nor within countries. Not all countries make the same changes to the same degree and not all women benefit to the same extent. Finally, on-paper changes may not translate into on-the-ground transformations, as laws and policies remain unimplemented, are implemented partially, or are applied in ways that actually undercut their equality goals.

What the international feminist blueprints and the domestic constitutional, legal, and policy changes do is lay the foundation for on-the-ground change. International frameworks are templates, representing women's vision for a better and more just world. Negotiating and codifying lofty gender equality goals constitutes a 'politics of aspiration', one in which transnationally networked actors forge alliances, hold meetings, issue demands, and ultimately write blueprints that, if followed, would transform their vision into reality.[11] Their efforts do lead to new norms and new policies, but on-paper changes cannot enact the on-the-ground transformation directly. Adopting gender quota laws that elect more women does not change sexist attitudes towards women politicians overnight. Adopting laws to sanction marital rape cannot reach into every bedroom and prevent every assault. Yet this book argues that these and other on-paper changes are nonetheless meaningful. Revised legal frameworks create clear references for the rights that exist and for the values and the behaviours that are and are not acceptable. They allow advocates to hold governments accountable for realizing these objectives in the long term. And they make a concrete difference to many women's lives. With the exception of women in countries experiencing dramatic reversals (e.g. Afghanistan with the 2021 return of the Taliban), women in most countries have more formal rights and freedoms in 2025 than in 1975.

As such, the book emphasizes an achievement-centred narrative of the women's rights era. The book focuses on the constitutional, legislative, and political reforms sought by women's rights advocates, articulated in international documents, and ultimately made by national governments via courts, parliaments, ministries, and the public administration. The chapters demonstrate how the past decades' reforms – however imperfect in their reach and however tenuous in a period of democratic backsliding – have depended on advocates' tenacity. Armed with the feminist blueprints they themselves wrote, and energized by the best practices exchanged at global conferences, women activists and their men allies have fought hard to change policy and practice. They have lobbied officials, written legislation, organized marches, and demonstrated in the streets. They have initiated court cases and written legal briefs, appeared in the press, and gained elected and appointed office.

Countless women from the Global North and the Global South dedicated their lives to writing the blueprints and pursuing the policy reforms recounted in this book. Many faced serious repercussions, including imprisonment and state violence, for challenging the patriarchal power structures that would keep women subordinate to men. Some literally gave their lives. Their individual names do not always appear in these pages, but in recounting the achievements of this era, this book celebrates women's success. The protagonists of the women's rights era fervently believed that on-paper changes mattered. Without advocacy and reform, no groundwork for transformation is laid.

Concepts and approach

This book focuses on women's movements' struggles for women's rights and for gender equality. This topic spans the globe: nearly every country has some individuals and some organizations working toward these goals, even if under adverse or threatening circumstances. Scholars, journalists, and other chroniclers have studied women's quest for gender equality extensively: some have looked in depth at histories in particular countries and regions, and others have examined one particular policy area within or across countries and regions, at one moment in time or across the years. These accounts document convergences and divergences: while many countries and regions adopt similar reforms during similar periods, women activists working at the international level and within their own countries still disagree about the meaning of women's rights and the policies necessary to bring about gender equality. These differences raise important questions. Does the diversity among countries and among women impede talking about women's rights as a singular concept? What does gender equality mean when feminists themselves disagree about how to achieve it?

Defining women's movements

This book uses expansive definitions of 'movements', 'rights', and 'equality'. To begin, 'movements' refers to any set of actors and organizations, working alone or in concert, that demand political and social change. This generous definition does not require movements to organize mass mobilizations. Demonstrations, protests, and marches are tactics of movements, but movements can also use other tactics, including less visible ones involving far fewer people – such as closed-door meetings between lobbyists and lawmakers.

Movements therefore can be small or large; be organized at and across different levels of government (e.g. local, national, regional, and international); encompass organizations and networks of different sizes; and their participants can have varied degrees of commitment and connectedness. Some activists may work full time for an NGO while others engage in advocacy via their day jobs in sectors such as journalism, law, business, and academia. Typically, key figures know each other: they meet at international conferences and they collaborate on certain actions. Policymakers, too, may form part of movements. They might themselves have participated in or led movements before entering office, or their sympathies align them with movements once in office.

For this reason, some scholars speak of 'advocacy networks' or 'policy networks' rather than movements, to highlight how government and movement leaders collaborate on certain issues. Actors within networks may indeed be more elite. When compared to organizations' rank-and-file members, individuals holding leadership roles may have more education and wealth, belong to majority social groups (e.g. be white women rather than women of colour), or simply have, by virtue of their professional positions, more access to resources and influence. Even Global South women may belong to their countries' elite. Since policy change depends on protagonists' coordinated efforts to persuade decision-makers, this book sees policy networks and advocacy networks as part of movements.

Importantly, movements are heterogeneous even when they pursue the same objective. Take the different groups that, in the United States, support women's access to legal abortions. There are WINGOs such as the Center for Reproductive Rights, national-level NGOs such as the Planned Parenthood Federation of America, and medical organizations such as the American Council of Obstetricians and Gynecologists (ACOG). There are scores of local NGOs such as the Fund Texas Choice group, which helps Texans travel for abortion access, and the Kentucky Health Justice Network, which advocates and funds abortions for all Kentuckians, but especially for immigrants and those who are Black, Indigenous, and trans. These organizations do sometimes coordinate their activities: the national ones, for example, all filed a 'friends of the court' brief when the US Supreme Court evaluated (and ultimately overturned) a federal right to abortion in 2022. They might also emphasize different priorities in their daily advocacy: the Kentucky Health Justice Network, for instance, tracks legislative initiatives that would limit women's and trans people's access to reproductive healthcare, whereas ACOG issues healthcare guidelines for abortion providers. Yet all these groups share a common goal: keeping abortion legal and accessible. Consequently, they all form part of the women's reproductive rights movement.

At their core, networks and movements are made up of committed individuals. This book refers to these individuals as proponents, protagonists, activists, participants, actors, or advocates, usually interchangeably. Some protagonists have leadership roles, which marks them as elite. In the opening anecdote, Hillary Clinton and Ambassador Melanne Verveer are elites. Most often, official records memorialize the names of the elite protagonists over the names of the rank-and-file members. Yet advocacy is always the joint work of elites and grassroots activists, even if all names and all tactics do not receive the same place within the historical record.

Defining women's rights, gender equality, and gender justice

This book treats women's rights and gender equality as broad goals towards which women's movements strive. Women's rights offer a pathway to gender equality: in adopting policy changes that advance women's rights, countries lay the groundwork for improvements in women's status and well-being, and gender equality becomes more probable. Still, protagonists may spiritedly disagree about exactly what 'women's rights' and 'gender equality' mean.

For instance, a classic debate exists about whether advocates should focus on women's difference from men or women's sameness with men. Take a policy question that divided the women's movement in a previous era: in the early twentieth century, labour laws in industrialized countries treated women differently from men, often by preventing women from working overtime or at night. This protectionist legislation ostensibly shielded women from overwork and ensured they could still care for their families. Advocates were divided over whether working-hour restrictions harmed or helped women. For reformers, treating women workers and men workers differently eroded gender equality: they argued that employers preferred hiring those who could work overtime and at night, so protectionist legislation made women less desirable employees and reduced their earning power. Defenders of protectionist legislation, by contrast, believed that women needed shelter from labour market competition. If women competed with men for overtime or nighttime work, employers would hire women but pay them less than men for the same shifts, and this wage discrimination would reduce women's earning power.

What united both camps was the shared understanding that legal and social structures create conditions in which women's lives diverge from men's lives. This divergence almost always makes women worse off relative to men. Protectionist legislation emerged because women, not men, were thought to be responsible for domestic work: the separate spheres mark a gendered division of labour, wherein men earn wages in public and thus carry out 'productive' tasks, and women nurture their husbands, children, and families in private and thus carry out 'reproductive' tasks. That these gender roles are phrased in heteronormative terms is the point: the separate spheres idealize roles corresponding to a traditional heterosexual family structure. While conservative thought leaders may champion women's reproductive tasks as the essential and ultimately prized duties of women, the fact remains that politics and economics treat women's private, domestic role as less valuable than men's public, productive role.

Countless laws and policies reflect and reify ideas about the separate spheres. Many of these discriminatory legal codes remain in force today; for example, many Middle Eastern and North African countries prohibit women from seeking employment without their husbands' permission. The point here is that women's movement actors broadly agree on the diagnosis even if they disagree about the cure. Whether by removing or by preserving protectionist legislation, both sides recognized that legal regimes and social structures fundamentally treat women as different from – and thus less than – men. Both sides wanted laws that could equalize women's access to employment and to wages.

As a concept, then, women's rights means that women cannot be treated as second-class citizens. This unequal treatment stems from patriarchy as an underlying social structure. Patriarchy is the hierarchical ordering of society by gender, with men and masculinity taking priority over women and femininity. Even as the roles, traits, and features that constitute idealized maleness and idealized femaleness vary according to countries' and groups' cultures and customs, the existence of gender as a hierarchical social structure that places men above women has what Karen Beckwith calls 'universal persistence'.[12] Patriarchy governs all contemporary societies. Everywhere, patriarchal ideas about gender and gender roles have become encoded into laws, and everywhere, the laws in turn reinforce the patriarchal norms.

What drew international women's rights activists together was their shared recognition that women, no matter their countries of origin or the circumstances of their birth, lacked equality relative to men. Women's movements have challenged historical and current manifestations of this subordination by reminding audiences that appeals to abstract rights too often exclude women. Early constitutions such as those written in the Americas during the late eighteenth and early nineteenth centuries established the basic rights of citizens (e.g. voting and holding elected office), but regarded neither women nor Indigenous peoples nor the enslaved as citizens. Battles to extend citizenship to women marked the suffrage movements of the late nineteenth and early twentieth centuries. Battles to include women's rights as human rights now characterize the struggle of the late twentieth and early twenty-first centuries.

Some advocates might prefer to say that they are seeking 'justice' rather than 'rights'. Consider again the US reproductive rights movements. Safe and legal abortion constitutes a women's rights demand, because abortion enables women to exercise control over sexual activity and reproduction, a control that patriarchy denies women. Measures guaranteeing abortion rights contribute to gender equality because, when women *do* exercise control over sexuality and reproduction, their status, dignity, autonomy, and life choices begin to resemble those of men. Yet some activists might prefer 'reproductive justice' over 'reproductive rights'. Protagonists like those in the Kentucky Health Justice Network might correctly point out that Native American women's disproportionate dependency on low quality public healthcare (and thus limited access to abortions) is not just unequal but *unjust.* Indigenous women suffer not only from gender subordination but also from systems of racialized segregation that result in chronically underserved Indigenous communities. Seeking 'justice' rather than 'rights' emphasizes how interlocking forms of oppression are themselves harms that must be repaired. Claims to gender justice recognize how gender – as a hierarchical organizing principle within society – intersects with other hierarchical organizing principles, including race, ethnicity, and class.

Yet whether women's organizations say that they are seeking women's rights, gender equality, or gender justice, they are seeking to subvert norms and laws that treat women as subordinate to men and as less deserving of human rights and legal protections. Terms such as 'gender equality' and 'gender justice' often become conflated in practice, used interchangeably by scholars and activists alike. This book analyses how women's rights create the normative and legal apparatuses that move countries toward gender equality, but gender justice would fit just as well.

Women's interests, gender, and feminism

This book covers the accomplishments of the women's rights era in two arenas: the international and the national. The book first reviews how women's rights activists shaped the era's feminist blueprints and then discusses how and when national governments respond. The book then turns to achievements in six policy areas: women and constitutional rights; women's participation in elections and government; education and workforce participation; family law and care work; reproductive rights; and violence against women. These six areas do not exhaust the realms in which women's rights reforms occur, but they capture the most prominent ones. Within these areas, women will not hold uniform preferences about their demands. Given this disagreement, some might question how these six areas constitute 'women's interests' – and whether 'women's interests' are feminist interests.

Women's interest in gender equality

In a foundational article, Maxine Molyneux argued that women's structural position in patriarchy gives rise to two kinds of women's policy interests. Molyneux had studied women's political participation in Nicaragua's Sandinistas, the Marxist-style rebel group that, in 1979, overthrew the dictatorship of Anastasio Somoza and governed for ten years. At issue was whether Nicaragua's socialist revolution, primarily organized to advance socioeconomic equality, could also advance gender equality.

As Molyneux and countless scholars before and after her acknowledged, while 'at a certain level of abstraction women can be said to have some interests in common, there is no consensus over what these interests are or how they are to be formulated'.[13] This lack of consensus emerges from women's heterogeneity. For instance, upper-class women surely lost when the Somoza dictatorship was abolished, as the Sandinistas appropriated private property, but lower-class women surely gained, as the Sandinistas redistributed wealth. Molyneux thus preferred the term 'gender interests' to 'women's interests', as gender interests capture the shared policy interests specifically tied to ending women's subordinate position within gender hierarchies (even as women's exact experiences within gender hierarchies are shaped by other identities, like race and class).

Molyneux further argued that gendered interests could be divided into *practical gender interests* and *strategic gender interests*. The former arise from women's position within the gendered division of labour embedded within the separate spheres. When women demand policies that help them fulfil their traditional gender roles – such as income support from governments in order to buy food and feed their children – women are pursuing practical gendered interests. These demands accept rather than challenge the gendered division of labour. However, when women connect their disproportionate responsibility for domestic work to gender inequality, and therefore demand the separate spheres' abolition, then they are pursuing strategic gender interests. These latter interests are what, Molyneux argues, many feminists see as 'genuine' women's interests – the policy demands that would not just improve women's experience within gender hierarchies but actually undo them. Following Molyneux, many scholars further emphasized the distinction between working within gendered systems and challenging these systems. Karen Celis and Sarah Childs, for instance, later divided women's interests into those that are *gendered* (that align with classical gender roles) and those that are *feminist* (that challenge classical gender roles).[14]

Yet the line between practical and strategic gender interests, to use Molyneux's terms, or between gendered and feminist interests, to use Celis and Childs's terms, is clear in theory but blurred in practice. Fighting for practical gender interests can radicalize women, as Molyneux recognizes. The very act of demanding policy change can lead women to discover their agency and to contemplate the sources of their problems in new ways. This pattern holds when women join social or political movements *not* based on gender, like Nicaragua's class-based revolution. Women find that gender roles become reproduced within the movement: women often end up doing much of the nurturing work for movements – such as organizing supporters and preparing food for marches – but face exclusion from the political work. In the US Civil Rights movement's 1963 March on Washington, for instance, Black women were originally excluded from the speakers' platform and only Black men formed the delegation received by then President John Kennedy.[15]

Women's initial activism within gendered hierarchies thus often turns into critiques of these hierarchies and efforts to dismantle them. Women's advocacy *itself* also challenges gender roles, as women position themselves as political subjects who claim public space, make public demands, and seek public resources. Since patriarchy relegates women to the private and apolitical realm, women raising their voices in public – especially to insist that governments attend to their needs – are enacting citizenship. Women's exercise of their citizenship rights contributes to gender equality, even if this exercise serves practical gender interests rather than strategic gender interests or feminist interests.

Moreover, many women making practical, gendered demands upon the state are not unaware of strategic, feminist claims. Women's movements often demand support for women's traditional roles, with full recognition and even opprobrium of the gendered hierarchies that create these demands in the first place. For instance, the COVID-19 pandemic helped women's movements to draw new attention to unpaid care burdens. Demands that governments increase funding for care services emerge precisely from women's critique of the gendered division of labour: women's movements argue that women's time poverty and livelihoods will improve only once governments provide more care services. Public provisioning of care offers women, especially socioeconomically marginalized women, more ways to support their families. Moreover, when the state pays for care, work that women perform for free becomes work that labourers perform for wages. In this way, even helping women to navigate their traditional roles has the potential to transform these roles, thus blurring the line between practical gender interests and strategic gender interests. Broadly speaking, conceptual distinctions between women's interests, gendered interests, and feminist interests – like conceptual distinctions between women's rights, gender equality, and gender justice – overlap in practice. What the underlying idea of interests conveys is that, as a subordinate social group, women benefit from efforts that erode their second-class status.

Being feminist without saying so

While women's interests or gender interests span policy areas, not all advocates making demands would describe themselves or their interests as 'feminist'. Turning feminism into a dirty word proves to be a nearly universal form of resistance to women's rights and to gender equality. Opponents undermine women's advocacy by casting aspersions on protagonists, such as by claiming that women's rights advocates are 'against men' or 'hate men', or that they break cultural taboos by being 'whores' and 'lesbians'. Such accusations do not just sting; they can ostracize women from their families and their communities, especially in conservative contexts. They can have a particularly chilling effect on minoritized women, who simultaneously combat prejudice from outside their community and sexism from within – while often feeling pressure from community members to prioritize the former. Women of colour who critique patriarchy within their communities are often reproached for making their men or their culture look bad and are thus accused of betraying the struggle against racism. Ultimately, accusing women of hating men, with whom they have genuine, affective relationships, foments a distasteful image of feminists and discourages women from joining a movement for women's rights, or even from using the label feminist to describe themselves.

This resistance strategy is not just individual-level name-calling. Governments resisting women's rights reforms frequently use 'feminist' to tar advocates as provocateurs, enemies of the nation, and even foreign spies. In Saudi Arabia, when Manal al-Sharif dared to violate injunctions against women's driving, security officials called her a 'traitor'.[16] In China, state security forces arrested six young women for organizing protests against street harassment and sexual assault. Interrogators called them 'whores', 'subversives', and 'foreign spies'.[17] When Iranian security forces detained filmmaker Asfar Sonia Shafie for her movie that showcases how access to education improved women's lives, they repeatedly asked her 'Are you a feminist?' and whether she received support from the US Counter Intelligence Agency.[18]

For many women leaders and activists, eschewing the feminist label may be strategic and even essential for survival. Many reproductive rights activists frame their demands not in terms of women's rights but in terms of helping women become better mothers. For instance, Ipas, an international women's NGO dedicated to reproductive rights, features stories from Global South women who became better at caring for their families because they could have abortions.[19] These narratives place women's demands for abortion access within their appropriate cultural contexts. In the long run, policy changes framed in conservative terms still increase women's autonomy and contribute to altering traditional gender roles.

The book's big-tent approach

The above examples echo the earlier point about shared principles. Even if women's rights advocates diverge in what they would term their interests, their priorities, and even themselves (e.g. whether they see themselves as feminists or not), they are united by their overarching commitment to improve women's lives by ending women's second-class status. The point here is neither to homogenize nor to essentialize women or women activists: women are not the same by virtue of their shared biology nor their shared second-class status. Women's diverse identities are further shaped by the countries, cultures, and epochs in which they live and by their position in social hierarchies based on organizing principles other than gender, including but not limited to race, ethnicity, socioeconomic class, religion, sexual identification, disability, and migrant status. This intersectional perspective cautions that gender hierarchies manifest differently across time and space. Yet across all contexts, gender hierarchies *do* exist. They shape women's lives in deleterious ways, no matter whether an individual woman recognizes them, dislikes them, or denounces them. Women thus have policy interests related to gender equality, even if not all women share these interests, prioritize these interests, or express these interests in uniform ways. Interests emerge from political, social, and economic structures, not from uniform recognition and agreement among the affected parties. Women's interest in and women's policy demands about gender equality emerge from the very real existence of patriarchy, not from all women's universal experience within this reality.

For this reason, this book takes two approaches to conceiving of movements, interests, and demands as belonging to women, gender, and feminism. On the one hand, the book contends that, scholarly debates notwithstanding, big-tent definitions are possible. Specifically, the book contends that *women's movements seek women's rights and gender equality* and that *women have a shared interest in and make demands about women's rights and gender equality.* On the ground, practical and strategic interests collide and intertwine. 'Gender' refers to the hierarchal ordering of society along patriarchal lines – and 'gender equality' to the disappearance of this hierarchy. 'Women' refers to the numerically largest gender group that has second-class status within this gender hierarchy. (Other gender groups, such as non-binary individuals, also have lower-tier status, but this book focuses on those actors who organize as and make demands as women; however, LGBTQIA+ identity constitutes an important intersectional dimension.) 'Feminist' slides in as well: even as some protagonists tie 'feminism' more closely to challenging rather than accommodating gender hierarchies, feminism generally seeks to undo gender hierarchies that are based on power and domination. 'Gender equality' and 'feminism' capture movement actors' understanding that women are differentially and adversely positioned within political, economic, and social structures, as well as the demands that would move these structures towards more equality.

On the other hand, two policy areas particularly produce more unanimity among women's rights protagonists relative to being labelled *feminist*: seeking reproductive rights and ending violence against women. These two policy areas directly affect whether or not women have safety and bodily autonomy. Policy reforms in these areas would thus remove the ultimate tool used to preserve the patriarchal gender order: force and the threat of force. As a result, the book uses 'feminist' especially when discussing these policy areas.

Opponents to gender equality are not part of women's movements

Conceptualizing women's shared interest in gender equality as the shared goal of women's movements also makes clear what women's interests and women's movements are not. Women's interests and women's movements are about dismantling patriarchy. They are not efforts to uphold the norms and laws that underpin patriarchy. Such countermovements do exist: many movements oppose gender equality and wish to preserve or reinstate patriarchal gender norms and heterosexual family structures. Scholars describe countermovements using different adjectives, including 'conservative', 'reactionary', or 'anti-gender'.

The US Quiverfull movement illustrates a movement seeking to preserve patriarchy. Laura Harrison and Sarah Rowley summarize Quiverfull as follows: 'Quiverfull members are evangelical Christians who eschew all forms of birth control as interference with God's divine plan. Women, in particular, are encouraged to sacrifice their bodies for unfettered reproduction and to submit to both God and their husbands, who are their earthly masters.'[20] Unlike the Nicaraguan women pursuing practical gender interests, who recognized that the gendered division of labour creates burdens that make women's lives difficult, Quiverfull women *valorize* this division as natural and just, as a divine gift to embrace rather than a socially constructed problem to fix. For Quiverfull women, patriarchy and the separate spheres reflect the correct political, economic, and social order.

These views are not particular to Quiverfull, but broadly shared among conservative religious groups across the Global North and South. Countermovements are just as internationally and transnationally linked as women's movements. Conservative, reactionary, and anti-gender groups hold their own international convenings and send advocates to mainstream international convenings. In the case of UN conferences, countries organized on religious lines – such as the Vatican and some Middle Eastern countries – offer easy access points through which women's rights opponents can gain influence over the proceedings.

Women hold key leadership roles and participate actively in conservative, reactionary, and anti-gender organizations. Not all women agree that women's second-class status produces harmful effects on women's lives, but, as already pointed out, unanimity among women is not the criterion for identifying women's interests. The presence of women in countermovements is therefore not a 'gotcha' that undermines the ability to talk about women's movements and women's demands. Nor do countermovements' claims to act for gender equality constitute a similar 'gotcha'. Many countermovements appropriate gender equality discourses in order to occult their true aims. As in the case of women's interests, what matters for defining women's movements is how the movement's objectives relate to existing political, economic, and social structures: women's movements would eliminate gender hierarchies and end women's second-class status, whereas countermovements would not.

One era but countless struggles

Gender hierarchies have universal persistence, but this does not mean that they have singular and uniform manifestations across time and place. Women's rights advocates are on the same side, but as a heterogeneous group, women's rights advocates within the same country and those collaborating across countries will spiritedly disagree about just exactly how patriarchy should be abolished. Rather than hold the women's rights era back, diversity and disagreement has propelled it forward.

Disagreement over priorities

Women disagree on policy design and policy goals precisely because they are not a homogeneous group. Intersectional perspectives examining how gender interlocks with other axes of oppression illustrate that seemingly contradictory policy demands nonetheless pursue similar gender equality aims. Take the US women's movement's decades-long fight to add an Equal Rights Amendment (ERA) to the US constitution. Some women of colour have questioned whether 'equal rights between men and women' can address how race and class affect Black women's lives. When the ERA faced a renewed ratification debate in the Illinois State Senate in 2018, Democrat Mary Flowers – one of Illinois's few Black women legislators – worried that an ERA requiring the same treatment for all women would prevent Black women from benefitting from affirmative action policies based on race.[21] Flowers shared the ERA proponents' goal of gender equality, but feared that the ERA would work against equality for racially minoritized women.

This division between movement protagonists happens not just within countries that have histories of racial and ethnic exclusion but between countries that are differentially positioned in global power hierarchies. At the world conferences on women, Global South activists argued that women's rights could not be satisfactorily achieved without simultaneously ending colonialism and extractive development models. Global North women prioritized equal workforce opportunities and equal pay, whereas Global South women viewed workforce inequality not only in terms of their individual inequality relative to men but in terms of their country's inequality within the global economic system. Global South women contended that economic equality meant addressing how their workforce opportunities were concentrated in exploitative jobs, including in export-oriented factories or as domestic workers. Likewise, demands for reproductive rights that focused exclusively on access to contraception and abortion rang hollow for Global South women. Many Global South women had not been denied access to contraception and abortion; instead, international aid programmes had coerced them into having fewer children. Women from Guatemala, Colombia, India, Peru, South Africa, and many other countries underwent forced sterilization in the 1960s and 1970s. For Global South women, family planning policies had harmed, not enhanced, women's bodily autonomy.[22] (Forced sterilization also occurred within Global North countries, with public health authorities from California to Scotland prescribing long-term birth control or performing hysterectomies on impoverished women and on non-white women without their consent.[23])

Disagreements over priorities infuse the global women's movement. Nitza Berkovitch deploys a collage metaphor to capture the movement's internal diversity: the global women's movement 'is not a mere aggregate of national women's movements nor is it an expression of one hegemonic power . . . a "collage" that keeps changing all the time is a suitable metaphor for this complex web of organizations'.[24] Within this collage, participants seek to hold each other accountable for articulating intersectional visions of gender justice; they have at times succeeded and they have at times failed; and they have at times reached impasses that have resulted in different groups' decision to branch out and pursue different objectives. Rather than identify certain understandings or certain claims as correct or incorrect, this book examines how women's specific demands emerge from their embeddedness in specific times and places. Rather than undermine the objective existence of a women's movement, these differences about the policies or goals that would advance gender equality enrich the women's movement's multiple manifestations.

Further, disagreements generate what some scholars have called productive tensions or energizing tensions. For instance, prior to the 1995 Beijing conference, the Women's Global Network for Reproductive Rights forced a paradigm shift in how feminist blueprints would frame contraception and abortion. At a 1984 international meeting on global women's health policy, members of organizations from the Global South literally tore up the initial declaration.[25] The rewritten version articulated that both withholding *and* forcing contraception and abortion were deleterious to women's reproductive rights. These efforts paved the way for the Beijing PfA's declaration that 'acts of violence against women also include forced sterilization and forced abortion [and] coercive/forced use of contraceptives'.[26] Here the contestation clarified and strengthened women's demands. Of course, disagreements among women activists should not be romanticized: these disagreements emerge from real harms, abuses, and misdeeds that reflect global, national, and intergenerational forms of injustice – from enslavement and colonialism to racial segregation and religious persecution. Nonetheless, working through these flashpoints has helped the women's rights era's feminist blueprints incorporate an intersectional ethos.

Disagreement over strategy

Another long-standing tension among movements and their protagonists relates to *how* gender equality should be sought and *who* can deliver it. Specifically, should women's movements make demands upon the state? Should they, as Mary Hawkesworth writes, 'engage the state'?[27]

By the state, scholars mean the permanent apparatus of government, its institutions and bureaucracies. The government forms part of the state: it consists of the collection of actors who control the state at a given time, meaning the chief executive (the president or the prime minister), their ministers, and all policymakers and staff. For women and feminists, as well as for members of other marginalized groups, the state constitutes an oppressive force: from failing to prohibit rape to restricting reproductive choice, the state makes and enforces laws and policies that encode patriarchy and violate women's rights.

The state can also unmake these rules. The quest for constitutional, legal, and political frameworks that improve women's status constitutes the main goal of the women's rights era – and the topic of this book. Women's movements have demanded that states repeal, undo, and rewrite the rules that keep women unequal. In doing so, women's movements have critiqued how existing constitutions, laws, and policies perpetuate gender hierarchies. This critique means that women's movements actually recognize the state's oppressive character. The changes they seek would lessen the state's oppressive character, making the state work for women rather than against them. Yet the very act of seeking policy change means accepting the state's legitimacy to regulate political, economic, and social life. In asking the state to encode new gender norms, women's movements implicitly (if not explicitly) accept the state's power to coerce citizens into following specific rules and adopting specific behaviours.

For this reason, some feminist activists disagree with engaging the state. Coercion is not consistent with their vision of feminism. More centrally, they argue that the state cannot shed its oppressive character and thus can never gain legitimacy. Leveraging state power to dismantle gender hierarchies constitutes a fool's errand, as US activist Audre Lorde explained in 1984 when she argued that 'the master's tools will never dismantle the master's house'. Lorde's words directly criticized white feminists' blinders vis-à-vis state power: the state might guarantee equality to privileged white women but not to women of colour, gay women, and women from other marginalized social groups.[28] For minoritized women, the state will always be an oppressive force. Lorde's sentence eventually took on larger meaning within feminist political thought, suggesting that *no* feminists should engage the state. If feminists seek freedom from dominance, Lorde's formula came to imply that the state can never be the answer.

At the same time, state power represents women's and marginalized peoples' best chance to attain rights and to exercise autonomy. At a basic level, when countries remove laws detrimental to women's rights and establish equality guarantees – when they eliminate restrictions on women's right to own property, for example – the material conditions of women's lives improve. Having women and feminist allies placed inside the state – as lawmakers, ministers, and executive branch staffers – also provides access points for movements to win changes and to later hold governments accountable for their implementation. Women holding positions of authority within the state often become first responders when governments attempt rollbacks, as women officials are able to raise the alarm and work to stall or thwart countermovements.

Further, contemporary best practices for advancing women's rights *do* attend to how hierarchies of difference interface with state power. Take the Spanish province of Catalonia's 2021–2024 National Strategy for Sexual and Reproductive Health. The strategy takes a holistic view, utilizing a rights-based approach and addressing not only abortion and contraception access but assisted reproduction, trans people, mental health care during and after pregnancy, obstetric violence, sexually transmitted diseases, reproductive health illnesses such as endometriosis, and the sexual health needs of younger and older people.[29] The plan's attention to marginalized groups, interlocking forms of oppression, and intertwined problems characterizes the Ministry of Equalities and Feminism's transformative approach. As then minister Tània Verge explains, policies introducing new rights and policies identifying and addressing the causes and consequences of systemic oppression are not 'the master's tools'.[30] Rather, such policies offer pathways to a more equitable world, pathways that only state power can make available.

The transformative aims of women's rights advocacy and reform

The women's rights era sought to change constitutions, laws, and policies in order to build more equal polities and societies. Yet there are no overnight routes to gender equality. Inequality between women and men ultimately rests on the values and beliefs of individuals, who are socialized throughout the centuries to conform to gender hierarchies that elevate men and masculinity over women and femininity. Ideas of what makes a 'good' man or a 'good' woman or what constitutes 'real' masculinity and femininity vary, but the ideas themselves are remarkably sticky.

Sometimes policy changes outpace social values. Take gender quota laws: when found in countries thought to hold very conservative ideas about gender, like Morocco and Sierra Leone, observers often ask: 'Are these countries "ready" to have so many women leaders?' Other times, policy changes lag or fall behind social values: large majorities in Hungary and Poland support legal abortion, for instance, notwithstanding recent governments' restrictions on access.[31] Essentially, public policy and social norms do not move in lockstep. Nor can gender equality be achieved by adopting a single policy change. Recall the length of the Mexico City conference and Beijing conference reports: 203 and 132 pages respectively. The sum total of the changes needed to achieve gender equality is massive, indeed.

Additionally, policies on the books may not translate into practices in the streets. Policy changes may not deliver their promised outcomes, largely because reforms on paper cannot immediately take effect or immediately alter attitudes and behaviours. Does having more women in office actually change citizens' views about the appropriateness of women's public and political roles? Does legalizing abortion actually make the procedure more available to women, especially marginalized women and poor women? When the answer to such questions is not an unequivocal 'yes', disillusionment sets in. When implementation falters and transformation remains unrealized, some wonder: what is the point of women's rights advocacy and reform?

This book poses two answers to that question. First, advocacy sets agendas, bringing diverse groups of women together in countless events and settings and generating shared visions and agendas for change. Advocacy establishes the feminist blueprints that contain templates for action and for reaching more equitable futures. Gender equality advocacy entails seeking discrete policy changes, but also aspiring to a better and more just world. Even when campaigns target identifiable policy changes in specific places (e.g. Nigeria's #ChildNotBride campaign against early and forced marriage), the campaign itself names the future it would like to see (e.g. the end of child marriage). As Natali Francine Cinelli Moreira and Kelly Komatsu Agopyan reflect, the women converging on Mexico City in 1975 *wanted to change everything*.[32] The fact that women's rights advocates managed to put this aspiration on paper, in the form of feminist blueprints, and to have this vision recognized by the United Nations and by most of the world's governments, is itself an achievement.

Second, these international frameworks have led national governments to adopt constitutional, legislative, and policy reforms. One remarkable outcome of the women's rights era is the commonality of changes despite countries' different histories, political regimes, legal systems, and cultures. Regions as different as Latin America, Southeast Asia, the Middle East, and Africa have adopted gender quotas for women candidates, created government ministries dedicated to women's affairs, and passed laws prohibiting gender discrimination in the workplace. Countries' varied histories, contexts, and politics help explain why these reforms flourish in some places and struggle in others. This book does not, however, examine whether policy implementation succeeds or fails. The book instead emphasizes the substantive and symbolic importance of policy adoption itself. Even underimplemented laws change at least some women's lives, giving some – or even many – women protections and opportunities they previously lacked. Constitutional amendments, statutes, and policies create mandates and establish avenues of accountability when implementation falters or fails to reach all women. Adoption is not sufficient, but it is necessary.

That said, the constitutional, legal, and political reforms that hasten gender equality do envision different transformations of the state and society. Mala Htun and Laurel Weldon extensively catalogued and compared governments' promotion of women's rights, arguing that different policy areas challenge different configurations of political, economic, and social power.[33] The policy areas this book examines – constitutional reforms, government and elections, education and workforce participation, family law and care work, reproductive rights, and violence against women – all matter for gender equality. Yet some invoke more profound transformations of everyday life than others. For some gender equality goals, attaining the perfect outcome – meaning that the reform is implemented such that no woman experiences discrimination or denial of her rights – requires greater political willpower, more state resources, and more comprehensive behavioural and attitudinal shifts among policymakers, bureaucrats, and private individuals. Said another way, adopting a reform is one thing; ensuring that this reform is not just implemented, but implemented because it reflects altered 'hearts and minds' about gender and gender roles, is another. This book describes the gap between adoption and implementation as the gap between the formal, legal changes that women's rights advocates can achieve, on the one hand, and the everyday changes to lived realities that women's rights advocates hope will follow, on the other hand. Said simply, the gap reflects how transformative the policy aims to be, meaning how many practices, attitudes, and values would need to change to bridge the distance between aspiration and reality in the long term.

The book argues, for instance, that enacting gender quotas presents a smaller adoption–implementation gap by comparison with legalizing abortion. Even countries where citizens hold conservative values have adopted gender quotas, as attitudes about women's public roles can shift more rapidly than attitudes about private roles (hence the persistence of the double day, where women join the paid workforce but still complete housework). The number of women in political office is also a discrete and countable metric, an outcome that countries can easily point to when demonstrating their commitment to international gender equality norms. Furthermore, implementing gender quotas usually requires singular entities – namely political parties – to make a change, and enforcing the change usually falls on a singular office – typically an election agency. The fewer the responsible parties, the shorter the distance between on-paper and on-the-ground change. Even if not every single man and woman truly believes that women have the right to hold political office, a government committed to implementing gender quotas can compel compliance.

Legalizing abortion, however, requires more profound transformations. First, attitudes about doctrinal issues like reproductive rights prove harder to shift than attitudes about women's public roles.[34] Second, even if abortion becomes legal, effective implementation involves far more responsible parties and far more measurable outcomes than in the case of gender quotas. Compliance with permissible voluntary abortion requires hundreds of thousands of medical providers, social workers, educators, judicial authorities, and other actors to ensure abortion access by providing information, opportunity, and services in culturally appropriate ways, at multiple touchpoints in medical, legal, and educational settings. Even governments committed to upholding abortion rights will need significant planning and technical capacity to reshape and monitor all these interactions. Assessing and ensuring outcomes – such as the number of women who receive the requisite pamphlets at certain moments in their healthcare journeys – also requires significant resources related to measurement, evaluation, and sanctioning noncompliant providers. In this case, those whose hearts and minds do not change – those who oppose women's reproductive autonomy – have many more opportunities to withhold access and services.

Two interrelated factors thus affect which policy areas present small or large gaps between aspiration and reality: the complexity of the reform and the depth of the hearts and minds shift that implementation requires. Figure I.1 arrays the book's six policy areas on a continuum from least to most transformative, beginning with reforms related to constitutional and political rights (e.g. gender quotas) and ending with reforms related to reproductive rights and violence against women. Importantly, the idea of an adoption–implementation gap ranging from least to most transformative is conceptual, not empirical. Neither the book nor Figure I.1 quantify the gap by assessing which regions or which countries are more successful at bridging adoption and implementation. Rather, Figure I.1 contextualizes why, in some policy areas versus others, observers may be less ready to accept the book's argument that formal, legal changes mean that women's status and lives have improved. The conceptual schema acknowledges that implementation, and thus visible progress, can and does fall short. The more the policy reforms require political willpower, attitudinal changes to underlying values and norms, and behavioural shifts in daily life, the more difficult it is to achieve 'perfect' results. Conceptualizing reforms relative to their transformative aims helps explain why scholars and commentators see stalled progress in some policy areas more than others.

That said, the idea that some transformations are easier to realize does not mean that adoption *itself* is easy to attain. All gender equality reforms face resistance at the adoption stage. Gender quotas might place women into positions of political power faster than legalized abortion guarantees women's bodily autonomy, but women in most countries needed to campaign intensely for gender quota adoption. Nor do reforms advance linearly, spreading from one policy area to the next. Rather, Figure I.1's placement of policy areas from less to more transformative captures how women's rights advocacy and reform do not implicate uniform kinds of on-the-ground change.

The book's structure follows Figure I.1. Chapter 2 reviews how transnational networks of women's rights activists leverage international organizations, especially the United Nations, to create normative frameworks and policy templates for gender equality. These documents comprise the feminist blueprints undergirding the women's rights era. Chapter 3 moves from the international to the national, examining how

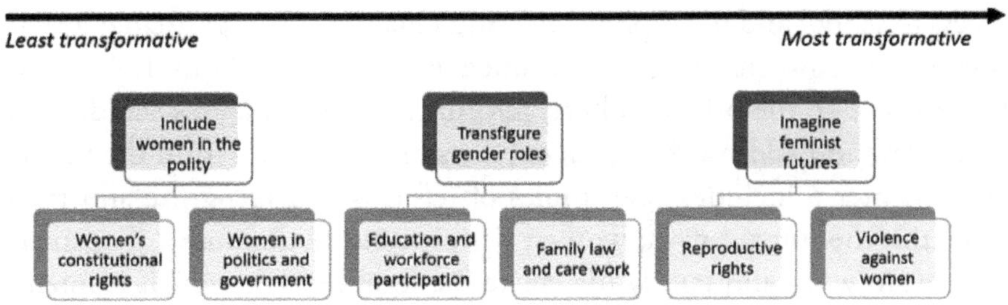

Figure 1 The Adoption–Implementation Gap: Conceptualizing the Transformative Aims of Women's Rights Advocacy and Reform. Drawn by the author.

and when governments adopt women's rights reforms and exploring whether democracies really outperform non-democracies in their commitment to women's rights. In doing so, Chapter 3 examines reforms that *include women in the polity*, discussing how women became recognized as citizens and how women influenced constitution writing.

Chapter 4 extends Chapter 3's analysis of reforms that include women in the polity, examining reforms that guarantee women access to and voice in politics, elections, and government. Adding more women to the state has progressed more rapidly than changes in other policy areas, given the more straightforward alignment between the policy objective and the actual change. While those in power may resist women's inclusion, bringing more women into political and public offices remains a straightforward numerical objective. The number of women candidates and officeholders can be tracked over time, which makes the achievement easier to identify. While activists rightly continue to push for greater diversity among the women (and men) who hold decision-making power, the gendered distribution of political leadership is vastly different in 2025 by comparison with 1975. Moreover, once in elected and appointed office, women have introduced practices and created agencies that elevate gender equality concerns within policymaking.

The next two policy areas aim to *transfigure gender roles*, meaning that they encompass reforms that would dissolve the separate spheres' gendered division of labour. Chapter 5 analyses women's entry into the public sphere beyond politics, namely via education and workforce participation, and Chapter 6 explores reforms that affect women's status in the private sphere. In the public sphere, reforms support women's access to school and to employment, and Chapter 5 pays particular attention to reforms ensuring that women enjoy equal labour rights and protections. In the private sphere, reforms equalize women's standing in family law and address the gendered division of labour within the home, and Chapter 6 includes case studies of reforms that recognize and even monetize the unpaid work women perform inside the home. Together, reforms to work and family life create the legal basis on which women's (and men's) roles are reconfigured over time. They articulate women's rights that were historically not enumerated – such as the right to own property – and create channels through which women can challenge their second-class status in the economy and in the home.

Lastly, there are two policy areas that *imagine feminist futures.* Feminists have consistently prioritized reproductive autonomy and freedom from violence. Chapter 7, on reproductive rights, and Chapter 8, on combating violence against women, examine these challenging areas of women's rights reforms. Realizing reproductive rights (including liberalizing access to abortion) requires shifting deeply held moral views. Ending violence against women necessitates transforming not just the attitudes of hundreds of thousands of state officials, from law enforcement officers to judges, but also the behaviours of the everyday people who commit abuse. Here feminist blueprints become especially important for articulating the freedoms and protections women ought to enjoy. National laws often reproduce feminist blueprints' aspirational content. Even when implementation ultimately falls dramatically short, activists can and do use international frameworks and national laws to hold governments accountable.

These types of change – including women within the polity, transfiguring gender roles, and imagining feminist futures – are not mutually exclusive categories. Women's presence in political leadership and their ability to choose when and how to become mothers also reconfigure gender roles, for instance. Rather, arraying policy areas from less to more transformative illustrates why some global regions have moved the needle more than others. All regions have tackled all policy areas to some degree, but they have not all pressed forward to the same degree. To situate this variation, each policy-focused chapter (chapters 4 to 8) follows a similar basic structure: the policy area and the issues at stake are explained; the particular feminist blueprints are summarized; and some of the era's more notable examples of advocacy and reform are highlighted, with attention to regional patterns. Chapter 9 concludes by assessing women's activism in the latter part of the women's rights era, a context marked by increased democratic backsliding and the rollback of previous decades' progress on women's rights.

No one chapter can wholly illustrate the diversity and richness of women's rights advocacy and reform in every corner of the globe. The chapters can only sample the variety of activism and reforms shaping each policy area. The case studies and individual stories that follow are neither exhaustive nor definitive, but are illustrative of how international and transnational organizing for women's rights produced policy reforms that materially and meaningfully altered women's lives. The takeaway message is that, during the women's rights era, women authored international feminist blueprints and leveraged these visions to change their countries' constitutions, laws, and policies. They imagined new worlds, changed policy, and won more rights and freedoms. This work was carried out by women, for women – and the protagonists and the achievements should not be forgotten.

TWO

International Advocacy for Women's Rights

In the early 1990s, Hillary Clinton was not the only first lady preparing for the Fourth World Conference on Women in Beijing. Egyptian First Lady Suzanne Mubarak and Nigerian First Lady Maryam Babangida wanted a coordinated African voice in Beijing.[1] They proposed that the then Organization of African Unity (OAU) create a women's unit. Initially conceived as a public relations body that would market African states' activities at Beijing, the Women's Unit became a focal point for African women's activism. From within the Women's Unit, protagonists like Nigeria's Yetunde Teriba, one of the Women's Unit founding leaders, and Senegal's Bineta Diop, the director and founder of the NGO Femmes Africa Solidarité, would negotiate, write, and secure an explicitly African women's rights framework.

In 2002, the Organization of African Unity became the African Union (AU). Diop manoeuvred extensively behind the scenes, converting the Women's Desk into the Women and Gender Development Directorate. In parallel, Teriba and Diop convened civil society organizations, including NGOs like Women in Law and Development in Africa (WiLDAF), the African Women's Development and Communication Network (FEMNET), Equality Now, and Akina Mama wa Afrika, to draft a women's rights charter. They combined forces with the Inter-African Committee on Traditional Practices Affecting the Health of Women and Children, which was then evaluating a potential convention against harmful practices. Together, these actors drafted and proposed the Protocol to the African Charter on Human and Peoples' Rights on the Rights of Women in Africa, known as the Maputo Protocol. Adopted by the AU in 2003, the protocol establishes a pan-African approach to women's rights, reflecting international norms but also censuring specific women's rights violations found in Africa, such as female genital mutilation and polygamy. As of its twentieth anniversary in 2023, 44 of 55 African states had ratified the treaty.

The Maputo Protocol exemplifies how the women's rights era's international convenings linked activists on shared agendas and fuelled change across the globe. The United Nations provided the platform, beginning in 1975 with the First World Conference on Women in Mexico City and the launch of International Women's Year (IWY), continuing through the International Women's Decade and its two additional World Conferences on Women (Copenhagen in 1980 and Nairobi in 1985), and capped by the Fourth World Conference on Women in Beijing in 1995. Each event generated a virtuous circle: the conferences' preparatory processes, actual convening, and aftermath allowed activists to assess progress and demand additional advances. Each world conference on women produced an advocacy document that would inform women's organizing. The conferences also propelled other blueprints forward: the Mexico City conference bolstered those authoring what would become the 1979 Convention on the Elimination of All Forms of Discrimination against Women (CEDAW) and the Beijing conference helped inspire not just regional initiatives such as the Maputo Protocol but specific instruments such as the 2000 UN Security Council Resolution 1325 on Women, Peace, and Security (UNSCR 1325). Women's international organizing also ensured that the UN 2015 Sustainable Development Goals (SDGs) included gender equality as goal number 5 (SDG 5).[2] All constitute what this book calls 'feminist blueprints', the international norms and policy prescriptions that women's rights advocates leverage when seeking country-level changes to constitutions, statutes, and policies.

Yet exactly how does the international arena, and its most central actor, the United Nations, work? The United Nations, like all international governance organizations, is a political body. Every action requires negotiation among diverse actors, including member-state representatives, staffers, and leaders of non-governmental organizations with consultative status (e.g. certain WINGOs). What the United Nations decides reflects complex political bargains – and even when decisions are reached, the United Nations can urge but not compel national-level action. The key drivers of feminist blueprints are movement actors. At the international level, these protagonists shape two outcomes: the normative frameworks that motivate policy change (such as the idea that women's rights are human rights); and the documents that list the policy objectives and provide concrete examples for achieving them (these documents may also bear names such as roadmaps, toolkits, handbooks, or plans, among other descriptors). Together, normative frameworks and prescriptive documents constitute the feminist blueprints that actors redact at the international level and then carry to the regional and national level, lobbying national and subnational governments to make changes.

In this way, the story of the women's rights era is a story about how women's rights advocates collaborate in interlocking arenas: the international, the regional, the national, and the local. As much as feminist blueprints are transmitted to individual countries, what happens within individual countries also shapes what actors convening in international meetings decide that the blueprints will say. Across the women's rights era, the documents' content shifted in response to global events and power struggles, depending upon which protagonists were in the room at which time.

The women's rights era was therefore neither conceived in an international bubble nor imposed upon passive national governments. The post-Second World War era ushered in a period of decolonization and democratization across the globe. Protagonists from decolonizing and democratizing regions (today called the 'Global South' but then called 'developing' or even 'third world' countries) hoped that international frameworks articulating human rights would support their quests for political independence. By the 1970s, many countries had experienced armed conflict and regime transitions. They had emerged from periods of colonial rule and military dictatorship and were seeking to (re)establish electoral democracy. Periods of democratization continued into the 1980s and the 1990s, especially following the 1989 dissolution of the Soviet Union, and in the 2010s, with the Arab Spring. Women participated actively in their countries' struggles: they joined resistance movements and rebel movements, including as armed combatants, and they participated in democratization and peace processes as human rights activists, constitution writers, and electoral candidates. Regime transitions became moments to realize women's rights. In Chile in the 1980s, women campaigning against the Pinochet dictatorship demanded 'democracy in the country and in the home'.[3] In the Soviet Union at the same time, women activists argued that 'democracy without women is no democracy'.[4] Of course, not every country shares the exact same history. Still, political ruptures shaped the women's rights era, as women active in their country's internal struggles brought their visions of development, democracy, and peace to international conferences.

This chapter reviews how the international arena, particularly the United Nations, generated feminist blueprints. The story starts with Global South women's insistence that the 1945 UN charter include the word 'women' when mentioning human rights. With this seed planted, a new generation of women could then convince the United Nations to convene the First World Conference on Women. From there, other benchmarks followed, including CEDAW, the 1995 Beijing PfA, which affirmed the normative connection between human rights and women's rights, and UNSCR 1325. These three documents remain the most prominent and influential feminist blueprints.

The international arena as a policymaking space

Chapter 1 defined 'movements' as any set of actors and organizations, working alone or in concert, that demand political and social change. Actors and organizations in the same policy space – such as those working on women's rights and gender equality – might not always agree, but they likely have professional ties. Protagonists often straddle arenas or government levels or move between them during their careers. An academic might consult for the United Nations while also conducting policy research in her home country. A WINGO leader may resign to work in her country's social development ministry, then later lead a different NGO. Academics, bureaucrats, elected officials, and NGO leaders and staffers sit on the same advisory panels for international and regional organizations and meet at the same international and regional conferences. As such, they often blur the distinction between insiders (those who work in government) and outsiders (those who pressure the government from the outside). Over time, these women professionals form dense and interconnected networks, which scholars Margaret Keck and Kathryn Sikkink call 'transnational advocacy networks'.[5] The networks focused on women's rights – what scholar Valentine Moghadam calls 'transnational feminist networks' – author international organizations' feminist blueprints.[6]

Using the international arena

Transnational advocacy networks have two targets. First, they have to persuade international organizations to act. In the case of the women's rights era, the United Nations had to be persuaded to launch the IWY and to convene the Mexico City conference. Second, networks shape the feminist blueprints and then carry them to the national level. International organizations' critics often portray national governments as mindlessly following supranational governments' directives, but national governments do not simply or unthinkingly acquiesce in international organizations' edicts merely because the organizations said so. In reality, national governments rarely spontaneously move to protect rights. Instead, domestic activists use international treaties, conference reports, and agenda-setting periods or targets – such as the IWY and the SDGs – as lobbying tools, usually translating and adapting normative ideas and policy proposals to their own contexts. Many of these advocates operate in subnational spaces, at the local level, meaning in certain cities, towns, or rural areas (hence the designation 'grassroots'). As Keck and Sikkink described, the United Nations' agenda-setting often 'boomerangs' from the international level to the local level, then back to the national level. In some cases, international norms stick at the local level first. The United States, for instance, has not ratified CEDAW, but local activists have successfully campaigned for some US cities to adopt the CEDAW Convention into their city charters.

That transnational feminist networks share the principles of gender equality does not mean that all protagonists uniformly agree on *how* these principles should translate into domestic policy. Transnational advocacy networks do not just lobby international organizations and national governments; they also negotiate *among themselves.* Take Global South women's efforts to include forced sterilization in conceptualizations of reproductive rights, as briefly recounted in Chapter 1: this understanding did not appear in the plan of action following the First World Conference on Women in 1975, but did enter the platform for action following the Fourth World Conference on Women in 1995.

Of course, the United Nations is not the only international organization setting norms and issuing blueprints. Nearly all international organizations convene events and produce documents to guide members' behaviour. Whether they are dedicated to economic growth, like the World Bank or the International Monetary Fund, or regional cooperation, like the OECD or the Organization for Security and Cooperation in Europe (OSCE), they all produce templates, toolkits, and other documents outlining the road to gender equality. The documents share a common language. They talk about gender equality and women's rights; they argue for gender mainstreaming (meaning adopting a gender perspective in all policy areas); and they explicitly cite key UN frameworks such as CEDAW, the Beijing PfA, and UNSCR 1325. As Sonia Palmieri and Julie Ballington explain, these feminist governance tools are wildly popular, 'evident not only in their number and publication by a range of transnational bodies, but also in the diversity of languages to which they are translated'.[7]

The United Nations' feminist blueprints thus offer policymakers across the globe a common language, one shaped and circulated by transnational feminist networks. For example, even a multilateral security organization like the North Atlantic Treaty Organization (NATO) boasts a Committee on Gender Perspectives that advises member nations on adopting gender mainstreaming and implementing UNSCR 1325. Regional organizations like the AU, the OAS, and the Association of Southeast Nations (ASEAN) have their own blueprints. The OAS issues 'model laws' for gender equality – template legislation for member states – including model laws for creating national care systems (Chapter 6) and combating violence against women (Chapter 8). ASEAN produces declarations and guidelines related to women's rights and gender mainstreaming, such as its 2021 Declaration of the Gender-Responsive Implementation of the ASEAN Community Vision 2025.[8] The AU has two plans of action for implementing the Maputo Protocol. Organizations beyond the United Nations thus play key roles in transmitting feminist blueprints from the global to the regional, national, and local levels.

How countries respond

Not all international organizations are created equal. Depending on the organizations' charters and membership terms, international organizations' edicts may be more or less binding on member countries. Most international organizations, including the United Nations (like the OAS, the ASEAN, and the AU), can cajole rather than compel. Transnational advocacy networks' use of feminist blueprints as domestic lobbying tools does not alone produce reform, as the success of pressure campaigns depends on myriad domestic factors, from government ideology to economic outlook.

Chapter 3 explores national-level reform processes in more depth, but one element worth noting here is that countries often adopt gender equality reforms to improve their international image. For example, countries adopting policies that elect more women become seen as more egalitarian and can attract more foreign aid.[9] Some international organizations exert particular leverage, namely, international financial institutions. The International Monetary Fund, for example, often conditions loans on countries making significant policy changes, like cutting welfare spending and deregulating markets. So, while countries do not passively and automatically accept international organizations' edicts, the international system does allow more powerful and wealthy countries to pressure less powerful and less wealthy countries into acting in certain ways.

Even the terms used to group countries imply some division according to international influence and prestige. As noted, advocates in the women's rights era's initial decades would have used binaries such as 'first world' or 'third world', or 'developed' or 'developing'. A more contemporary approach groups countries on the basis of whether their wealth, market dominance, level of democracy, or historic influence places them in the Global North (meaning they have these features) or the Global South (meaning they do not). Still, the division remains imperfect. The Global South is itself diverse, comprising middle-income countries with significant regional or even international clout (e.g. Brazil, Mexico, India, and South Africa) alongside lower-income countries and fragile or failed states. And some countries may not fit this schema at all: the Gulf states, for example, are wealthy but not democratic and not large market economies.

Countries sharing the same geopolitical milieu also diverge in their policy frameworks – even when they ostensibly should not. In organizations like the European Union, where policy mandates are ostensibly binding, countries still do not blindly follow the edicts. Social movements matter for accountability. When Central and Eastern European countries joined the European Union in 2004, the ascension process required them to adopt all EU directives, including those related to gender equality, such as gender mainstreaming and revising discriminatory national laws. When the European Union began admitting countries that did not have the requisite gender equality provisions in place, national chapters of the European Women's Lobby insisted that gender equality not be deprioritized within the ascension process.[10] This process highlights both how even similar countries resist complying with international norms and how transnational advocacy networks play key roles in monitoring (non)compliance.

International organizations' reporting mechanisms provide further scaffolding for advocacy work. Exact processes vary, but the general setup is that a committee or group within the international organization functions as an oversight body, requiring countries to report on their progress at regular intervals. In the United Nations, different bodies follow the different documents. Over at the UN Office of the High Commission for Human Rights, the Committee on the Elimination of Discrimination against Women monitors CEDAW implementation. Within the UN Economic and Social Committee, the Commission on the Status of Women (CSW) oversees countries' take-up of the Beijing PfA. Both monitoring bodies collect reports. In the CSW's case, the body convenes annually and each year has a 'review theme' (the area in which countries should report on existing progress) and a 'priority theme' (the area in which countries should set goals for future progress). Countries send formal reports, but NGOs can submit shadow reports. The latter serve as important counterweights to governments' often upbeat or sanitized accounts. The monitoring process thus constitutes another advocacy channel, allowing women's organizations to highlight gaps and demand more change.

In summary, the international arena is a complex, multifaceted site of policy contestation, articulation, and action. International governance organizations like the United Nations create spaces wherein differently situated and differently resourced countries and actors look to leverage outcomes. These processes are messy, fraught with complex power differentials, and shaped by often dark histories of geopolitical conflict. Yet they allow transnational movements to form and pursue policy goals.

The origins of the women's rights era

The IWY galvanized a global women's rights movement, but the transnational feminist networks nurturing this movement had important roots in the nineteenth and early twentieth centuries. International suffrage meetings brought activists together, like the 1902 Washington DC meeting between suffragists from Australia, Canada, Chile, England, Germany, Norway, Russia, Sweden, Turkey, and the United States.[11] Latin American women demanded not just political rights like suffrage, but labour rights like equal pay and maternity leave and social rights like public healthcare.[12] They converged in multiple regional meetings, like the Pan-American Women's Leadership Conference in Baltimore in 1922. In the Middle East, women leaders campaigning for suffrage, access to education, and reforms to marriage, divorce, and inheritance laws met at regional conferences in Beirut, Jerusalem, Damascus, Baghdad, Cairo, and Tehran between 1928 and 1938.[13] In Asia, Indian suffragists convened the All-Asian Women's Conference in Lahore in 1931. The Asian meeting stressed the 'western' feminist concerns applicable to Asian women – education and freedom of movement, for instance – but also added concerns related to the preservation of Asian cultures and traditions.[14]

Many women also joined the anti-fascist and peace movements formed during and after the First World War. At the Paris Peace Conference in 1919, French suffragists convened a parallel Inter-Allied Women's Conference (IAWC). Men were meeting to negotiate ending the First World War, and the IAWC wanted woman suffrage and women's fundamental rights in the home, in economy, and in society included in the Versailles peace treaty.[15] Women from the Americas, Europe, the Middle East, and Asia all attended the IAWC. They did not successfully persuade men leaders to mention women in the Treaty of Versailles, but they returned home even more committed. For the IAWC's non-western delegates, the cause of women's political and economic rights was woven into their participation in anti-colonial and nationalist movements. While Latin America had attained independence decades earlier, Middle Eastern and Asian women were seeking both political liberation and women's rights.[16] In Egypt, for instance, women returning from Paris participated in anti-colonial movements and women's movements. After Egypt's independence in 1922, they sought voting rights, equal access to secondary and tertiary education, and revisions to family law that would raise the marriage age and limit unilateral male divorce.[17]

Decades before Clinton spoke the immortalizing phrase 'women's rights are human rights', women's transnational advocacy networks were leveraging international meetings and regime transitions to make rights-based claims. Women advocates wanted women's rights to become constitutive parts of the postwar, postcolonial order. Transitions are moments of such significant rupture that they open opportunities for significant political change. Why not let men *and women* vote in a newly independent country? While advocates do not always succeed in influencing the transition – witness women's failure in Paris in 1919 – the momentous occasion means they must try. Women protagonists received another opportunity with the political rupture following the Second World War. As countries set out to create a new, durable international body to govern the globe, women knew that this international body would only support women's rights if women were included from the start.

Women at the UN's Founding

At the 1944 Dumbarton Oaks conference in Washington, DC, statesmen from the Big Four – the United States, the United Kingdom, the Soviet Union, and China – drafted a preliminary UN charter. No women were present and, perhaps unsurprisingly, the document contained not one word about women's rights or women's inclusion in the new global institution.[18] The following year, women comprised just six of the 850 delegates to the United Nations Conference on International Organization in San Francisco.[19] Three would fight to undo Dumbarton Oaks' oversight: Brazil's Bertha Lutz, the Dominican Republic's Minerva Bernardino, and Uruguay's Isabel Pinto de Vidal.

Alongside other veterans of the Pan-American women's movement, Lutz and colleagues had pioneered the use of international law to compel countries to protect women's rights. In the 1930s, they coauthored a Women's Rights Treaty, which read: 'The Contracting States agree that upon the ratification of this Treaty, men and women shall have equal rights throughout the territory subject to their respective jurisdictions'. They also produced a Women's Nationality Treaty, which forbade governments from revoking women's citizenship if they married non-nationals (at the time, men retained their citizenship upon marriage to non-citizens, but women did not). In Montevideo, Uruguay, at the Seventh International Meeting of American States, four countries signed the Women's Rights Treaty and all signed the Women's Nationality Treaty. Flush from these victories, Lutz – who had attended the 1922 Pan American Women's Leadership Conference and the 1933 Montevideo conference – said that Latin American feminists would 'be the most helpful in advancing women's rights' in San Francisco.[20]

Lutz, Bernardino, and Pinto de Vidal did not work alone. They found key allies among some delegations' technical advisors, especially Amalia de Castillo Ledón (Mexico) and Jessie Street (Australia). They drew further support from delegates and advisors committed to human rights. Delegates from third-world countries and NGO representatives dedicated to fighting racial, ethnic, and religious discrimination all saw human rights as critical to their fights against colonialism, imperialism, and racism. The leaders of the US National Association for the Advancement of Colored People (NAACP), for instance, became key supporters of Lutz's proposals. These advocates formed what Lutz called the 'gulf stream' of demands for justice at the San Francisco conference.[21] Just like the ocean current that flows up the Americas' eastern coast, activists from across the Western Hemisphere allied to insist that the San Francisco charter contain robust statements about human rights – including women's rights.

Specific UN charter passages are traced to their efforts.[22] The preamble, drafted by the Pan-American feminists and their allies and formally introduced by the Latin American delegations, ties human rights and women's rights together: 'We the people of the United Nations determined to reaffirm faith in fundamental human rights, in the dignity of the human person, in the equal rights of men and women and of Nations large and small.' Lutz and colleagues also secured that 'sex' would be among the protected characteristics listed: Article 55 reads that the United Nations shall promote 'universal respect for, and observance of, human rights and fundamental freedoms for all without distinction as to race, sex, language, or religion'. They also ensured that women could not easily be shut out of drafting again, with Article 8 reading: 'The United Nations shall place no restrictions on the eligibility of men and women to participate in any capacity and under conditions of equality in its principal and subsidiary organs.'

Finally, Pan-American feminists created the CSW. Lutz co-drafted the CSW proposal with Indian delegation head Arcot Ramaswami Mudaliar. Like other individuals and organizations engaged in anti-imperial struggles, Mudaliar saw the human rights framework as facilitating colonial resistance. Lutz and Mudaliar's proposal was formally introduced by the Brazil delegation and ultimately passed. The CSW would be located within the Economic and Social Commission (ECOSOC) and would prepare reports on 'the political, civil, and economic status and opportunity of women with special reference to discrimination and limitations placed upon them on account of their sex'. The following year, as the ECOSOC and the CSW organized, the CSW's formal mandate expanded to include 'promoting women's rights in political, economic, civil, social and educational fields' and making recommendations on 'urgent problems requiring immediate attention in the field of women's rights'.[23] When the commission convened in 1947, two of the original protagonists – Australia's Jessie Street and Mexico's Amalia de Castillo Ledón – became member-state representatives. Fifty years later, the CSW would begin monitoring implementation of the Beijing PfA.

The road to Mexico City

Global South women ensured that the United Nations' founding vision of human rights explicitly included women. Lutz and allies viewed incorporating the words 'women' and 'women's rights' as essential for repealing discriminatory laws. Just as with the Women's Nationality Treaty, which stipulated that countries' rules about how one gained and lost citizenship needed to apply to men *and women* equally, they viewed specifying 'women' as necessary for ensuring that women were not left behind. Yet not all women viewed saying 'women' and 'women's rights' as important. Some prominent US and British women, by contrast, feared that special mentions and specialized bodies such as the CSW would actually cleave women's rights from human rights and undermine women's ability to have their distinctive concerns addressed. This tension shaped the United Nations' initial years, especially as the new international body turned to writing the Universal Declaration of Human Rights (UDHR). Then US First Lady Eleanor Roosevelt presided over the mostly all-male drafting committee, but contended that 'human rights' included women and thus women needed no separate mention. The Pan-American feminists disagreed. Having reached a stalemate, Bernardino, de Castillo Ledón, Street, and others lobbied Indian activist Hansa Mehta, one of two women on the UDHR's drafting committee. Thanks to their efforts and Mehta's intervention, statements where 'man' or 'men' appeared as stand-ins for 'people' were revised to say 'human beings'. [24]

These tensions – where women disagreed about the universality of terms such as 'man' and 'human' or about attaining equality via recognizing women's sameness or difference – reflected larger divides among countries at the time. The CSW, like all other international bodies, would become an arena through which negotiating the issue at hand in fact meant navigating geopolitical divides. In the 1950s, for instance, debates on whether and how the CSW should call for equal pay for equal work became caught up in Cold War politics. Across the East, communism championed women's economic emancipation and sent millions of women into the workforce. US women viewed this wage labour not as emancipatory, but as compelled – and consequently opposed an equal pay for equal work resolution. Still, the CSW attained some early milestones, including the Convention on the Political Rights of Women in 1952, various conventions related to eliminating inequality in family law, and the Declaration on the Elimination of Discrimination against Women in 1967.

The CSW also unanimously advanced the IWY proposal in 1972, which included the provision for an international world conference on women. The initial push came from the Women's International Democratic Federation (WIDF), a WINGO with consultative status to the CSW. The WIDF represented Eastern Bloc countries, and its counterpart before the CSW was the Western Bloc-led International Council of Women (ICW). The organizations' rivalry notwithstanding, the IWY proposal received East–West support: the CSW's Romanian delegation advanced the IWY proposal and the Finnish delegation seconded it. The proposal then advanced to ECOSOC and then to the UN General Assembly (GA), where different countries advanced competing proposals and wrangled over the form, format, and location of a conference.

Ultimately, ECOSOC and then the GA approved the IWY to operate under three overarching priorities: equality, development, and peace.

This greenlight did not, however, settle the question of the conference. As the preparatory process unfolded from 1972 to 1974, wrangling continued. The choice of location proved a major challenge. Hosting offers from countries not clearly aligned with the Cold War's East–West polarities – such as Australia, Colombia, Mexico, and Iran – brought challenges. On the one hand, hosting the conference in neither the West nor the East avoided conflating gender equality with either democracy or communism. On the other hand, less wealthy nations faced considerable logistical and financial challenges, as well as their own imperfect records of democracy and human rights. When the GA approved Mexico's bid, many Mexican feminists reacted with outrage, viewing President Luis Echevarría's manoeuvre as capturing undue gender equality acclaim.[25] After all, Echevarría led a one-party state that managed dissent by either co-opting interest groups or resorting to outright oppression. Yet with the decision made, feminists across the globe would seize the moment.

The UN Decade for Women

The CSW may have persuaded the United Nations to declare the IWY in order to assess progress on women's rights, but that did not mean that the United Nations prioritized women's issues. The United Nations under-resourced the IWY and the Mexico City conference from the start, allocating just eight staff members to plan the conference, in comparison with the 125 allocated to the 1974 Bucharest World Population Conference.[26] Money would come from a UN 'voluntary fund', to which member states but also individuals could donate. Advocates scrambled to raise money from countries, wealthy individuals, and everyday women, giving fundraising a 'bake sale' character.[27] Finnish diplomat Helvi Sipilä – who had seconded the CSW resolution and would ultimately chair the Mexico City conference – suggested that every Finnish woman give one mark.[28] As women saw it, the United Nations' under-resourcing reflected the body's overall failure to take women's interests seriously (perhaps fulfilling the fears of those women who had feared that special mentions of women would actually result in deprioritizing their interests). Yet planning for the IWY drew attention to the United Nations' neglect and galvanized women even more. The United Nations may have intended to reduce the women's year and its conference to a historical footnote, but this strategy backfired. As UN staffer and IWY planner Susan Jane Kedgley observed, '[t]he UN made the mistake of discussing something that has grassroots interest and support – IWY could go down in herstory as the only UN-proclaimed year anyone can remember'.[29]

The Mexico City conference, convened from 19 June to 2 July 1975, featured two events: the official meeting of delegates representing 133 countries and the parallel NGO forum, where 6,000 civil society leaders and members convened to lobby delegates and to meet among themselves. True to Kedgley's predictions, NGO forum attendees marked the largest number of non-official participants attending a UN world conference to date.[30] The delegates would confirm a draft plan of action previously hammered out at the United Nations. Through these pre-conference interactions, countries across the globe – from the United States to Jamaica to Iran – tried to place their imprint on the document. The policy debates once again reflected the geopolitical conflicts of the day. For instance, would development be framed primarily in economic terms, leading to policy recommendations centred on increasing women's role in the industrialized workforce? Or would it – as some Global South countries and humanitarian organizations insisted – also conceptualize development in human and moral terms and recommend women's roles in disarmament and decolonization?[31]

These and other debates continued in Mexico City, especially in the lively NGO forum. Some policy areas, such as increasing women's political participation and ending sexism in education, did generate agreement. But others, such as prostitution and gay rights, generated conflict. Some disputes were existential, such as the ever-present disagreement on whether gender equality meant erasing differences among men and women or working within them. Others revolved less around the principle and more around whose perspectives should frame the issue. For example, most attendees agreed that women shouldered disproportionate unpaid care burdens in the home – but Global South women wanted to add a capitalist critique recognizing poor women's exploitation as underpaid domestic workers. Disunity among women was high, but historian Jocelyn Olcott argues that such spirited clashes were explicitly sought. As Olcott explains, the Mexico City gatherings 'had been designed precisely to encourage First World participants to listen to Third World participants . . . Forcing these encounters had been the highest priority for everyone involved in organizing these events, and participants consistently reported encounters across divides of ideology, experience and geopolitics.'[32] An NGO forum event on health and nutrition, for instance, featured a West German government minister, a Mexican nutrition specialist, a Peruvian gynaecologist, and the chief nursing officer for the Nigerian healthy ministry. For 14 days, diverse women cacophonously argued about politics and policy.

The global conflicts that divided NGO forum participants similarly divided member-state delegates. The resultant Mexico City Declaration and Plan of Action, written by delegates but with little activist input, attempted to satisfy everyone. Articles cover all aspects of women's lives. They reflect the imprint of first-world feminists – who emphasized ending sexism in the workforce and society – but also the imprint of third-world countries – which tied women's advancement to 'ending colonialism, neocolonialism, imperialism, foreign domination and occupation, zionism, apartheid, racial discrimination [and] the acquisition of land by force'.[33] Countries also appended resolutions about current conflicts, such as statements acknowledging Palestinian women's 'right to return to their homes and property from which they have been displaced'.[34] Addressing the NGO forum, conference secretary-general Helvi Sipilä stressed activists' role in carrying the Plan of Action forward. Sipilä said: 'The UN is nothing when it comes to implementation. We cannot change your laws, your education, your economic plans. You are the ones who elect people to the parliaments and the municipal councils where all the decisions are made . . . Let us create a network of women for the future. This is not the end – it is the beginning.'[35]

Sipilä's word proved prophetic. Reviewing first-hand accounts from delegates, NGO forum participants, and journalists, Jocelyn Olcott finds that women from all corners of the globe described the Mexico City conference in rapturous terms. Participants remembered not the disunity and the acrimony, but the momentum and the energy. In attendees' own words, the IWY became 'the greatest consciousness raising event in history'.[36] Returning home, women formed new NGOs, developed alternative feminist media, and launched street actions and policy campaigns. From women's environmental organizations in Kenya to women micro-entrepreneurs' self-help groups in India, groups dedicated to women's interests boomed. Women activists built networks at home – but also abroad. For example, women peace activists from the United States, Australia, and Thailand travelled to attend the 1976 Women's Peace March organized by women from Northern Ireland and the Republic of Ireland.[37]

Back at the United Nations, the General Assembly endorsed the Mexico City Declaration and Plan of Action and proclaimed 1976–1985 as the UN Decade for Women. The GA invited member states to declare one day a 'United Nations Day for Women's Rights and International Peace', which led to 8 March as International Women's Day (a day that still serves as a focal point for international and domestic activism).[38] The GA also institutionalized the voluntary fund, which became the UN Development Fund for Women (UNIFEM), located within the UN Development Programme (UNDP). Momentum also built around an international bill of rights for women, contemplated by the CSW as early as the 1960s, but given new life by its endorsement in Mexico City. Longtime CSW members Annie Jiagge of Ghana and Leticia Ramos Shahani of the Philippines had authored earlier versions of the text, which had advanced through ECOSOC and the GA in rough parallel to the IWY initiative.[39] Following Mexico City, a working group within the CSW – led by Shahani – revitalized the document and reworked the draft. The final document became the 1979 CEDAW.

A Second World Conference on Women marked the IWD's midway point, convened in Copenhagen in 1980. At the official meeting, member states presented CEDAW and adopted a Programme of Action. At the NGO forum, 7,000 people gathered, more than in Mexico City. The Copenhagen Declaration and Programme of Action followed the Mexico City approach by incorporating all countries' priorities, but added concrete recommendations.[40] These specific steps included adopting national strategies to improve the status of women 'at the national, local, and family levels'; setting 'quantitative and qualitative targets' that should 'especially seek to remove the gap between the attainments of men and women, between rural and urban women, and between all women in underprivileged population groups'; and establishing 'national machinery preferably at the highest level of government, where appropriate, should be established'.[41] Most notably, the Copenhagen conference report laid out a clear definition of what gender equality meant: not only the elimination of legal discrimination, but also the achievement of equal rights, responsibilities, and opportunities for women in development.[42]

The UN Decade for Women closed with the Third World Conference on Women in Nairobi in 1985. Attendance marked the explosion in women's organizing since Mexico City: 157 country delegations (up from 133) and 14,000 NGO attendees (double the number from Copenhagen). The Nairobi conference occurred during a period of global austerity, with neoliberalism drastically reducing all countries' investments in social services. Against this backdrop, Nairobi witnessed what scholar Sarah de Jong calls an important breakthrough moment in North–South cooperation. The high presence of African women, the greater presence of Global North women of colour, and the shifting fortunes of Global North women under neoliberalism combined, opening new space for fruitful dialogue.[43] Global North women, faced with economic retraction at home, became more receptive to Global South women's argument that fighting patriarchy could not be separated from fighting economic inequality. For their part, de Jong recounts, Global South women became more receptive to Global North women's emphasis on fighting sexism, sexual harassment, and violence against women (priorities that some Global South women previously had discounted relative to fighting imperialism and colonization). Famed Indian economist Bina Agarwal, who participated in the NGO forum, described the mood in Nairobi as 'celebratory'.[44]

The official member-state convening produced the Nairobi Forward-Looking Strategies for the Advancement of Women (FLS), again emphasizing the three themes of equality, development, and peace. The Nairobi FLS expanded on the Copenhagen conference report's definition of gender equality, worth quoting at length:

> Equality is both a goal and a means whereby individuals are accorded equal treatment under the law and equal opportunities to enjoy their rights and to develop their potential talents and skills so that they can participate in national political, economic, social and cultural development and can benefit from its results. For women in particular, equality means the realization of rights that have been denied as a result of cultural, institutional, behavioral and attitudinal discrimination. Equality is important for development

and peace because national and global inequities perpetuate themselves and increase tensions of all types.[45]

This sweeping definition transformed the FLS into a big tent, encompassing nearly all policy demands related to women's rights, from guaranteeing women's 'basic right to control their own fertility' to eliminating family codes that treat adult, married women as minors with fewer rights than adult, married men.[46] Taking the documents from Mexico City, Copenhagen, and Nairobi as a whole, the UN Decade for Women produced feminist blueprints that incorporated countries' and activists' diverse and disparate concerns.

Women's rights are human rights

In a virtuous circle, the UN Decade for Women created transnational feminist advocacy networks, and transnational feminist advocacy networks shaped the UN Decade for Women. Organizing continued after the decade closed. Reflecting on US feminism in the 1990s, historian Lisa Levenstein writes: 'The movement had grown so rapidly it was impossible to keep track of all the organizations and initiatives.'[47] Her description captures developments elsewhere, with feminist organizing increasing in every region.[48] Social scientist Sonia Álvarez called this moment Latin America's feminist NGO 'boom' (though not without worry that activists' increasing professionalization would inhibit grassroots movements' autonomy).[49] Internationally, the FLS had called for a Fourth World Conference on Women, to be held before 2000. Plans did not initially materialize, however, as the burgeoning number of feminist advocacy groups focused on preparing for other UN conferences in the queue: the 1992 Conference on Environment and Development in Rio de Janeiro, the 1993 Human Rights Conference in Vienna, and the 1994 International Conference on Population and Development in Cairo. The CSW finally called for the Fourth World Conference on Women in 1993, slated for Beijing from 4 to 15 September 1995.

The Rio, Vienna, and Cairo conferences proved important precursors to Beijing. One WINGO formed in Nairobi's aftermath – the Women's Environmental and Development Organization (WEDO), founded by US congresswoman Bella Abzug – pioneered the concept of the Women's Caucus. Since Rio, Vienna, and Cairo were not dedicated women's conferences, feminists knew that their inclusion was not guaranteed. The Women's Caucus created a formal mechanism to bridge the NGO forum and the official convening: each conference day, NGO forum participants, representing both Global South and Global North countries, convened and presented their demands to member-state delegates. At Cairo, the Women's Caucus met not just during the conference, but during every international and national preparatory meeting, giving women activists unprecedented influence over the draft and final plans of action. Their organizing changed the conversation. For example, while the feminist blueprints to date underscored women's reproductive choices, mainstream approaches to population and development still promoted poverty amelioration via controlling third-world births. Thanks to the Women's Caucus, the final Cairo Programme of Action abandoned the population control framework guiding development. The Cairo Programme of Action stated: 'Advancing gender equality and equity and the empowerment of women, and the elimination of all kinds of violence against women, and ensuring women's ability to control their own fertility, are cornerstones of population and development-related programmes'.[50]

While Cairo advanced the normative framework undergirding women's reproductive rights, Vienna reiterated the connection between women's rights and human rights. For women activists, violence against women (VAW) was *the* link between human rights and women's rights. VAW had emerged as a consensus issue in Nairobi, as Global North and Global South women began sketching commonalities across their different fights, from Indian women protesting dowry deaths, to Middle Eastern women working against female genital mutilation, to US women denouncing rape and murder.[51] VAW, women activists realized, stemmed from women's shared experiences of oppression. Yet VAW was neglected by male-led human rights organizations, who argued that such abuses were not human rights crimes because they were private crimes, perpetrated by individuals and not by governments. Feminists across the globe pushed back. In 1988, Filipina women fighting the Ferdinand Marcos dictatorship launched a Women's Rights Are Human Rights campaign, asking how their men colleagues could fight against torture without taking seriously the torture women experienced at the hands of men. In 1991, founder of the US Center for Women's Global Leadership (CWGL) Charlotte Bunch raised funds for the first Women's Global Leadership Institute, which brought together anti-VAW activists from across the globe. This disparate group of women left New Jersey's Rutgers University with a plan: promote women's rights as human rights at the upcoming Vienna conference.[52]

To do so, women at Vienna staged a Global Tribunal on Violations of Women's Human Rights, organized by the CWGL and other WINGOs. The tribunal featured testimonies from women representing 25 different countries, who described surviving human rights abuses ranging from domestic violence to political persecutions. The tribunal was convened as if it were an actual court, with women lawyers representing different regions and four international judges who heard the testimonies and issued judgments.[53] The tribunal then presented its judgments and recommendations to the official delegates – alongside a petition with 270,000 signatures demanding human rights for women. When presenting the tribunal's results to the delegates, Women's Caucus member Mary Kazunga of Zambia called for a minute of silence. Charlotte Bunch and Niamh O'Rielly recall: 'With her stopwatch held high in the air, she brought the delegates to a standstill and then asked them to remember all the women around the world who had died or been badly injured by domestic violence during that minute.'[54] As a direct result, the Vienna Declaration's preamble asserted that 'the human rights of women and of the girl-child are an inalienable, integral, and indivisible part of universal human rights'.[55]

Clinton's now famous Beijing keynote elevated this victory two years later. The emphasis on women's rights as human rights deliberately built on feminist activists' international campaigns, consciously pushing forward the framework that feminists developed via national struggles against dictatorships and political oppression.[56] Clinton introduced a list of gendered abuses, each prefaced with the same phrase, 'it is a violation of human rights when women. . .'. Her list included denial of family planning, forced abortions and sterilizations, trafficking and forced prostitution, genital mutilation, domestic violence, and wartime rape. She wrapped up with: 'If there is one message that echoes forth from this conference, it is that human rights are women's rights and women's rights are human rights.'[57] The significance of the US representative's saying these words cannot be overstated. By 1995, feminist transnational advocacy networks had socialized not just each other, but powerful countries into recognizing what their Pan-American predecessors had recognized 50 years prior: women's rights are human rights. Clinton's speech brought women's inclusion at the United Nations full circle.

It is this framing that makes the 1995 World Conference on Women and the resultant Beijing PfA the most important referent for the global women's movement today. The previous world conferences on women had located gender equality within economic and human development, but Beijing tied gender equality to human rights. This pivot happened at the largest convening to date, with 189 government delegations and 35,000 NGO forum participants (a five-fold increase from Mexico City) converging on this understanding. Still, like in previous conferences, consensus coexisted alongside struggle. Geopolitics continued to shape debates, as women were united by their common experiences of neoliberalism and economic austerity but divided by region-specific crises, like the collapse of communism in the East. Still, the balance of power had shifted to outside the West. The consensuses achieved on women's human rights in general, but also on women's specific rights, like sexual and reproductive rights and inheritance and property rights, 'were forced primarily by delegates who were neither white, nor liberal'.[58] The consensus achieved on women's human rights, while perhaps obvious in 2025, marked a radical reframing of gender equality for 1995, one crafted by Latin American, Caribbean, Pacific, and African countries.

The Beijing PfA also offered a more coherent, succinct vision than its predecessor documents, coming in at a modest 132 pages (by comparison with its predecessor documents, at over 200 pages). Its mission statement (re)introduces human rights language, reading '[e]quality between women and men is a matter of human rights and a condition for social justice and is also a necessary and fundamental prerequisite for equality development and peace'[59] and reaffirms the 'fundamental principle set forth in the Vienna Declaration' and repeats that 'the human rights of women and the girl-child are an inalienable, integral, and indivisible part of human rights'.[60] Most centrally, the PfA organizes its recommended actions into 12 'critical areas of concern', an advance on its predecessor blueprints' kitchen-sink approach. The policy areas are: women and poverty; education and training of women; women and health; violence against women; women and armed conflict; women and the economy; women in power and decision-making; institutional mechanisms for the advancement of women; human rights of women; women and the media; women and the environment; and the girl child. The PfA also builds on the FLS's inclusion of specific steps, such as calling on governments to adopt national action plans that outline their plans for PfA implementation.[61]

With no fifth world conference on women (see Chapter 9), the PfA remains the globe's guiding feminist blueprint. The CSW monitors implementation and has marked each five-year anniversary via special convenings. The first five-year review, in 2000, occurred via a special session of the UN General Assembly. In 2025, the Beijing +30 process entailed countries and regions undertaking national and regional reviews, respectively. Women activists used the Beijing +30 framing to take stock and set new targets. Documents submitted to the CSW illuminate how the process of international norm setting and domestic policy change works. To mark Beijing +30, Australia, for instance, reported introducing new paid leave for those experiencing domestic violence.[62] Samoa highlighted its 2023 revisions to labour laws requiring equal pay for men and women.[63] Mozambique described significant progress on girls' education.[64] The international review process thus constitutes another mechanism through which feminist blueprints identify targets and spur policy change.

Women, peace, and security

The world conferences on women ceased after Beijing, but feminist blueprint-making did not. The adoption of UNSCR 1325 follows the pattern of collaboration between member states and transnational feminist networks. This process occurred within perhaps the United Nations' most important decision-making body, the UN Security Council (UNSC).

The UNSC consists of five permanent members with veto power – Russia, China, the United States, the United Kingdom, and France – and ten elected members. The latter are distributed regionally, occupy the council for two-year terms, and lack veto power. As such, the UNSC's balance of power tilts towards the permanent Big Five members while offering less powerful countries opportunities to exert some influence.

The UNSC mainly responds to countries' threats or breaches of international peace, primarily by issuing sanctions and deploying peacekeeping missions. As such, the UNSC historically takes a militaristic, masculine approach to security that has invited feminist critique. From failing to prosecute rape as a war crime to excluding women from peace negotiations, traditional security approaches neglect women's and girls' gendered experiences during war. They also neglect women's right to participate in – and have their needs addressed by – reconciliation and reconstruction.

At a 1998 CSW meeting, women from conflict zones met to assess the implementation of the PfA's critical area of women and armed conflict. They coalesced on advocating for a UNSC resolution on the topic.[65] At the 2000 CSW meeting, activists formalized an NGO Working Group on Women, Peace, and Security, which would draft and promote the resolution's passage.[66] Though the core NGOs were based in New York and London, the working group included Femmes Africa Solidarité as a founding member.[67] Coordinating figures bridged North and South, including women peace activists from conflict-affected countries such as Sierra Leone's Isha Dyfan.[68]

The Beijing +5 process helped mobilize member states. In 2000, Namibia presided over the GA (and thus the Beijing +5 process) and was in the second year of its two-year term as an elected UNSC member. In its first year, Namibia successfully sponsored the first-ever Security Council resolution on children and armed conflict. Namibia reportedly wanted a similar history-making resolution for its second year.

Then Namibian Minister of Women Affairs and Child Welfare Netumbo Nandi-Ndaitwah is credited with conceiving that Namibia could sponsor a UNSC resolution on women. She reports drawing inspiration from her own country's role in promoting women in peacebuilding.[69] Indeed, the UN peacekeeping mission to Namibia had been recognized as among the first to include women in significant numbers, with women comprising 40 to 50 per cent of staff.[70] Namibia's idea gained steam in May 2000, two months after the CSW's March 2000 meeting, when the capital Windhoek hosted a seminar assessing women's equal participation in UN peacekeeping missions. The seminar produced the Windhoek Declaration and the Namibia Plan of Action, which stated that women had been denied inclusion in peacebuilding and that gender equality 'must permeate the entire mission, at all levels, thus ensuring the participation of women and men as equal partners and beneficiaries in all aspects of the peace process'.[71]

The NGO Working Group formed an alliance with Namibia, alongside other supportive member states holding UNSC elected positions at the time – namely, Bangladesh, Jamaica, and Canada. Two women from Namibia's UN mission led the drafting and negotiations, Selma Ndeyapo Ashipala-Musavyi and Aina Iiyambo. They collaborated extensively with and relied on research and evidence provided by the NGO Working Group and by UNIFEM.[72] The UNSC scheduled the resolution's debate for late October. The day prior, Jamaica's UN Ambassador Patricia Durrant chaired an Arria Formula meeting designed to apply pressure on UNSC members. In Arria Formula meetings, UNSC members invite interlocutors to informal and confidential expert sessions. Durrant's speaking roster featured women peace activists and NGO leaders from conflict-affected countries, including Dyfan, Luz Méndez from the National Union of Guatemalan Women, Faiza Jama Mohamed from the Africa Office of Equality Now, and Inonge Mbikusita-Lewanika of the Organization of African Women's Peace Movements. Dyfan spoke about the sexual violence committed in Sierra Leone not just by men combatants but by UN peacekeepers themselves. Méndez spoke about peace accords' needs for women's support and thus their imperative to incorporate women's voices.[73]

The UNSCR 1325 on Women, Peace, and Security passed unanimously on 31 October 2000. The resolution is a succinct four-page document that locates its motivation in the Beijing PfA alongside other, more specific declarations about women and peace, such as the Windhoek Declaration. Its 18 provisions include exhortations for member states to increase women's representation in all 'institutions and mechanisms for the prevention, management and resolution of conflict'. The UN Secretary-General is urged to appoint more women as special envoys and to expand women's role in UN peacekeeping operations.[74] Overall, UNSCR 1325 emphasizes three themes: women's *participation* in peace and security; women's *protection* (especially but not only from sexual violence); and *mainstreaming gender* into all peace and peacebuilding efforts. Despite verbs such as 'urge' and 'recommend', UNSC resolutions are binding on all UN members.

To further institutionalize the UNSCR 1325 mandate, beginning in 2004, the UNSC required all member states to produce National Action Plans (NAPs). Over 60 countries have filed NAPs, including those currently or previously affected by conflict (e.g. Ukraine and Bosnia) alongside those participating in peacekeeping (e.g. Belgium and Austria). Regional governance organizations such as the AU, ASEAN, the League of Arab States, the Pacific Islands Forum, and the European Union have crafted regional action plans. Once again, these documents serve as important touchpoints in activists' ongoing efforts to translate UNSCR 1325's objectives into reality. Further bolstering the UNSC's WPS agenda are an additional seven UNSCR resolutions issued between 2008 and 2015 that reaffirm the UNSCR 1325's original principles.

As with all feminist blueprints, realizing UNSCR 1325 is complex. Some critics suggest that UNSCR 1325 reifies rather than challenges militarized forms of peacekeeping.[75] Echoing Audre Lorde's caution that the master's tools cannot dismantle the master's house, these feminists see policing as fundamentally incompatible with peace. Other critiques centre on whether local women's organizations can meaningfully influence NAPs, whether the protection pillar cements perceptions of women as exclusively victims, and whether the mainstreaming pillar falls victim to tick-box exercises wherein countries promote women without substantively empowering them. Some argue that even tick-box exercises fall short: for example, only one woman participated in Yemen's 2019 Peace Talks and the resultant accords contained no gender-sensitive language.[76]

Yet advocates highlight that UNSCR 1325 and its follow-up resolutions help institutionalize and operationalize WPS ideals. For example, Nepal invited war widows' groups to consult on the country's NAP, and the resultant document became the first NAP to expressly address war widows' needs and rights.[77] Similarly, Heidi Hudson concludes, on the basis of her analysis of NAPs in Kenya, Liberia, Nigeria, and Uganda, that the documents' mix of radical and conservative visions of 'women' and 'gender' is not a failure, but an advantage: ambiguity allows UN gender officials and African women's organizations to push more feminist interpretations over time.[78] In Colombia, UNSCR 1325 guided grassroots feminists organizing during the peace process. A network of nine women's groups, calling themselves Coalition 1325, convened a National Summit of Women for Peace in the capital Bogotá in 2013, the year before the commencement of the official peace negotiations in Havana, Cuba. The summit successfully pressured negotiators into creating a gender subcommittee in Havana.[79] The 2016 Colombian accords became the most gender-inclusive peace agreement produced to date.

Women and the United Nations in the new millennium

The action plans from the first three world conferences on women, CEDAW, the Beijing PfA, and UNSCR 1325 provide the women's rights era with its feminist scaffolding. The latter three constitute the guiding documents of UN Women, which replaced UNIFEM in 2010.[80] UN Women's creation elevated women and gender equality within the UN apparatus. Whereas UNIFEM was a subsidiary of UNDP and could not even distribute its own funds without UNDP approval, the executive director of UN Women is a UN Under-Secretary-General who reports directly to the UN Secretary-General.[81] Some critics lament that UN Women has moved away from UNIFEM's emphasis on development, which meant designing and implementing projects across the globe, and towards the more technical work of articulating international norms, writing policy toolkits, and conducting and disseminating research on best practices.[82] Yet UN Women's regional and country offices still provide direct support to women in politics, NGOs, and social movements via convenings, capacity building, training, expert consultations, and research.[83]

Upon their adoption in 2015, the SDGs became UN Women's fourth guiding document.[84] Here, too, feminist transnational advocacy played a key role. Since the early 2000s, the United Nations had granted 'major groups' – international alliances of civil society organizations – access to official UN meetings and negotiations. The Women's Major Group, formed in 1992 for the Rio Conference on Environment and Development, focused on injecting women's rights into the 2012 United Nations Conference on Sustainable Development (known informally as Rio +20).[85] This conference fed into the SDG development process. The Women's Major Group gained access to the high-level policy forums and open working groups, meetings in which national governments hammered out the new global development goals.[86] The Women's Major Group's objective was fully transformational: their guiding statement read: 'We do not want to be mainstreamed into a polluted stream. We call for deep and structural changes to existing global systems of power, decision-making, and resource sharing.'[87] Ultimately, SDG 5 includes nine targets and fourteen indicators for countries to achieve. Though some feminist critics argue that 'governance by indicators' reduces gender equality to quantitative metrics that countries can easily game, Sara Rose Taylor finds that UN Women implements a multi-method and nuanced approach to SDG assessment and measurement.[88] UN Women, she argues, seeks data and stories that honour the human rights framework, acknowledge women's structural discrimination, and critique political systems or cultural beliefs that justify or ignore women's oppression.

The processes of redacting and utilizing feminist blueprints thus does not unfold seamlessly. Importantly, however, Global South actors enjoy considerable influence in international fora, both historically and today. After all, it was Latin American women who ensured women's inclusion in the UN charter. It was collaboration between Global South and Global North women that, 50 years later, enshrined the women's human rights approach that informs the Vienna Declaration and the Beijing PfA. And it was Global South women, especially women from conflict-affected zones, who conceived of and lobbied for UNSCR 1325. Finally, it was Global South women who brought these ideas back home, shaping regional feminist blueprints like the AU's Maputo Protocol. As historians Elise Dietrichson and Fatima Sator argue, acknowledging Global South women's influence over feminist blueprints moves beyond a superficial dichotomy of the North's power and the South's powerlessness and inspires 'a more global ownership to gender equality'.[89]

Ultimately, international governance organizations, and specifically the United Nations, provide important platforms through which women's rights advocates articulate their aspirations for a better world. Reflecting on the Vienna and Beijing conferences, Charlotte Bunch suggested that the process mattered as much as the resultant documents: 'it is about women building a movement and utilizing the space that the UN brought to us . . . to affect ideas and policies more broadly'.[90] In the contemporary era, UN Women fosters this space. The agency sustains lobbying at the United Nations while supporting gender equality advocacy across the globe, adding what Rose Taylor calls a 'feminist voice' that unites actors within, adjacent to, and outside the United Nations system.[91] The stories in this chapter indeed reveal the global character of these voices and these aspirations, challenging countermovements' claims that international gender equality norms undermine their countries' cultures and histories. The women's rights era shows that ideas about gender equality are very much homegrown.

THREE

Political Regimes and Constitutional Rights

Until 2018, women in Saudi Arabia could not drive cars. Women long had sought the right to drive, however. In the 1990s, women in Riyadh drove in protest; they were arrested, their passports confiscated and their employment terminated.[1] In 2007, women's rights activist Wajeha al-Huwaider presented the Saudi king with a petition to lift the driving ban.[2] In 2008, she posted a video of herself driving, saying: 'Many women in this society are able to drive cars, and many of our male relatives don't mind.'[3] In 2011, she filmed a fellow activist, Manal Al-Sharif, behind the wheel and again helped circulate the video online. The video shows Al-Sharif driving, accompanied by al-Huwaider and a male companion, Ahmed. As she drives, Al-Sharif tells al-Huwaider and Ahmed: 'I'd like to get my son a treat.' The video then includes Al-Sharif's grocery store visit.[4] Two days later, Al-Sharif was arrested. Her drive and subsequent arrest attracted international attention but no policy change, and the women who defied the driving ban after Al-Sharif were also arrested. Six years later, in 2017, Saudi Crown Prince Mohammed bin Salman announced that women would be allowed to drive.

The crown prince's pronouncement suggests that Saudi women's campaign eventually worked. According to this book's framework, advocacy led to reform. Women applied pressure on the Saudi government, leveraging international ideas about equality while still recognizing local norms. Al-Huwaider stressed that men 'do not mind' their women relatives' exercise of autonomy. Al-Sharif's drive complied with Saudi Arabia's male guardianship system (her friend Ahmed came along) and Al-Sharif executed a stereotypically feminine task (getting her son a treat). The government eventually responded. Mohammed bin Salman made an on-paper change expanding women's social mobility and opportunity within a highly patriarchal society. Researchers Inmaculada Macias-Alonso, HaRyung Kim, and Alessandra L. González found that lifting the driving ban facilitated women's access to employment, generating a virtuous circle wherein women's extra income outweighed family members' negative perceptions of their driving.[5] More permissive norms allowing women to drive and work thus co-evolved. Saudi women spoke positively about their newfound independence. One commented: 'It's very exciting. I feel more independent because I can go to my work by myself, and come back by myself.'[6]

Other observers doubt, however, that Saudi women actually emerged victorious when faced with an autocratic government. After all, authoritarian leaders like Mohammed bin Salman, son of the king and recognized as the de facto leader, do not need to respond to activist pressure. The sceptical argument holds that the crown prince's decision to lift the driving ban does little to recognize Saudi women as rights bearers. Sceptics make two points. First, prominent women's rights activists were arrested *after* the 2017 proclamation, including many driving activists (except for Al-Sharif, who by this time lived in Australia).[7] The activists remained imprisoned after the 2018 lifting of the ban. Many were tortured.[8] This state violence constituted a significant warning to Saudi women openly challenging the patriarchal political system.

Second, the crown prince's decision formed part of his Vision2030 agenda, a plan to modernize Saudi Arabia by opening the economy and attracting foreign business. This agenda implies that lifting the driving ban constitutes a cynical gesture, one aimed at making Saudi Arabia appear more modern and thus more palatable to the outside world. The crown prince's calculus points to *genderwashing*, government leaders' use of gender equality reforms to give their regimes a veneer of egalitarianism they may not necessarily deserve. Elin Bjarnegård and Pär Zetterberg argue that autocrats especially gain from genderwashing, as they leverage the international norms connecting gender equality to democracy to make their regime seem not just more egalitarian, but more democratic than it actually is.[9] Autocrats, then, face strong incentives to adopt gender equality reforms, but such changes might not come with any willpower for carrying them out. Imprisoning women's rights activists after lifting the ban bolsters arguments that lifting the driving ban offered mere window dressing. So do the practical barriers that women face to actually getting their license, including expensive tests affordable only to privileged Saudi women, alongside the persistence of the male guardianship system that affects all women. Together, these rights violations give the lie to the accolades piled on the Saudi royals for their (supposedly) newfound enlightenment about women's rights.

A similar two-sided coin appears when assessing women's inclusion in government. As part of their democratic transitions, many post-conflict countries adopted gender quotas, measures that set aside certain proportions of candidacies or parliamentary seats for women. Rwanda constitutes one well-known case. The country's civil war began in 1990 and culminated with genocide against the Tutsi population in 1994. Following the peace settlement, all political parties adopted gender quotas in some form. The Rwandan Patriotic Front (RPF), which now dominates post-conflict electoral politics, has used gender quotas to bring record numbers of women into government. In the first post-conflict elections of 2003, women attained 48.8 per cent of seats in the lower house.[10] That same year, the parliament approved a new constitution, which mandates that women hold at least 30 per cent of seats in all elected decision-making bodies. The constitutional gender quota – alongside other gender equality provisions – entered because women's civil society organizations such as Collectifs Pro Femmes / Twese Hamwe liaised with the Women's Parliamentary Group and the constitutional drafting commission to ensure the inclusion of women's rights provisions.[11] In 2008, with the new constitution in force, women's presence in the lower house increased to 56.3 per cent, which made Rwanda the first country in the world to attain a majority-female legislature.[12] Rwandan women MPs also passed other women's rights laws, including statutes equalizing inheritance and property ownership between men and women and sanctioning gender-based violence and workplace harassment.[13]

President Paul Kagame's RPF clearly exceeds the constitutional targets for women's parliamentary representation. In 2025, Rwandan women held 63.8 per cent of parliamentary seats, the highest in the world.[14] Yet Rwanda's democratic transition has not succeeded. Expert Jennie Burnet explains: 'The RPF orchestrates elections, suppresses the independent media, and retains control over most civil-society organizations. While the parliament is majority female, most of these women are card-carrying members of the RPF or its coalition partners . . . Thus most of these women owe allegiance to the RPF rather than to the constituencies who elected them.'[15] In other words, since Rwandan women parliamentarians owe their position to the RPF and ultimately to Kagame, their loyalty overrides their legislative independence and initiative: they themselves have become the window dressing.[16] On this reading, Rwanda offers another instance of autocratic genderwashing. Women's presence gives Rwanda a democratic veneer, allowing Kagame to cement Rwanda's image as a gender-equality pioneer among African nations while drawing attention away from electoral fraud, corruption, and his own refusal to cede power.[17]

The Saudi Arabia and Rwanda stories capture key tensions in the relationship between women's advocacy for gender equality, on the one hand, and government responsiveness, on the other. What factors tip governments into making women's rights reforms? The fact that governments, particularly autocratic ones, undertake genderwashing raises further questions about leaders' commitment to gender equality. How should researchers assess leaders' motivations: does a principled commitment to gender equality not matter, so long as the reform is adopted, or does window dressing transform adoption into a farce? Whether Saudi Arabia's lifting of the driving ban and Rwanda's gender equality milestones constitute a genuine or a pyrrhic victory depends on how researchers and observers weigh strategy against principles. Those sceptical about leaders' underlying commitment rightly point out that words on paper are cheap, and that domestic and international audiences should not be duped into praising governments that say one thing, but do another. Audiences especially should not be fooled when the governments are autocracies, which by definition hold a terrible record on human rights.

Governments may thus pursue feminist blueprints' policy objectives for their own ends. This chapter explores this proposition, considering when, how, and why governments respond to women activists' domestic policy campaigns. The chapter begins with a primer on government design and how political scientists classify political regimes (meaning, how they distinguish between democracies and autocracies). The chapter then turns to the dynamics underlying policy adoption. The main takeaway is that genderwashing remains common in democratic and autocratic regimes alike. Few leaders adopt gender equality reforms only because they hold principled commitments to gender equality. All political regimes resist international norms and women's advocacy for some time, *until* women's demands align with leaders' strategies and incentives. Shifts in objectives, like the desire to attain foreign approval or attract new voters, open windows of opportunity for policy reform. Women's rights advocates will seize the moment because, window dressing or not, inscribing the reform on paper moves the status quo and establishes a vision for the future. The chapter concludes by examining one key way advocates leveraged opportunities during the women's rights era: in the constitution-writing processes that occurred as part of the era's democratization wave. By gaining seats and voices at the drafting tables, women could ensure that political regimes' foundational documents recognize women as citizens, as rights bearers, and as full and equal members of the polity.

Governments, regimes, and rights

How governments make decisions about policy depends on how they arrange themselves, meaning which institutions of political authority exist, which powers are accorded to each institution and its leaders, and the rules according to which each institution operates, including rules governing how leaders are chosen and removed. Governments usually divide power horizontally, across some number of national decision-making institutions, and vertically, by some number of subunits, such as provinces and municipalities. These divisions matter for how activists pressure from the outside and how decision-makers enact change from the inside. Activists and advocates can present the ideas, but leaders inside the institutions actually enact the change.

Governments' horizontal division of power determines their *political regime*, by which political scientists mean whether the country is or is not considered a democracy. Many believe that democracies offer better prospects for protecting human rights, including women's rights. As Chapter 1 noted, the women's rights era coincided with the third wave of democratization. Roughly speaking, a first wave of democratization occurred in western and northern Europe and the Americas in the late eighteenth and early nineteenth centuries; the second wave in the aftermath of the Second World War; and the third wave beginning in the 1980s, with the transition of Latin American countries from dictatorship and of Eastern European, Central European, Balkan, and Eurasian countries from communism. Certain postcolonial Asian and African countries also transitioned in the second and third waves. Some scholars consider the

Arab Spring, which began with Tunisia's democratic revolution in 2010, as part of the third wave or as marking a later, fourth wave. Democratic transitions matter because, in the international system, democracies and democratic ideals carry significant moral weight. Democracy offers citizens equality and rights not offered in autocratic systems. Yet as the chapter's opening illustrations show, progress on women's rights also happens in non-democratic systems. To understand why requires first reviewing (1) the basics of how governments divide power and make policy, (2) what distinguishes democracies from other political regimes, and (3) the persistent gap between aspirations and realities.

Divisions of power

Countries make policy at the national or subnational level. The institutional design of the subnational level varies substantially, depending on how countries vertically divide their powers. For instance, Canada and the United States are federal countries with certain policy powers granted to provinces and territories (Canada) and states and territories (the United States); subunits then elect to devolve further powers to lower government levels, such as cities and towns. Unitary countries also devolve power to provinces, regions, or municipalities. The United Kingdom is considered a unitary country, but still devolves significant powers from Westminster to Scotland, Northern Ireland, and Wales.

These vertical divisions of power offer activists options. Depending on the policy area, subnational governments have complete autonomy or, if they must follow the central government's lead but no national mandate exists, subunits can set their own policies until such an edict arrives. Take marriage equality in the United States: before the US Supreme Court legalized same-sex marriage in the 2015 *Obergefell v Hodges* case, states set their own rules. This possibility meant that marriage equality activists could undertake what scholars call 'venue shopping': they could start by winning their desired reform in receptive subnational jurisdictions. Progressive and more LGBTQIA+-friendly states such as Massachusetts and Washington legalized same-sex marriage well before 2015. Venue shopping constitutes a state-by-state strategy, an approach some US marriage equality activists preferred for building momentum towards a national change. As noted in Chapter 2, international norms often stick first at the subnational level. Researchers thus argue that vertical divisions of power benefit gender equality activists – but only when subunits are more progressively minded than national governments. Again taking marriage equality as an example, before the *Obergefell* decision, some US states looked to forestall marriage equality, with states like Arkansas, Georgia, and Kansas banning all unions other than those between a man and a woman. Venue shopping thus cuts both ways, benefiting both progressive movements and their opponents.

Most countries also divide power horizontally, into branches. The standard branches are an executive branch, led by a chief executive (e.g. a president, prime minister, or monarch); a legislative branch, meaning some collegial decision-making body where members are usually elected (e.g. a legislature, congress, parliament, or assembly); and a judicial branch. This book focuses primarily on the national level and considers women's rights reforms made by any branch. The primary actors are usually legislatures, but women's rights reforms also come via decrees and rules made in the executive branch and legal decisions issued by high courts such as supreme or constitutional courts. Crucially, countries vary dramatically in whether their horizontal branches of government are co-equal, meaning that branches can check and balance each other's powers, or whether one branch dominates the others. Saudi Arabia is among a handful of countries with no legislative branch, but in other monarchies, such as Morocco and Kuwait, separate legislative branches exist but defer extensively to the monarchy.

Understanding how countries design their national political institutions matters for understanding how and when countries make reforms. The greater the horizontal division of power, the more democratic the country: decision-making power becomes more diffuse, allowing for checks and balances, and advocates count on more policymaking venues. The fewer the horizontal divisions of power, the less democratic the country: fewer checks on political authority and more policy power concentrated into fewer hands facilitate autocrats' dominance. Advocates tailor their strategies on the basis of their country's political arrangements, targeting the branch and the leaders with decision-making power. In a monarchy like Saudi Arabia, activists seeking women's right to drive petitioned the royal family whereas in a federal democracy like the United States in the 2000s and 2010s, marriage equality advocates targeted the state and federal legislative and judicial branches.

Democracies and rights

The broad distinction between democracies, on the one hand, and autocracies, on the other hand, shapes possibilities for women's rights reforms (and for any other reforms). Researchers have several reasons for believing that democracies' institutional design makes them better at recognizing and protecting human rights, including women's rights. First, democracies are more permeable to activists because, by definition, democracies empower citizens to have voice and roles in government. The mechanism for empowering citizens is almost always regular elections, in which citizens can choose their governments, voting leaders in and out of office. Regular elections allow for competition between different factions, which present their policy proposals for periodic evaluation. Competition in turn enables *political pluralism*, the flourishing of diverse ideas and groups. Democracy encourages elected officials to care about what citizens want, as unpopular, unresponsive, and unaccountable leaders or their parties will lose the next elections. Democracies are therefore open to policy contestation and susceptible to public pressure in ways in which autocracies are not.

Second, democracies empower citizens to have a voice and a role in government because their founding principles entail some formal recognition of equality among citizens and some recognition of citizens' basic rights. Recognition and rights form the legal basis that allows citizens to participate in elections and to pursue policy change. A minimum definition of democracy, then, means guaranteeing the political rights necessary to hold free and fair elections: the right to freely organize, to voice opinions, to persuade others, to contact leaders, to vote and to stand for office.

The idea that citizens enjoy political equality constitutes the bedrock principle of modern democracies. In the European monarchies of the medieval and Renaissance eras, monarchs were considered divinely ordained, which meant that their subjects could never be their political equals. The European Enlightenment, which unfolded during the seventeenth and eighteenth centuries, upended this thinking by asserting equality among all men (or at least among men of sufficient income and stature). Enlightenment philosophers challenged the divine right of kings, shaping the first wave of democratization in both the Old World (Europe) and the New (the Americas). European countries created parliaments and curtailed monarchs' powers. The Americas gained independence and established new republics. New political elites wrote new founding documents. The US constitution's Bill of Rights, added in 1789, contains the minimum set of individual rights needed to sustain self-government, such as the right to assembly and a free press. At the time, such enumerated rights still only applied to those then considered citizens – essentially, white property-owning men.

Two struggles followed this first wave of democratization: expanding who counts as a citizen, to include all men alongside women, formerly enslaved peoples, and Indigenous peoples, and expanding the menu of rights. Constitutional amendments, statutes, and high court rulings would be required to grant equal status and protection to these groups. In Canada, for instance, women became recognized as 'legal persons' in 1929 via a decision from the Judicial Committee of the Privy Council of Great Britain, then Canada's highest court of appeal. The 1982 Canadian Charter of Rights and Freedoms, part of Canada's constitution, later recognized equality between men and women as a founding principle. (The United States, by contrast, has yet to ratify an equal rights amendment.)

As countries transitioned to democracy during the second and third waves, their founding documents reflected more modern sensibilities. Contemporary constitutions generally do not limit legal personhood and citizenship to men. Relative to the US constitution's Bill of Rights, twentieth- and twenty-first-century constitutions also include much more expansive lists of rights, including rights to public goods and services like clean water and healthcare. As discussed later in this chapter, a major achievement of the women's rights era has been incorporating women into constitution-writing processes and ensuring that contemporary constitutions both recognize women as citizens and enumerate women's rights. The more countries formally recognize citizens' rights and equality, the stronger their democratic foundations.

Theory versus practice

This very stylized presentation collapses enormous nuance. Many countries do not claim to be democracies, but still enumerate citizens' rights. For example, communist countries (discussed in more depth below) also list extensive citizen rights in their constitutions. And in those countries that claim to be democracies, the formal recognition and rights in their founding documents – their foundational principles – are rarely fully realized in practice. The 2003 Rwandan constitution, for example, guarantees 'freedom of thought, opinion, conscience, religion, worship and the public manifestation thereof' (Article 33) and freedom of the press (Article 34), but Kagame does not respect these rights. Reporters without Borders documents multiple instances of Rwandan journalists who investigate or criticize the government and subsequently face intimidation, harassment, violence, imprisonment, and exile.[18]

Governments' failure to match on-paper visions with in-practice realities is a general phenomenon. This gap leads many political scientists to further contend that democracy exists in degrees rather than kind. An enormous body of political science scholarship classifies and measures political regimes, focusing on their stated structures and divisions of power *and* on their actual behaviour. This categorization process generates significant debate among scholars and policymakers alike. Two broad approaches are discernible: researchers either treat political regimes as binary, classifying countries as democracies or autocracies, or adopt a granular approach, creating scales where countries can be ranked as closer to or farther from a perfect democracy. The latter approach leads researchers to create new categories for countries that are neither perfect democracies nor pure autocracies. For instance, many countries promise free and fair elections on paper but deviate in practice. Scholars offer various names for these in-between cases, such as hybrid regimes, competitive autocracies, or electoral autocracies. In 2025, El Salvador and Hungary exemplify these in-between cases.

Yet efforts to categorize and rank countries by their quality of democracy have long ignored the criterion of whether women enjoy political equality with men. As Lisa Baldez points out, were women's rights taken seriously, the very idea of democratization's first wave would disappear, since no first-wave country granted women the right to vote.[19] This gender-blind approach persists today.

Take the Economist Intelligence Unit rankings. In 2024, its report listed 25 countries as 'full democracies', including Japan at position 16 and Mauritius in position 19. Yet that year in Japan, women occupied just 15 per cent of parliament, and in Mauritius, barely 18 per cent. Both countries fall in the bottom tier when ranked by women's political representation in national decision-making bodies. Both countries recognize women's rights to vote and to run for office, but neither actively supports these rights' exercise. Unlike Rwanda, neither has mandatory gender quotas that help women stand for election and thus attain more seats. In Japan, strong patriarchal norms push women towards family and childrearing and away from high-powered careers in politics and adjacent fields such as business and law. Japanese women cannot even legally retain their own surname upon marriage. Similarly, in Mauritius, Sheila Bunwaree finds that male political dominance remains so entrenched and patriarchal norms so strong that even some politically active women ultimately decide that 'it is best that women conform to traditional family roles and steer clear from politics'.[20] Mauritius's 2006 constitution makes no reference to gender equality and its electoral law even uses male pronouns to refer to candidates and officials.[21] For the Economist Intelligence Unit, whether women actually participate in free and fair elections on equal terms with men does not matter for whether or not countries are a 'full democracy'.

This gap between democratic theory and democratic practice has several implications. First, most countries fall short of their democratic ideals. These shortcomings appear especially evident when examining members of groups historically not considered citizens and not granted rights. Do these groups now enjoy these rights on paper? Can they exercise their rights in practice? Even if women now have the on-paper right to vote and stand for election, they clearly face barriers to doing so on equal terms with men. Second, scholars and observers rarely consider these gendered dynamics as important when classifying countries as democracies, even as democracies theoretically seem better poised to not just encode but also implement women's rights. On the one hand, gender-blind definitions of democracy obscure the many ways in which gender inequality persists. Since democracies are presumed equal by virtue of being democracies, countries like Japan and Mauritius escape scrutiny for their poor women's rights record. Countries like Rwanda and Saudi Arabia, by contrast, receive no benefit of the doubt and must resort to flashier – and perhaps hollower – gender equality reforms. On the other hand, while feminists might criticize labelling Japan and Mauritius as full democracies when women's political representation remains so low, calling Rwanda a democracy merely because it has gender-equal political representation seems unsatisfying given the Kagame regime's obvious circumvention of free and fair elections.

These considerations shed light on the tensions introduced in the chapter's opening anecdotes, which raise questions about whether and how leaders' motivations affect the significance accorded to women's rights reforms. The possibility that leaders leverage gender equality reforms as window dressing could initially appear less applicable to democracies, given their structure of political contestation and underlying rights protections. In theory, reforms adopted by democracies happen when women's rights protagonists emerge victorious in the competitive marketplace of ideas; since the victory was fairly won, and since democracies recognize equality among citizens and allow for government accountability, women's rights reforms in democracies offer genuine possibilities for closing the adoption–implementation gap and achieving long-term transformations. By contrast, autocracies have no underlying commitment to equality nor do they care about accountability, so women's rights reforms in autocracies have little chance to meaningfully change women's lives or alter citizens' hearts and minds. Yet democracies might not deserve these higher expectations. As already suggested, democracies theoretically offer women more formal protections and freedoms, but in reality, adopting women's rights reforms has rarely been their main concern.

Women's rights across political regimes

Without getting too entangled in the measurement debates around quantifying and qualifying democratic regimes, this book follows most political scientists in adopting the minimum approach: democracies must practice elections in contexts where elections are free (there is broad participation without restriction or coercion) and fair (there is open competition without malpractice or manipulation). This approach would in fact count Japan and Mauritius as democracies, and Rwanda as a non-democracy. Women in Japan and Mauritius have equal political rights on paper, but face significant obstacles to running for and holding office on the same terms as men. It is precisely this distance between democracy's promise of equality and its on-the-ground treatment of historically discriminated against groups that women's rights protagonists seek to leverage. They argue that adopting women's rights reforms brings democratic regimes closer to a richer, more substantive version of democracy.

When and why democracies adopt women's rights reforms

As described above, democracies are designed to permit advocacy and to respond to public pressure. At the same time, democracies do not just have one decision-maker: in creating checks and balances across and within institutions, democracies have multiple veto players.

Women's rights advocates in democracies need to craft majorities, which means winning the hearts and minds of majorities within the general public and within elected assemblies. Even high courts, which technically make decisions according to constitutions and case law and not according to public sentiment or elected officials' preferences, often weigh majority opinion when deciding monumental cases. Famously, US Supreme Court Justice Ruth Bader Ginsburg, reflecting on the court's 1973 decision legalizing abortion, commented that she would have preferred if a consensus around legal abortion had emerged more gradually, with more states acting before the Supreme Court imposed a mandate.[22] (Ginsburg herself did not join the court until 1993.) In Ginsburg's view, gradual change would have helped the court's decision to stick.

Yet democratic governments do not leap into action even when political or public majorities appear convinced. Political scientists note that elected officials often hold more extreme views than members of the public. In most democracies, political parties work as intermediaries between voters and governments. Strong parties have stable identities – brands – that communicate their positions in clear, easy-to-understand ways. To attain political office, individuals must join parties and must therefore follow the party's position on issues. Such positions are not fixed forever – party members can and do work within the party to shift its platform – but party dynamics can lead elected officials to firmer views on issues where the public sees shades of grey or remains confused, divided, or uncertain. Additionally, those who gain access to elected officials – the very advocates this book focuses on – are the most committed and most motivated representatives of their group. Advocates must, by definition, believe in the rightness of their cause, again expressing firmness. Policymakers' perspectives on issues are therefore further influenced by those most committed to clear sound bites: their party, other politicians, and lobbyists.

Elected officials in democracies are also inherently risk-averse. Their survival in office depends on the electorate's favour. Voters may *say* they support a reform, but voters might also change their minds once they receive it. After all, plenty of baubles look attractive on the shelf but fail to produce joy once purchased. Elected officials and their parties deeply fear such buyers' remorse. Women's rights reforms especially risk regret. Since they touch deeply seated cultural, social, moral, and religious views, risk-averse elected officials need strong reasons to move the status quo with respect to women's roles in society.

Democratic governments, then, do not simply adopt women's rights reforms because they have democratic ideals to fulfil. Reform happens when activists' demands and governments' strategies align. These *windows of opportunity* open when some element of the political situation shifts such that elected officials realize that meeting activist demands furthers their own goals. These windows of opportunity take different forms. Sometimes windows open in response to tragedies, shocking events so outraging that elected officials' cost of inaction becomes higher than leaving the status quo alone. For example, brutal murders of women and girls have led countries to pass femicide laws, with the resultant laws often named after the victims. Other times, women's rights reforms offer governments a win when they need one. In her analysis of why Argentina became, in 1991, the first country to adopt a statutory 30 per cent quota for women candidates, Melody Ellis Valdini concludes that then President Carlos Menem hoped the positive press would detract from an unfolding corruption scandal.[23] Women legislators had written and introduced the quota bill and women activists showed their support by filling the galleries during the chamber debate, but it was Menem's middle-of-the-night phone call to party leaders that tipped voting majorities to the women's side.

As president of Argentina, Menem pursued a socially conservative agenda (see Chapter 7), a record that makes his last-minute support for the gender quota bill surprising and bolsters Valdini's argument that Menem sought a public relations win. However, gender scholars do not find that left-wing leaders have better track records, even though left parties' entrance into government should open more windows of opportunity for women's rights advocates. After all, left parties generally hold more egalitarian views and even campaign on issues important to marginalized constituencies.

Still, left governments in democracies rarely proactively initiate gender equality reforms. Analysing 15 years of left governments in Latin America, from 1998 to 2015, Merike Blofield, Christina Ewig, and Jennifer Piscopo coined the term 'reactive left'.[24] First, they found that, despite the seeming alignment between left ideology and gender equality, left parties rarely campaigned explicitly on women's issues. Left parties instead emphasized classic left issues – such as income redistribution and workers' rights. Second, once in office, left parties needed to be pushed on gender equality: women's rights reforms only happened when women's movements remained mobilized and reminded presidents and lawmakers that responding to their demands mattered for maintaining domestic support. For instance, Bolivia's indigenous movement contributed to electing the country's first Indigenous president, Evo Morales, in 2006. Morales did not proactively address women's demands, but he eventually created a special executive branch office to represent Indigenous women – but only after Indigenous women maintained significant pressure on his government, reiterating their importance as representing one half of his Indigenous electoral base.[25] Left governments are thus more likely to be accountable to women's movements demands, but do not necessarily initiate reforms in the absence of pressure.

Comparing women's rights reforms in democracies and autocracies

A savvy reader will note that democratic leaders' reasons for adopting women's rights reforms often resemble the autocrats' reasons in this chapter's opening accounts. Like Rwanda's Kagame, Argentina's Menem hoped gender quotas would deliver a public relations win, drawing attention away from other misdeeds. Similarly, Morales's reasons for including Indigenous women within his administration echoes Crown Prince Mohammad bin Salman's reasons for allowing Saudi women to drive. Both chief executives needed to convince observers that their regimes were more women-friendly than they actually were. Morales needed to cement his image as leading an Indigenous refashioning of Bolivia's democracy. The crown prince cultivates an image as a modernizing and even democratically minded monarch. Further, Morales and Mohammad bin Salman combined public relations flash with hollow substantive commitment. Morales's Office for Depatriarchalization lacked resources and stature, and Mohammad bin Salman oversaw the arrest, detention, and torture of women activists who defied the driving ban. Morales also, subsequently, took policy actions that harmed rather than helped Bolivian women – such as forcing the legislature to repeal the decriminalization of abortion.

In short, genderwashing occurs across regimes. Democratic regimes also pursue women's rights reforms strategically, to improve evaluations of their governments and to look more egalitarian than they actually are. Reforms that governments believe they can control are more easily granted, as indicated by this book's schema that arrays reforms from least to most transformative. With gender quotas, not all women will become candidates, and even if they do, party loyalty still constrains their actions. Not all Saudi women will start driving themselves to work, and even if they do, the male guardian system prevents them from becoming financially independent. These reforms do not transform the everyday patriarchal norms and practices that constrain women's lives. In managing their image, all political regimes ultimately favour words over deeds, meaning that their adoption of women's rights reforms often does not come with deep-seated commitments to realizing these rights.

Yet adoption does shift the formal status quo. In non-democracies, on-paper changes can even be easier to obtain than in democracies. Non-democratic regimes vary in their structure, including monarchies (like Saudi Arabia), one-party states (like Rwanda or communist countries), or military regimes (like Myanmar). All these regimes have fewer veto players than democracies. Advocates in autocracies do not need to craft political majorities or sway most voters' views; they need only convince a few decision-makers, such as a crown prince, a party leader, or a military general. If autocrats see women's rights reforms as useful for their ability to maintain a good image, they will respond to international normative frameworks and women's policy demands. That said, when women's policy demands exceed what the autocrat perceives as in his interest to grant, women in autocracies face much steeper activism costs than women in democracies. That women continue to press for their rights despite risks of reprisals suggests that reforms intended as mere window dressing still reflect women's policy priorities and can lay the groundwork for meaningful transformations. When Saudi Arabia's driving ban was lifted, women hailed it not as an ending, but a 'good beginning' – 'the first few steps of freedom'.[26]

Women and communist regimes

One type of non-democratic regime requires special mention: communism. Generally, communist countries are one-party states led by the communist party, with decision-making concentrated in the party's core organ, the politburo. The chief executive (president or premier) presides over the party. Communism centres on achieving socioeconomic equality, where the state distributes all public goods and employment so that, in theory, citizens' material inequalities disappear. The central mechanism for erasing class divisions is a command-and-control economy. Under communism, citizens' access to all goods and services is centrally managed, with items such as housing, employment, education, healthcare, and even groceries all distributed via rations, quotas, and mandates.

Setting aside that actual communist regimes rarely produce classless utopias, communist leaders' desire to prove that command-and-control economies can generate the same growth as capitalist economies affects women's lives in several concrete ways. First, to achieve productivity, communist governments need to harness every worker – including women. Communist regimes support or even require women's university enrolment and their workforce participation, even providing free childcare and generous maternity leave to help women combine work and family and maintain their labour force participation. Second, most communist governments are secular and even hostile to religion. Communist constitutions eliminate many doctrinal restrictions on women's rights and roles, offering guarantees of equality in inheritance, divorce, and child custody.[27] Some communist governments even make birth control and abortion widely and freely available.

When the United Nations convened the First World Conference on Women in Mexico City in 1975, much of the world was divided between democracy and communism. Two communist federations – the Soviet Union and Yugoslavia – then contained most of the countries throughout Eastern Europe (e.g. Poland and the Czech Republic), Central Europe (e.g. Hungary), the Balkans (e.g. Croatia), and Eurasia (e.g. Uzbekistan and Kazakhstan). Eastern Bloc women's lives diverged dramatically from Western Bloc women's lives. Communist governments sent Eastern Bloc women to school and to work. They eliminated gender-segregated spaces and forbade customary practices such as women's seclusion or bride kidnapping. Reactions to these political and social changes varied: some women found them empowering, whereas others found the abrupt, overnight end to customary practices disruptive and even traumatic.

These Cold War differences shaped the early decades of the women's rights era. The Mexico City, Copenhagen, and Nairobi world conferences on women occurred prior to the 1989 collapse of the Berlin Wall and unravelling of the Soviet and Yugoslav regimes. Kristen Ghodsee notes that, while the conferences fostered a transnational global sisterhood, they also reflected Cold War fault lines.[28] For Western Bloc countries, capitalist free markets and open societies would liberate women from patriarchy, whereas for Eastern Bloc countries, state-managed economies and the elimination of class-based inequality already had achieved this end. US feminists wanted to discuss the legal barriers women faced in universities and the workplace; Eastern Bloc feminists did not face such barriers and instead wanted to critique the imperialist, colonialist, and Zionist attitudes of the West. The 1980 Copenhagen conference report even acknowledged that communism's command-and-control economies had generated gender-equal outcomes: 'In the countries with centrally planned economies a further advancement of women took place in various fields . . . A high level of employment, health, education and political participation of women was achieved in countries with centrally planned economies'.[29]

Yet communist countries' claims about achieving women's liberation were not necessarily true. Official delegates to the world conferences on women would need government approval, so women attendees would have represented the party line. At the same time, numbers certainly supported communist countries' claims, with women attaining parity or near-parity in education and workforce participation in most communist countries.[30]

Women living under communism and feminist scholars raise important critiques, however. The Soviet Union and Yugoslavia no longer exist, but China, Cuba, Laos, Vietnam, and North Korea still have communist governments. Echoing patterns seen with democracies but also other autocracies, communist regimes do not adopt women's rights reforms because they care about women's rights, but because doing so advances their economic objectives. Moreover, women's higher participation in politics, education, and the workforce does not undo gender hierarchies – and may even reinforce them. Communist countries did not and have not ended occupational segregation along gender lines: women largely occupy feminized segments of the labour force, such as education, retail, the service sector, and light industry, which also means that they earn lower wages than men.[31] Historically and today, communist parties' politburos incorporate almost no women, while women fill the bottom tiers as rank-and-file members. Take China: the 24-member politburo usually had one or two women members, but in a 2022 membership refresh, not a single woman joined this exclusive club. In the same refresh, the party's second-most important tier, the 205-member central committee, contained just 5 per cent women.[32]

Communism also fails to challenge the gendered division of labour within the private sphere, with women still performing most domestic chores and care work. Women in the West often speak of the double shift – meaning waged work during the day and domestic chores at night – but women living under communism have confronted a triple shift – waged work during the day, domestic chores at night, *and* mandatory party activity. The former Soviet and Yugoslav countries thus cloaked themselves in a gender-egalitarian mantle not matched to women's day-to-day realities. Many women living under communism grapple with paradoxical forces: state policies encourage or even force them to work, but also to become mothers, and traditional patriarchal attitudes do not change as fast as education and economic policies change. Ultimately, communist countries materially improve women's lives while placing unreconcilable demands on their time and labour.[33] Consequently, women's employment and political engagement often declines in post-communist democracies, as many exhausted women gratefully shed some of the participatory obligations that communism forced upon them.

Women, democratic transitions, and constitution writing

Not all countries are democracies but, for most of the women's rights era, the number of democracies steadily increased. Democratic transitions occurred as communism ended across the Eastern Bloc and as countries in Latin America, East Asia, Africa, and, later, the Middle East emerged from different combinations of civil war, armed conflict, colonialism, dictatorship, and one-party rule. Not all transitions looked alike and not all countries ultimately succeeded (as seen with Rwanda). Still, many countries underwent the process, which included writing new constitutions. Between 1990 and 2015, 75 countries undertook constitutional reforms after undergoing a transition from authoritarianism or armed conflict.[34] These countries span the globe, from Colombia, Brazil, and the Philippines to Macedonia, Nepal, Tunisia, and Senegal.

Many other countries also revised their constitutions during the women's rights era. Longstanding democracies like Canada updated their founding documents and emerging democracies like Mexico underwent protracted transitions from one-party rule. For example, Canada added the 1982 Canadian Charter of Human Rights and Freedoms to its constitution. Mexico made successive constitutional reforms in the 1990s and 2000s in order to permit more electoral competition. Old and new democracies alike, including Iceland, Ireland, Chile, Liberia, and the Ukraine, also formed constitutional review bodies or attempted to write new constitutions (even if they did not succeed). In short, the women's rights era was replete with countries undertaking constitution writing in order to improve their democratic foundations.

Contemporary constitution writing follows more inclusive and participatory norms when compared to the first and even second waves of democratization. While 1975 marked the first year that the international system, via the United Nations, identified women as a distinctive group with distinctive interests, most countries had by then formally granted women citizenship. Equal citizenship means, in turn, an equal stake in constitutional processes. The resolutions from the 1975 Mexico City conference call for women's equal participation in democratic constitutions, and UNSCR 1325 makes the same call for women's participation in post-conflict decision-making, which includes constitution writing. Ideas about inclusive and participatory constitution writing also emerged because, for post-conflict countries, it was systematic exclusion that had fuelled the civil wars in the first place. During the women's rights era, small groups of all-male propertied elites writing founding documents in secret were largely (though not wholly) artefacts from previous centuries. Most constitution-writing bodies in the late twentieth and early twenty-first centuries have instead been constituent assemblies with several hundred members, usually convened via popular election.

For women in new democracies, their role in their country's democratic transition strongly shapes their claim to seats at the constitution-writing table. Many women participated as combatants in countries' civil wars and liberation struggles, taking up arms alongside men to forcefully oust dictators or colonists. Even when they did not fight, women joining armed groups filled critical roles, such as gathering intelligence, acting as informants, guarding hostages, and keeping camp. Many women also participated in pro-democracy movements and peace movements, facing arrest, detention, and torture for their activities, just like their male counterparts. Women's contribution to armed groups and to democracy and peace movements often made them more aware of gender inequality – especially when they found themselves bearing the same risks but without receiving the same recognition, benefits, or leadership opportunities within the liberation movement itself.

Women's own demonstrated capacity as fighters, activists, and leaders thus did not initially translate into actual access to decision-making following democratic transitions. For instance, women comprised nearly 40 per cent of active combatants within Nepal's communist insurgency, but no women representatives from the Communist Party of Nepal participated in the 2006 peace negotiations.[35]

Democratic transitions and constitution writing create breaks with the past, but patterns of male political dominance remain hard to shake. To claim their rightful space as political and social equals, women democracy and peace activists from the former Soviet Union through Southeast Asia to Latin America have used a common refrain: 'democracy without women is not democracy' or 'without women, there is no democracy'.

When Colombia opened its constitutional process in 1991, the Feminist Collective of Bogotá launched a national campaign called Women in the Constitutional Assembly with the slogan 'Democracy in the nation and in the house'.[36] Women's mobilization to denounce their exclusion and demand their inclusion fuelled demands for founding documents to address women's rights and for women actors to guarantee this outcome by actually participating in the constitution-writing processes.

Democratic transitions and constitutional reform processes thus offered women's rights activists a significant window of opportunity, a moment to influence their countries' founding documents. As the women's rights era unfolded, women successfully gained access to more and more constitutional processes. Among the 75 countries undertaking constitutional reforms between 1990 and 2025, women averaged about 10 per cent of constitution-writing bodies convened in 1990, but 25 per cent to 30 per cent of those convened between 2010 and 2015.[37] Women's mobilization proved critical in all cases. For instance, following the complete exclusion of women from Nepal's peace talks and the subsequent Constitution Draft Committee, women's organizations led widespread protests, forcing the reconstitution of the committee with four of 16 women members. The committee then approved an interim constitution that outlined provisions for elections to a constituent assembly, with a mandate that one-third of the constituent assembly candidates be women.[38] Women secured 33 per cent of seats in Nepal's first constituent assembly (2008–2010) and then 29 per cent of seats in Nepal's second (2013–2015). In 2011, Tunisia became the first country to mandate gender parity for its constituent assembly elections, and in 2020, Chile became the first country to require gender parity among the candidates *and* among the final delegates (though, due to reasons other than women's representation, Chile's draft constitutions were not ultimately approved).

Women shaping constitutions

Women's role in constitution writing matters. Women constituent assembly members have worked with women's civil organizations to represent women's issues. In Nepal, women challenged a proposal that would require both parents to hold Nepalese citizenship in order to pass this citizenship on to their children, arguing that the measure discriminated against single women and women married to foreigners. Women organized protests, petitions, and even hunger strikes – though they ultimately did not succeed. Still, with one-third of the seats in both constituent assemblies, Nepalese women secured other victories. The 2015 Nepalese constitution gives women equal right to lineage (an important element in an otherwise patrilineal society) and the right to participation in all state structures and bodies on the basis of proportional inclusion.

In her analysis of the 44 African constitutions rewritten since 1990, Aili Tripp finds that constitutional processes taking place in the aftermath of conflict resulted in constitutions with stronger women's rights protections than those taking place in the absence of conflict.[39] While the vast majority of African constitutions reworked between 1990 and 2025 contain clauses stipulating equality between men and women, many post-conflict constitutions also address women's rights in relation to customary laws that govern family life, property and inheritance, and reproduction (see Chapter 6). Post-conflict constitutions also usually include gender quotas for women's election to parliament. Tripp notes that post-conflict constitutional processes proved more open to international, democratic norms about individual rights and women's rights, and were more likely to question citizens' longstanding reliance on traditional authorities such as tribal chiefs. Most importantly, post-conflict constitutional processes unfolded alongside significant organizing from autonomous women's movements. Women's movement leaders had themselves participated in their country's conflict and its peace processes, which also connected them to UN officials and WINGOs. African women protagonists were familiar with and had even shaped the global language of women's rights (see Chapter 2), which they then brought back to their countries' constitutional processes.

Kenyan women, for example, participated actively in their country's pro-democracy movement. The constitutional process opened in 1997, leading to the Constitution of Kenya Review Commission and the National Constitution Conference, and restarted in 2008, with a Committee of Experts and a Parliamentary Select Committee co-authoring the drafts.[40] During the first process, the parliament's cross-party Women's Political Caucus brought women's concerns forward, lobbying the Inter Parties Parliamentary Group to include women's demands such as gender quotas in the constitutional review. When the parties could not agree on the constitutional process's ground rules, the Women's Political Caucus, led by Caucus coordinator Jane Ogot, restarted and managed the negotiations. The Women's Caucus's efforts secured the inclusion of eight women on the Constitution of Kenya Review Commission, four from parliament and four representing civil society groups. In the second process, pressure from women's organizations ensured that women once again formed part of the bodies, winning three of nine seats on the expert committee and five of 26 seats on the parliamentary committee.

In both processes, women at the drafting tables worked closely with women's organizations to present a unified front, one that transcended ethnic divisions to focus on women's rights. Unity does not mean that all women agreed – but women knew that, were they to appear divided, the men constitution writers would use women's discord to deny women's claims. During the second process, a larger Women's Consultative Group, formed to engage the broader peace process, held a 'spitting session' in which women from different organizations and different ethnicities aired their grievances. This spitting session cleared the air and allowed women to find common ground. Atsango Chesoni, a human rights attorney for Kenya's Federation of Women Lawyers (FIDA) who participated in both processes, explained: 'We were able to come together and to support whatever was going on to ensure the women's agenda.'[41] Chesoni emphasized the importance of collaboration between women inside the constitutional process – such as herself and her two women colleagues on the 2008 Committee of Experts – and women outside – meaning women's organizations that kept pressure on all drafters. Together, these women insiders and outsiders developed clever strategies. For instance, when they identified a male ally among the drafters, they sent a woman from his ethnic group or region to lobby him, in order to avoid inflaming ethnic or regional tensions and to more easily build rapport.

As a result of women's efforts, the 2010 Kenyan constitution included key provisions related to women's rights. These included women's and men's right to equal treatment, equal opportunities, and non-discrimination; affirmative action programs for minorities and marginalized groups in government, education, economic opportunities, and employment; the mandatory elimination of gender discrimination in law, customs, and practices related to land and land ownership; and the statement that any law, including customary law, inconsistent with the constitution would be void. Further, women secured their long-sought gender quotas, with a mandate that no more than two-thirds of elective public bodies be of the same gender and a requirement that the government enact legislation to promote women's representation in parliament. FIDA expressed disappointment that women did not succeed in encoding other rights, such as equal marriage rights and reproductive rights. However, the constitutional clause making customary law subordinate to the equality and non-discrimination clause laid important groundwork for tackling these demands later. For instance, Kenya's 2013 Matrimonial Property Act and 2014 Marriage Act equalize men's and women's rights in marriage and Kenya later became an important leader tackling period poverty.

Tunisia constitutes another instance where women members of constitution-writing bodies translated their presence into influence.[42] Following the gender parity requirement for women candidates in the 2011 constituent assembly elections, 27 per cent women joined the constituent assembly that sat from 2012 to 2014. On the inside, women delegates formed a caucus, and on the outside, leading women's organizations such as the Tunisian Association of Democratic Women (ATFD) and the Association of Tunisian Women for Research on Development (AFTURD) worked to establish common ground among activist women.

Echoing developments in Nepal – but with more success – women quickly mobilized against a draft provision that referred not to women's and men's equality, but to their 'complementarity'. Though some women delegates and activists aligned with the Islamist parties supporting the complementarity measure, feminists did not. The latter feared that complementarity would embed women's traditional roles into the constitution, undermining women's ability to claim equality. Women's groups organized a mass sit-in in front of the National Constituent Assembly's building. Six to seven thousand women joined protest marches. Outrage outside the assembly helped women delegates inside the assembly remove the complementarity clause from later drafts. In perhaps the most celebrated accomplishment of women's participation in Tunisia's drafting process, the Tunisian constitution of 2014 ultimately states that 'all citizens, male and female, have equal rights and duties'.[43] Other women's rights provisions include women's and men's equal rights to work, decent working conditions, and fair pay; the state's obligation to eradicate violence against women; and gender parity between women and men in all elected assemblies.

Women, regimes, and rights

This chapter opened with two instances where women fought for reforms that would expand their rights, only to finally succeed when men leaders saw the potential public relations benefit of granting their request. The Saudi Arabian and Rwandan cases are far from unique. In democracies and non-democracies alike, political leaders – who remain mostly men – have been quick to appropriate 'their' accomplishment in advancing women's rights. Such behaviour exemplifies what many feminist activists and scholars call genderwashing: governments adopt women's rights reforms when doing so appears convenient, allowing them to appear equality-minded, but then do not support – or even actively undermine – these reforms in practice.

To some extent, genderwashing does work. Observers are often quicker to credit men leaders' largesse than they are to credit women activists' hard work. Take Mwai Kibaki, the president who promulgated Kenya's 2010 constitution: when he died, a retrospective on his legacy applauded *him* for advancing gender equality – rather than the women parliamentarians, experts, and lawyers who organized, lobbied, and fought throughout Kenya's multi-decade constitutional process.[44] Kibaki even received these accolades despite having attempted to overturn the constitution's gender quota (an effort that ultimately did not succeed).[45]

Fortunately, determining women advocates' success or failure does not depend on leaders' underlying commitment to gender equality principles and effective implementation. Asking governments or leaders to genuinely embrace gender equality sets the bar too high: *all* policy adoption happens because those with decision-making power see the reform as being in their own interest. A window of opportunity that aligns advocates' demands with leaders' incentives is simply how politics works. No matter the reasons underlying government acquiescence, putting the policies on paper encodes formal rights and lays the groundwork for future transformations.

Further, women often lose their reform bids more than they win them, which signals that policy adoption to advance women's rights remains incredibly difficult, incentives for genderwashing notwithstanding. In Nepal's and Kenya's constitution-writing processes, for instance, women faced severe, and sometimes impenetrable, headwinds when challenging customs related to family, divorce, children, and reproduction. Following this book's schema, governments more readily grant reforms related to women's inclusion in the polity: while changing foundational principles provokes consternation, laying out these aspirations requires the fewest alterations to actors' day-to-day behaviour. Yet even then, men leaders look to contain the damage, from Morales making his new executive branch office representing Indigenous women toothless to Saudi Arabia imprisoning women's rights activists to remind all women about the costs of defying patriarchy.

Ultimately, women's rights reforms happen because women activists name the problem and fight for its redress. Windows of opportunity and genderwashing incentives explain why reforms happen *in a particular moment*, but not why the reform entered the agenda in the first place. Political leaders' lack of underlying commitment explains why implementation lags – but does not undermine the achievement of adoption itself. Words on paper *do* matter. Saudi women cannot drive without the policy changing, and Rwandan and Kenyan women cannot introduce women's rights legislation without seats in parliament. If encoding women's rights were a purely costless step for governments to take, they would have responded faster and more comprehensively to 50 years' worth of feminist blueprints. Instead, women wage a near-constant battle to advance and must take their wins when offered – even if political elites offer them for impure reasons. Without such pragmatism, far fewer constitutions and statutes would consider women's rights at all.

FOUR

Elections and Government

At the start of the women's rights era, women held 10.9 per cent of the seats in the world's national parliaments.[1] Fifty years later, they held 27.2 per cent.[2] This increase is among the most identifiable improvements in women's status from 1975 to 2025. Chapter 3 introduced the primary mechanism underlying women's increased political representation: the widespread adoption of gender quota policies. Gender quotas are formal mandates that women must constitute a certain percentage of parties' candidates for national legislative offices (candidate quotas) or hold a certain number of seats in the parliament (reserved seats). Gender quotas also apply to subnational governments and even to political executives. In Latin America, for example, Colombia, Ecuador, and Bolivia all require gender-equal representation (gender parity) among cabinet members. Costa Rica further requires gender balance among candidates running on a single ticket for the dual vice-presidency and for mayorships and vice-mayorships. Over 100 countries currently apply statutory gender quotas to their national legislative branch, making gender quotas central to countries' democratization processes and *the* most popular electoral reform of the late twentieth and early twenty-first centuries.

Women's political representation matters in and of itself, for ensuring women's access to political decision-making power, but also for the women's rights reforms that follow. As Chapter 3 showed, women in constitutional assemblies used their presence to insert women's rights principles into their countries' new founding documents. Women elected to parliaments have introduced and fought for other reforms, from sanctioning violence against women to protecting property rights. This story of women transforming policy from the inside recurs throughout the women's rights era (and in this book). Reforms can be demanded by those outside the government, but they are made by actors *in* government. Not all women policymakers agree on policy priorities or solutions, but it is usually women's rights protagonists within government who lead on women's rights reforms (even if the final decision, the votes, or the approval comes from men political leaders). Women's presence in government is thus fundamental for women's inclusion in the polity, for women's access to decision-making power, and for women's realization of their rights as full and equal citizens. Women's presence does not guarantee women's rights reforms, as myriad other factors intervene in the policymaking process, but women's presence constitutes a critical enabling condition.

Conceiving of women's presence in government as foundational may seem at odds with this book's claim that including women in the polity constitutes the least transformative set of women's rights reforms. Recall that a small gap between adoption and implementation does not imply that the reform itself faced no resistance. Quotas advocates, who are mostly women, have faced opposition from political elites, mostly men, at every step of the process. Gender quotas challenge the historical, entrenched pattern wherein men hold the majority of political decision-making posts in any regime (what scholars call 'male political dominance'). Allocating these decision-making posts also constitutes a zero-sum game: the number of viable candidacies and the number of elected or appointed offices are fixed quantities, so allocating more posts to women means fewer posts for men. As the stories of gender quota adoption show, men elites did not easily yield their access to these posts or their decision-making power.

Rather, the book's schema that arrays policy areas from least to most transformational captures the size of the qualitative distance between the reform's objective and its achievement. Gender quotas are mechanically straightforward to implement. Their target is a quantifiable, discrete metric and the responsible entities are clear and identifiable. Parties nominate candidates, and simply counting the number of women candidates or women parliamentarians reveals if parties complied with the target. In most cases, the quota statute includes sanctions, such as fines or rejection of non-compliant lists, and election authorities merely need to enforce quota laws as written. This rather direct line from the on-paper change to the real-world transformation contrasts with the indirect line in other women's rights policy areas (as elaborated in Chapter 1). In the case of gender quotas, individual men politicians may resent women's presence and continue to hold sexist attitudes, but electoral authorities and courts can induce parties' compliance virtually overnight.

The relative ease of moving from setting targets for women's political representation to actually electing or appointing more women explains why the book treats reforms that include women in the polity as less transformational than reforms in other policy areas. Bringing more women into political and public office constitutes a more straightforward task than breaking down the public–private divide, guaranteeing reproductive rights, or ending violence against women. The classification emerges not because women's inclusion is not symbolically and substantively important (it most certainly is), but because achieving this objective requires relatively lower execution, enforcement, and monitoring costs and a relatively lower need for hearts and minds to shift (though hopefully they will). When it comes to women's political inclusion, moving from adoption to implementation constitutes an identifiable change, one that requires the smallest number of responsible parties to act and the smallest number of behaviours to change. To be achieved, women's political inclusion therefore requires only modest levels of political willpower, while also being foundational for justice.

This ease may further explain why quotas became a popular tool for autocratic genderwashing, as the Rwanda case suggests (see Chapter 3). Gender quotas first emerged among new democracies, demanded by women activists frustrated over having their contributions to pro-democracy and peace movements ignored once electoral politics resumed and men seized the lion's share of candidacies and posts. Yet gender quotas quickly became appropriated by non-democracies: since quotas generate a numerical change in the distribution of political power that implies greater democratization, autocrats leverage this association to make their regimes look more egalitarian *and* more democratic than they actually are.[3] The world rankings of countries by the number of women in parliament reflect quotas' popularity across political regimes. Of the top ten countries in 2025, seven use statutory gender quotas: three non-democracies (Rwanda, Nicaragua, and the United Arab Emirates) and four democracies (Mexico, Andorra, Costa Rica, and Bolivia).

An important distinction thus emerges between including women in political institutions' headcount and ensuring that women exercise full decision-making power. Gender quotas ultimately only affect women's political equality in numerical terms, not substantive ones. Countless other factors shape whether and how women representatives and officials can influence policy. Some factors remain tied to political regimes. Can women parliamentarians, ministers, and other officials truly influence policymaking in autocratic regimes? (Can men, for that matter?) Since authoritarian regimes demand loyalty, repress dissent, and maintain power via coopting some and coercing others, do individuals who voluntarily participate make untenable moral and political compromises? Some activists might point out that this question resonates even within democracies, since electoral politics is exclusionary, hierarchical, and combative. They might argue that even democratic politics creates winners and losers, and that systems designed to punish losers cannot produce justice because, yet again, 'the master's tools will never dismantle the master's house' (see p. 23). Moreover, men's long-time political dominance means that governments and political institutions are designed to resist women's entrance. From salty debates that last until dawn to campaign promises made then broken, political structures and practices accommodate men's lives and embody a stereotypically masculinized ethos of aggression and manipulation. The fear that women can never attain substantive equality in institutions created to dominate and exclude leads many women to eschew formal politics.

The authors of the women's rights era's feminist blueprints did not take this view, however. For them, women's political empowerment, understood as access *and* influence, constituted a fundamental demand, a matter of justice, and an essential right, no matter the democratic or autocratic quality of their country's political regime. They well understood that the first challenge would be gaining entrance, and that the next challenge would be gaining power. Women have sought reforms on both fronts, seeking policies that would bring more women into political leadership, and then policies that would transform political structures and practices such that women could become efficacious actors. In this latter process, women have designed and secured mechanisms that raise their collective influence and cement their gender equality concerns within government decision-making. For instance, women parliamentarians have founded women's caucuses and secured mandates requiring that countries mainstream gender equality considerations into all legislation and policy.

Bringing more women into government

Women's rights protagonists are practically unanimous in prioritizing women's equal participation in decision-making. The reports from the first three world conferences on women – Mexico City, Copenhagen, and Nairobi – each mention women's participation in decision-making over 30 times. CEDAW also clearly states that countries must 'take all appropriate measures to eliminate discrimination against women in the political and public life of the country' and to ensure that women can vote and access decision-making posts 'on equal terms with men'.[4] CEDAW laid the initial groundwork for gender quotas by clarifying that measures targeting women did not introduce inequality between men and women. Article 7 explains that 'temporary special measures aimed at accelerating de facto equality between men and women . . . shall in no way be considered the maintenance of unequal or separate standards'.[5] Policies privileging women for purposes of correcting imbalances – like guaranteeing women but not men a certain percentage of candidacies or legislative seats – therefore could not be regarded as discrimination against men. The 1995 Beijing PfA took this principle further, dropping the understanding of such policies as 'temporary' and underscoring the importance of targets and measures. Countries must

> Commit themselves to establishing the goal of gender balance in governmental bodies and committees, as well as in public administrative entities, and in the judiciary, including, inter alia, setting specific targets and implementing measures to substantially increase the number of women with a view to achieving equal representation of women and men, if necessary through positive action, in all governmental and public administration positions.[6]

CEDAW inspired women's activism around gender quotas, but this paragraph in the Beijing PfA would shape decades of advocacy and undergird the spread of gender quotas across the globe. The feminist blueprints were clear: bringing more women into government, particularly the legislative branch, would require more than just waiting for women's political representation to catch up. It would require affirmative action.

Gender quota adoption and reform

Women in Latin America and Europe would initiate the global wave of statutory gender quota adoption. Most countries would primarily adopt candidate quotas or reserved seats for the national legislature, though some countries would also extend gender quotas to cabinets, the public administration, and the judiciary. Costa Rican women emerged as early protagonists.[7] Their CEDAW ratification campaign inspired presidential candidate Óscar Arias to openly court women voters. Arias made gender equality central to his campaign and, after his 1986 election, he appointed women to top posts. Victoria Garrón de Doryan became vice-president and Rose Marie Karpinsky became president of the National Assembly. They worked alongside former ministers Carmen Naranjo and Elizabeth Odio, Inter-American Court of Human Rights judge Sonia Picado, and First Lady Margarita Penón to draft a gender equality law. The 1988 proposal contained five sections, spanning politics, society, economics, the judiciary, and violence against women. The political rights section required that parties practise gender balance when nominating men and women for the National Assembly and local councils, that political parties have gender balance in their party assemblies, and that parties allocate 25 per cent of their public campaign funds to activities supporting women's political participation. Vice-minister of culture Mimi Prado explained the women drafters' rationale: 'We knew that to ask for 50% of the political power was to ask for a lot, but in addition we left it in the law as a point of negotiation and strategy. As women, we couldn't ask for 25% or 30%. Why? . . .We couldn't ask for less than we are'.[8]

Ultimately, Costa Rican feminists proved to be ahead of their time. Women legislators were forced to withdraw the gender parity requirements as part of the legislative negotiations to pass what became the 1990 Law of Real Equality for Women. (The 25 per cent funding requirement remained.) Argentina instead earned accolades for becoming the first country to pass a candidate gender quota law: in 1991, women legislators and women's movement representatives won their multi-year campaign for a 30 per cent gender quota law. Costa Rica would ultimately come second, introducing a 40 per cent candidate quota in their 1996 electoral reform. Overall, 12 Latin American countries and two European countries, France and Belgium, adopted legislative gender quotas in the

1990s.[9] From there, the quota wave became a tsunami, with candidate quotas becoming especially popular after the Fourth World Conference on Women.[10] By 2015, 63 countries had adopted legislative gender quotas and another 31 had adopted reserved seats, spanning every global region.[11] By 2025, additional countries joined these ranks, bringing the number of statutory gender quotas for national legislatures to well over 100.

Nearly all gender quota laws are passed by legislatures or constitutional assemblies. In the Latin American and European democracies starting the trend, legislatures are not rubber stamps for chief executives. Gender quotas generated fierce debate and opposition from lawmakers across the ideological spectrum, as evidenced by how many quota bills failed in their first attempts (as in Costa Rica, but also in Uruguay, India, and Wales). Why, then, would men legislators eventually vote 'yes' to giving up their candidacies or seats to women?

Gender and politics scholars have spent decades examining this puzzle, identifying several factors that together explain why men legislators would seemingly vote against their own interests. First, gender quotas' popularity in the 1990s dovetailed with the third wave of democratization (Chapter 3). Women protagonists fumed about women's ongoing political exclusion in new democracies: in Latin America, for example, women led anti-dictatorship and peace movements but won under 10 per cent of seats in their country's first democratic election after the regime transition.[12] Frustrated at being left behind, women argued that mechanisms guaranteeing their political representation were essential to building genuine democracies. Women accused party leaders of being dinosaurs, prehistoric relics whose sexist attitudes had no place in contemporary democratic life.[13] Even in longstanding democracies such as Belgium, women party members leveraged parties' declining voter support to bolster quota demands.[14] Committing to gender quotas means committing to bringing in new faces, allowing parties to woo voters back with a fresh approach. Yet if just one party adopts an internal gender quota (often called a voluntary party quota), that party gains an advantage over its competitors: parties therefore have incentives to accept quota laws that bind everyone to the same rules.

Second, initial gender quota laws were rather toothless. Many of the proposals fell back from gender parity to one-third, with 30 per cent becoming the de facto international standard. Other laws passed with loopholes baked in. Take Costa Rica's 1996 reform: the quota law did not stipulate where parties needed to place women candidates on their electoral lists. Parties could then comply with the letter but not the spirit of the law, clustering women candidates in the lowest – and therefore least electable – positions. This toothlessness underscores a potential link between gender quotas and genderwashing: men political leaders could reap all the public relations benefits of seemingly embracing gender equality while paying few actual costs. Indeed, Malu Gatto finds that the men legislators most likely to support quotas have less ambition to remain in politics, making their 'yes' votes less personally costly.[15]

Many gender quotas did not remain toothless for long, however. Even initially weak quota laws brought greater numbers of women into office, and these women in turn sought stronger measures. Nearly half of quota-adopting countries passed at least one reform after implementing the initial law.[16] In Mexico, the 30 per cent gender quota for legislative candidates adopted in 2002 became a 40 per cent gender quota in 2008 and gender parity in 2014. Argentina and Costa Rica, too, eventually raised their candidate quotas to gender parity. Reforms also eliminated the loopholes men legislators deliberately wrote into earlier versions of the laws, introducing requirements for women's placement in electable list positions and competitive districts and including harsher sanctions for noncompliance. Reforms also expanded quotas vertically, to subnational legislatures, and horizontally, to other government branches. In 2019, Mexico became the first country in the world to adopt the reform known as 'gender parity in everything', which is a constitutional amendment that requires gender parity in the executive, judicial, and legislative branches at the federal, state, and municipal levels. For the 2021 and 2024 elections, Mexico's national electoral institute added candidate quotas for Indigenous peoples, LGBTQIA+ people, disabled people, Afro-Mexicans, and Mexicans living abroad, with a mandate for gender parity *within* each group.

As Costa Rica's Mimi Prado had intuited, women could initially seek gender parity in decision-making but negotiate for less – and then come back later demanding more. In Mexico, a legislator recalls that, when negotiating the 2014 parity reform, an annoyed male colleague asked her: 'What more do you women want?' She recounts shrugging and replying calmly: 'We want it all.'[17] Such private grumbling notwithstanding, male elites felt considerable outward pressure to support gender quota reforms. Gradual changes moved the status quo slowly, making any public refusals from men legislators seem unreasonable – especially when their women colleagues would swiftly call press conferences calling them sexists (as happened in numerous cases). Ultimately, embracing statutory gender quotas allowed men leaders to publicly parade their democratic and egalitarian credentials, a win that overrode whatever private distaste they often had.

Gender quotas in non-democracies

Quotas also evolved within authoritarian countries, as women's groups in certain countries found that pressing for more women in politics, while not necessarily popular among men elites, did not invoke the same outright state repression as other feminist demands. In China, mobilization would come from the All-China Women's Federation (ACWF), the women's wing of the Chinese Communist Party (CCP).[18] In 1990, against the backdrop of China's preparations for hosting the Beijing Conference, then ACWF head Chen Muhua approached her female colleague Lü Feng, then head of the party's personnel division, the Organization Department. Chen knew that the ACWF could not alone alter the CCP's promotion rules, and that the Organization Department would need to agree. Chen and Lü established an initial modest target: at the county and township level, all party branches and governments would need to have at least one woman in the next three to five years. The ACWF also launched programs to train women for holding leadership posts, so the CCP could not claim 'there were no women' (a common protest heard from party leaders across the globe).

The ACWF then aimed to expand the 'at least one woman' principle to all government levels. Chen and the ACWF argued that China, as host of the Fourth World Conference on Women, needed to demonstrate its commitment to women's political representation. In 1995, one month before the Beijing conference, the State Council issued the 'Outline for Women's Development in China', which acknowledged that women's decision-making inclusion 'should improve' and 'be aimed for'. While the outline fails to set clear targets for women's inclusion, the commitment's issuance by the State Council gave the idea more weight than the

ACWF's exhortations alone. That same year, the CCP's legislative organ, the National People's Congress, amended the electoral law to say 'the proportion of women deputies should gradually increase'.

The Beijing conference introduced the ACWF to international advocacy tactics. In other countries, women underscored their demands with research into the problems and solutions for women's political underrepresentation, and they used this research to urge their countries to adopt policies found in nations they considered role models or peers. The ACWF did the same, founding its first think tank, the China Women's Research Society (CWRS), in 1999. The CWRS published research on the barriers Chinese women faced when participating in politics. Its leader, Peng Peiyun, travelled internationally to learn about other countries' experiences with gender quotas. And, as women had done elsewhere, the ACWF and the CWRS leveraged disappointing election results to argue for quotas' importance. When the 2003 elections to the National People's Congress saw the number of women delegates drop, the unfavourable attention created a window of opportunity for the ACWF and the CWRS to propose a 30 per cent gender quota for the National and Local People's Congresses. Their proposal did not succeed, but in 2007 the National People's Congress commanded that, for its next elections, the proportion of women elected should be no less than 22 per cent. This gender quota only applied in 2008, however. Subsequent State Council guidelines for elections to the national and local people's congresses have referred only to the proportion of women gradually increasing. Xinhui Jiang and Yunyun Zhou conclude that the CCP ultimately installed these measures due to 'its need for an improved international image'.[19] Tepid commitments notwithstanding, China did not wish to appear too out of sync with the global quota tsunami.

Even in the context of authoritarian regimes, then, women's mobilization remains fundamental for gender quota adoption. In China, the CCP channels all contestation, but Chen, Lü, Peng, the ACWF, and the CRWS mobilized within these constraints; had they not acted, gender quotas would not have emerged. Similarly, Moroccan women's groups pushed for gender quotas, even as Morocco remains an authoritarian system with limited political freedoms.[20] In Morocco, different political parties do compete for parliament, but parliamentary authority remains subservient to the king. Following patterns of quota mobilization seen in other countries, Moroccan women's rights activists and women party members first proposed gender quotas in the 1990s, quoting both CEDAW and the Beijing PfA in their demands. In 2002, a window of opportunity opened as King Mohamed expressed an interest in electoral reforms. The Network of Women Partisan Leaders seized the opening and proposed a 30 per cent gender quota. They did not succeed, but party leaders agreed to reserve 30 of 325 seats in the House of Representatives for women. Following the Arab Spring uprising in 2011, and to appease protestors' demands for greater democracy, the king conceded more electoral reforms. The number of reserved seats expanded to 60, 18 per cent of the lower house. An additional 30 seats were reserved for candidates under 40; they were initially only available to men, but opened to women in 2016. In Morocco as in China and as in the democratic cases, gender quotas gradually expand as women's demands meet leaders' incentives to appear responsive and egalitarian.

Levelling the playing field for women in politics

Statutory gender quotas are well suited to tackle women's numerical under-representation in politics – but only modestly able to tackle the norms and practices that contribute to women's under-representation in the first place. Gender quota laws enforce women's right to be elected. Yet, as with all women's rights reforms, realizing this one right does not mean that other practices and structures magically become supportive and enabling environments. Women politicians face countless barriers, from sexist attitudes about who makes a 'good' political leader to working hours incompatible with family life. An entire development industry exists to support women seeking and holding political office. Development initiatives include education, training, and mentoring programmes for women candidates and women politicians, alongside recommendations for reforms that would level the playing field between men and women and ultimately make politics more welcoming to women. Nearly universally, within-country reform efforts come from elected women themselves, with support from international organizations such as UN Women and the Inter-Parliamentary Union (a professional body representing the world's legislatures) and local women's organizations. Many policies seem quite commonsense – such as parliamentary codes of conduct sanctioning sexual harassment – but only happened within the last decade of the women's rights era.

The electoral playing field

One popular set of measures, often contained within statutory quotas or issued by countries' electoral authorities, address the funding imbalances between women and men candidates. In many countries, political campaigns are publicly financed (though candidates can also separately raise money from private donors). Gender quota laws guarantee women certain proportions of their parties' candidacies, but not necessarily the resources to mount a competitive campaign. In Brazil, gender quotas apply but have not significantly boosted the number of elected women, in part because political campaigns remain quite costly and women candidates raise less money than men. A 2015 reform tackled women's campaign resources, requiring that parties allocate between 5 to 15 per cent of their Party Fund to their women candidates (the Party Fund holds the public money each party receives for its election campaign). In 2018, Brazil's Supreme Court ruled the cap unconstitutional, determining that parties must allocate at least 30 per cent of any public monies to women (which applies to the Party Fund and other special public election funds). In 2022, the judicial decision became a constitutional amendment.[21]

Other measures offer incentives rather than mandates or combine both. In Chile, for instance, parties receive higher public reimbursements for every woman candidate they elect. In Brazil, the state double counts women candidates when calculating how much money each party receives. Though neither measure places money directly in women candidates' hands, they reward parties that nominate but also materially support women's campaigns. In South Korea, women's organizations looking to strengthen the quota law introduced similar measures. South Korea's 2000 gender quota law contains no sanctions for noncompliance. In 2002, the group Korean Women's Political Solidarity proposed and secured the Women's Nomination Subsidy, which gives political parties extra public funding if they fill the 30 per cent candidate quota for women running in single-member districts.[22] Like gender quotas themselves, policies rewarding parties for nominating or electing women (or both) have diffused across the globe, appearing in Europe and the

Balkans (Bosnia and Herzegovina, Croatia, Moldova, and Romania), in Africa (Ethiopia, Mali, Niger, and Togo), and in the Pacific (Papua New Guinea and the Solomon Islands).[23]

Seemingly gender-neutral campaign funding rules also negatively impact women candidates, making them targets for reform. In the United States in 2018, Gretchen Shirey wanted to run for congressional office. Yet Shirey – like countless women in the United States and elsewhere – found that family responsibilities put her off. She told reporters, 'I had thought about it [running] for much of the year, but I decided that with two small children, I wouldn't be able to do that'.[24] Shirey then decided to run, but realized that the US Federal Election Commission (FEC) did not allow campaign donations to be spent on childcare. She petitioned the FEC, arguing that, had she not become a candidate, she would not have needed childcare, which made childcare a campaign expense. Two dozen Democratic members of Congress wrote to the FEC in support, arguing that ruling in Shirey's favour would allow other women and working parents to run.[25] The FEC agreed – but had Shirey not asked, the rule would never have changed.

The legislative playing field

For the women and men who enter political office, political spaces become their workplaces. Political institutions traditionally included only men, and so their structures, procedures, and practices accommodate masculine norms and men's lives. This male default remained largely unnoticed until women entered and called attention to problems and challenges – even basic ones, such as the absence of women's bathrooms.

In the legislative branch especially, women have confronted workplaces that operate as old boys' clubs, with all the requisite infrastructure to sustain male socializing – such as men's gyms, saunas, and locker rooms. Gender experts within international organizations, themselves usually women, have worked with consultants and activists to write blueprints for 'gender-sensitive parliaments'. These documents focus on empowering women within parliament to attain leadership positions and influence legislation (discussed below). They also outline changes to legislative buildings, rules, and cultures that would better accommodate women, from family-friendly working hours to sanctions for sexual harassment. These latter procedural and cultural changes would make parliaments more inclusive for all under-represented groups, but Sonia Palmieri and Lenita Freidenvall note that 'responsibility for institutional change continuously falls on the shoulders of women'.[26] Since men benefit from workspaces designed for them, they have fewer reasons than women to seek reform, and since the status quo protects their privilege and authority, they have more reasons to resist women parliamentarians' and women staffers' demands.

Take reforms that would make legislatures more parent-friendly. In many countries, parliamentarians are not considered employees, so their jobs fall outside their country's standard employment regulations. As a result, legislators in many contexts have no statutory entitlement to parental leave. Many parliaments may also have internal procedures saying that 'strangers' – that is, people who are neither lawmakers nor staff – cannot access the chamber floor; others even have rules explicitly barring infants and children. Though men are also parents, men legislators would traditionally have women spouses carrying out childrearing tasks, a gendered division of domestic labour that renders matters of parental leave or children at work largely invisible to men. Yet women legislators may not have stay-at-home spouses. They could be single parents. They also could be breastfeeding.

In 2021, UK Member of Parliament (MP) Stella Creasy confronted both the absence of parental leave and the ban on infants in the chamber. She sought maternity cover for when she needed to appear for sessions and votes in parliament, but was rejected. As she explained, the chamber authorities reasoned – incorrectly in her view – that 'democracy demands no one else can substitute for me'.[27] After giving birth, Creasy arrived on the chamber floor with her infant son in a sling. The Speaker reprimanded her, asking her to leave.[28] Despite the resultant media attention, the United Kingdom has yet to introduce parental leave for MPs. However, a group of committed women MPs and their male allies fought to overturn perceptions that MPs have no substitutes, introducing a proxy-voting scheme that allows MPs who are new mothers, new fathers, and adoptive parents (as well as those who are ill) to have another MP vote on their behalf. Ministers can receive parental leave and MPs can hire replacements (locums) for their constituency service. Children still cannot visit the Westminster chamber floor, though Australia and New Zealand now allow MPs to bring their infants and children into the plenary. Other key family-friendly reforms include on-site childcare, now offered in the United Kingdom, Australia, and New Zealand (among other places). Yet none of these reforms was easy to achieve. In Australia, 'women from all political parties had continuously lobbied for a childcare centre over a period of 20 years' – only winning in 2008.[29]

The failure to see parliamentarians as 'regular' workers creates another vacuum relative to workplace misconduct: women legislators are not protected by countries' statutes prohibiting and sanctioning workplace harassment, including sexual harassment. The #MeToo wave (see Chapter 8) also reached politics, with women members and women staffers coming forward to denounce abuse not just from voters but from their own colleagues (and, in the case of staffers, from the lawmakers themselves). For the United Kingdom, Christina Julios summarized the behaviour underpinning the nickname 'Sextminster': 'Elected representatives seemed to have violated women's rights and wellbeing by indulging in unsolicited acts such as: groping, inappropriate touching, making unwanted passes, initiating sexual chatter, making misogynistic comments, sending improper text measures, using sexual overtones, and pressuring women into unwelcome sexual behaviour.'[30] Nor is the problem confined to the Global North. In Latin America, women candidates and elected officials denounced this problem well before #MeToo, mobilizing against not just sexual harassment but also physical attacks and even assassinations. Calling this phenomenon 'violence against women in politics', women in countries such as Bolivia raised global awareness about the risks women politicians faced for challenging male political dominance, a risk made especially acute for Indigenous and other marginalized women.[31]

Once again, women identified, named, and proposed solutions to problems that affected them as women. Efforts in Canada also predated #MeToo, when two women MPs made allegations of sexual harassment and, in doing so, uncovered that the Canadian parliament had no guidance whatsoever for preventing, responding to, or sanctioning sexual misconduct. In 2014, Canada adopted a sexual harassment policy focused on staffers and then, in 2015, one focused on MPs. Only in the wake of #MeToo, however, did the Australian, New Zealand, and UK parliaments adopt sexual misconduct policies.[32] In the Global South, women politicians built on their success in mobilizing for quota adoption and reform, turning their sights to violence against women in the political workplace. In the 2000s, Bolivia, Mexico, Costa Rica, and Tanzania are among those countries passing laws to sanction violence against women in politics.

From gender-equal parliaments to gender equality policy

Gender-sensitive parliaments aim to alter workplace practices and cultures to eliminate gendered barriers that keep women from exercising decision-making power. Gender and politics scholars have long researched how women legislators do not enjoy substantive political equality within legislative chambers, largely because men legislators work to keep women outside the inner circles where the actual political decisions are made. When women are excluded from parties' and chambers' leadership structures and assigned to less prestigious committees and projects, for instance, they cannot influence law and policy to the same degree as men.

Women politicians counteract their exclusion from old boys' clubs by forming their own alliances. Women's caucuses are cross-party groups in which women legislators identify shared priorities, draft policy proposals, strategize about advancing proposals, and strengthen their own professional ties. Caucuses may be formally recognized by parliaments, or they may operate informally. As of September 2025, Inter-Parliamentary Union data show that women's caucuses exist in 92 of the world's legislatures, in every global region and across democratic and non-democratic regimes.[33] Parliamentary caucuses also exist within regional legislative bodies, for example the Network of Women in the Parliamentary Assembly of Portuguese Speaking Countries, and they might become transnational alliances of women MPs, like the Central Asian Women Leaders' Caucus that unites women legislators from Kyrgyzstan, Kazakhstan, Uzbekistan, Tajikistan, and Turkmenistan.[34] Caucuses help women legislators network with each other, creating counterbalances to the old boys' clubs within parliaments. They also provide access points for women's NGOs, consulting and holding events with women in civil society.

Women's caucuses develop and promote women's rights legislation. In Uruguay, 15 women legislators representing three different parties announced the formation of the Women's Bench in 2000.[35] The Women's Bench has since sponsored dozens of bills, among them

Uruguay's 2009 30 per cent quota law – ensuring that Uruguay would finally join the ranks of its Latin American peers, most of which adopted gender quotas much earlier. The Women's Bench members emphasize a common agenda, described as 'issues affecting women's lives and their ability to freely exercise their rights as citizens'.[36]

The focus on achieving consensus characterizes nearly all women's caucuses, even in countries with less established democratic traditions. In Kyrgyzstan, a post-Soviet country that maintained a fragile multiparty democracy from the 1990s until the early 2020s (before an authoritarian reversion), women parliamentarians created the Forum of Women MPs in 2011.[37] The Forum later sponsored eight laws on women's rights, in policy areas transcending partisan divides.[38] As a former Kyrgyz woman MP summarizes, '[t]he good thing about this caucus of women is that it allows us to go beyond our political differences, overcome the ideological contexts', and it 'unites women from different parties and from majoritarian districts. The Forum is the place for the gender agenda, the place where important issues like quota and violence against women override [the] political agenda.'[39] Indeed, in 2017, the Kyrgyz Forum for Women MPs won amendments to domestic violence legislation that strengthened victim protections and improved police and judicial responses. In 2019, the forum successfully promoted legislation that expanded the 30 per cent gender quota to local council elections.[40]

Women's caucuses have proved influential even in authoritarian settings. In Uganda, where the chief executive's party dominates congress and legislators remain co-opted and constrained, Ugandan women MPs still have found room for manoeuvre. For instance, the Ugandan Women's Parliamentary Association (UWOPA) is credited with advancing several pieces of gender equality legislation in the 2000s, including a prohibition on female genital mutilation, stronger penalties for sexual offences and domestic violence, and the removal of taxes on commodities important to women, such as nappies and cooking fuel. The UWOPA also won an internal reform, guaranteeing gender parity among parliamentary committee chairs.[41] Echoing her Kyrgyz colleague, a Ugandan woman MP said that the UWOPA 'makes it easy for us to lobby, for us to speak together'.[42] Through women's caucuses, women find strength in numbers.

The promises and pitfalls of gender mainstreaming

Gender mainstreaming constitutes another measure that prompts parliaments and governments to consider gender equality. Like many other policy approaches and ideas covered in this book, gender mainstreaming gained popularity through international policy conversations on gender and development and via the four world conferences on women. The 1995 Beijing PfA mentions bringing women's interests into the mainstream over 30 times, notably stating: 'Governments and other actors should promote an active and visible policy of mainstreaming a gender perspective into all policies and programmes, so that, before decisions are taken, an analysis is made of the effects on women and men.'[43] In 1997, the UN Economic and Social Council put forward the gender mainstreaming definition still used today:

> Mainstreaming a gender perspective is the process of assessing the implications for women and men of any planned action, including legislation, policies or programs, in all areas and at all levels. It is a strategy for making women's as well as men's concerns and experiences an integral dimension of the design, implementation, monitoring and evaluation of policies and programs in all political, economic and societal spheres so that women and men benefit equally, and inequality is not perpetuated. The ultimate goal is to achieve gender equality . . . GM does not replace the need for targeted, women-specific policies and programs or positive legislation.[44]

The idea of gender mainstreaming proved wildly popular across the globe. By 2022, researchers Kelsi Caywood and Gary Darmstadt counted over 170 distinct policy actors or geographic areas (countries or regions) enacting gender mainstreaming in some form – and these were just the ones covered in the academic literature![45]

For the legislative branch, gender-sensitive parliament toolkits include recommendations that gender mainstreaming be formally adopted into the policymaking process. Not all legislatures have specialized committees charged with gender issues, and even when they do, the very point of gender mainstreaming is that *everyone* needs to consider gender equality. Gender mainstreaming generally mandates work in one of two ways: there can be measures enacted within the parliament's rules to require legislators and staffers to practice gender mainstreaming as part of their work drafting, evaluating, amending, and passing legislation, or there can be laws passed by parliament that require all government entities to mainstream. Fiji illustrates the former. As of 2014, the parliament's standing orders require the chamber's six committees to 'ensure that all matters are considered with regard to the impact and benefit on both women and men equally'.[46] Fiji also constitutes one case where the mandate originated not with women parliamentarians, but with an international consultant, brought in to advise Fiji's reinstallation of parliament following a 2006 military coup that left parliament suspended for eight years. Still, the woman Speaker of the House in the 2014–2018 parliament, Dr Jiko Luveni, became a passionate advocate for the gender mainstreaming mandate. Luveni worked with the UN Development Programme to produce a gender mainstreaming guide, which she then used to train committee chairs.[47]

Beyond Fiji, gender mainstreaming appears in the European Parliament, via the Committee on Women's Rights and Equality, which can introduce gender mainstreaming amendments to any proposal (though the other committees are not obligated to accept them). In Italy, a procedural requirement mandates that all draft laws contain a 'gender impact assessment'. In Chile, the lower house contains a department charged with tracking laws' development and implementation, and staffers developed and began applying a gender impact assessment tool in 2022.[48] These examples merely sample the myriad mechanisms through which parliaments worldwide, often with technical support from international organizations, design mechanisms and procedures that empower legislators – usually women – to introduce gender equality concerns.

Elsewhere, parliaments have passed laws binding all government institutions – including themselves – to gender mainstreaming. In these cases, gender mainstreaming becomes what Jennifer Piscopo, Nancy Cohen, and Natalia Vega Varela call 'a whole-of-government approach'.[49] Canada, Spain, and Belgium all have legislation or executive branch orders enacting government-wide gender mainstreaming mandates, which include applying gender lenses to understand whether budgets advance gender equality. Canada also has a standalone gender budgeting law. Australia and Italy, too, have specific rules for applying gender scrutiny to the budget. In all, the OECD reports that 23 of its 38 member countries practised some form of gender budgeting by 2023.[50]

In Mexico, a cross-party group of women legislators fought for years to introduce gender budgeting. Women lawmakers founded the bicameral Committee on Gender Equality in 1998, through which they successfully intervened in budget cycles to reallocate monies to maternal, sexual, and reproductive health programmes for women, shelters for women victims of violence, and microcredit for women entrepreneurs.[51] These revisions proceeded ad hoc, without any formal process, until 2006, when Mexico amended the federal budget act to include an obligatory gender perspective. Beginning in 2008, women legislators were able to attach an annex to the budget that lists which of the budget's earmarked expenses promote equality between men and women. In 2012, Mexico again reformed the Federal Budget and Revenue Responsibility Act, to clarify that the annex's earmarked items are protected and cannot later face reductions.[52] These reforms fall short of granting the Committee on Gender Equality full gender budgeting powers, but they allow the women legislators to itemize and protect programs and services benefiting women.

Still, the Mexican experience anticipates the main criticism of gender mainstreaming: that it becomes a technical, evaluative, and often post hoc exercise that ticks boxes without meaningfully altering policy. Further, its box-checking nature means that the tasks can easily be sidelined, dumped on already marginalized parliamentary women's committees or ministries' gender experts. The actual reports then vanish into the ether while governments, again indulging in genderwashing, tout their gender mainstreaming processes before international organizations. These critiques are valid. Still, women legislators, policymakers, academics, experts, and civil society activists at the international and national level pour considerable energy into first winning gender mainstreaming and gender budgeting reforms and then implementing them. As with all aspirational politics, gender mainstreaming requirements create on-paper mandates that help women's rights protagonists advocate new policies, track how a policy affects women's lives, identify where and how a policy can be improved, and attempt to shift more resources towards implementing existing gender equality policies.

A similar story emerges with respect to women's policy agencies (WPAs), another key achievement of the women's rights era but one also subject to potential manipulation by governments more interested in show than substance. Women's policy agencies are dedicated executive branch offices charged with introducing gender equality perspectives across government alongside coordinating the implementation of existing women's rights legislation. In the anglophone, Nordic, and European countries, WPAs pre-date the women's rights era, with many established in the 1960s. For example, Canada's Royal Commission on the Status of Women, established in 1967, created the federal agency Status of Women Canada in 1976. The UN Decade for Women inspired countries beyond the Global North to adopt WPAs – even if just to showcase this achievement in Mexico City, Copenhagen, or Nairobi. By 1990, over 100 countries had some form of WPA, though many newly created agencies were rarely located near the apex of government decision-making power.[53] Recall the Office for Depatriarchalization created by Evo Morales in Bolivia: for all its flashy title, the office remained under-resourced and under-staffed, located within a vice-ministry (Chapter 3). The 1995 Beijing PfA acknowledged the exponential growth in these 'national machineries for the advancement of women' but also identified their deficits, stipulating that governments must locate WPAs 'at the highest possible level in Government' and provide them with sufficient resources and opportunities to influence policymaking.[54]

Ultimately, WPAs – like women's caucuses – become important advocacy spaces. They create platforms through which women in the state form ties and collaborate with elected women and women's civil society organizations. Some governments do elevate their WPAs: Status of Women Canada is now Women and Gender Equality Canada, and its head holds cabinet minister rank. When governments actually give WPAs stature and authority, the agencies can and do facilitate the adoption of women's rights policies. Laurel Weldon finds, for instance, that democratic countries are more likely to pass and implement strong anti-violence against women legislation when they have (1) WPAs that have the independence, resources, and channels to coordinate with women's organizations and (2) autonomous women's movements.[55] When well-funded and steered by feminists, WPAs can positively influence gender equality policy.

Including women in the polity

Countries diverge in their histories, cultures, and political regimes, but the women's rights era shows remarkable uniformity in the reforms adopted to raise women's political representation and include gender perspectives within policymaking. Across the globe, women activists have sought gender quota laws, demanded reforms to parliamentary and party procedures, formed women's caucuses, and shaped gender mainstreaming mandates. These successes do not mean that the reforms themselves have worked equally well everywhere – gender quotas underperform in some countries and gender mainstreaming rules are not always robustly followed. Still, women protagonists at the four world conferences on women converged on these demands, which proved straightforward enough for governments to adopt *and* implement. In many cases, men political leaders acquiesced because they knew that the damage could be contained: gender quota laws could be designed with loopholes, and women's policy agencies could be created but then underfunded and buried within sub-ministries.

At the same time, these reforms take fundamental steps to include women within the polity, eroding male political dominance from the inside. Women seize even the most tepid window-dressing reforms, turning each advance into a bigger win. When male opponents designed loopholes, women came back again to close them. Moreover, these reforms are not sought 'just' by elite women in political parties and elected office. Feminists marching in Latin America carry banners that read 'without parity there is no democracy' and 'parity now!'. In Cameroon in 2022, 20,000 women marched to denounce the electoral code's weak recommendation that parties should take gender into consideration. Instead, they demanded an effective gender quota law.[56] In Nigeria, in 2025, over 1,000 women marched on the capital Abuja, demonstrating support for the quota bill that would reserve 35 per cent of parliamentary seats for women. 'We want the legislature to work for women', a protest organizer said.[57] These demands from women citizens underscore the fundamental importance of formal measures that include women within the polity: without women in parliaments and government, the underlying patriarchal structures cannot fall. To achieve their political inclusion, women protagonists continue going to war against the male dinosaurs who deny them their rightful place – and they largely keep winning.

FIVE

Education and Workforce Participation

Casimira Rodríguez migrated from an Indigenous rural community in Bolivia when she was 13 years old. She went to work for a middle-class family in the city of Cochabamba, living in their home, working 18 hours a day. She had been offered schooling in exchange for domestic work, but instead the family kept her in 'slave-like conditions' for two years. She never received a pay cheque.[1] In 1985, at the age of 21, she helped to found the group that would later become the Cochabamba's Domestic Workers' Union, seeking to formalize domestic work such that girls and women could not be exploited and abused.[2]

Thousands of kilometres away, at about the same time Rodríguez formed her union, 12-year-old Kalpona Akter went to work in one of Bangladesh's garment factories. Her father was ill and there was no money for food, so she traded school for 16–18-hour workdays on the factory floor, where women comprise the majority of the workforce.[3] Bangladesh's garment factories provide clothes for familiar global brands such as H&M, Zara, Marks and Spencer, Primark, and the Gap, but labour conditions are notoriously poor. About 80 per cent of Bangladeshi garment workers have experienced or witnessed sexual violence and harassment.[4] Akter became a union organizer, founding the Bangladesh Centre for Worker Solidarity in 2000. She spoke out when the Tazreen Fashions fire killed 112 workers in 2012, and again when the Rana Plaza factory killed 1,133.[5] She has led garment factory workers in multiple strikes and has been arrested several times. Over 2023, 2024, and 2025 women garment workers have continued to strike over low wages, poor working conditions, and abuse in factories.

A world away, US states are passing salary history bans – laws prohibiting future employers from asking applicants how much they made in their previous jobs. That women are paid less than men for the same employment is well known and well documented, and salary history bans contribute to closing the gender wage gap. If employers are benchmarking new employees' salaries against their previous ones, non-disclosure lowers the risk that women start a new job with a lesser salary than men. In 2016, Massachusetts passed the United States' first salary history ban. As of 2025, the bans exist in 22 US states and many US counties and cities.[6] The motivation, as then Massachusetts state senator Pat Jehlen recounted, was a 1991 failed lawsuit brought by women cafeteria workers who sought equal pay with men janitors, on the grounds that they did similar work. At the time, the Massachusetts Supreme Judicial Court ruled against the women.[7] Yet while working-class women may have inspired Jehlen, professional-class women are thought to be better positioned to benefit from salary history bans, as they have more opportunities to negotiate their salaries. A salary history question could seem laughable to domestic workers like Rodríguez or garment workers like Akter, who have few options and so must take the cut-rate wages offered by predatory employers. Indeed, the End Salary History movement, promoted by the UK Fawcett Society and founded by London-based businesswoman Shobaa Haridas, primarily targeted large corporations and their professional employees (even as these corporations employ workers at all levels, from executives to cleaning staff).[8]

Still, Rodríguez, Akter, Jehlen, and Haridas share similar objectives. They want women to access dignified paid employment, to receive a fair wage equal to that of men, and to receive equal treatment at work and equal opportunities for promotion and advancement. Chapter 1 noted that the separate spheres ideology constitutes a fundamental structuring force of patriarchy: this is the idea that men perform paid 'productive' labour outside the home and women perform unpaid 'reproductive' labour inside the home. Of course, individual families' abilities to live up to this ideology vary greatly by socioeconomic status, cultural norms, and other factors. As economically marginalized women have long noted, *not* working for wages has never been an option. Upper-class families may glorify the stay-at-home mother, but minoritized women – whether migrant women, women of colour in the Global North, or impoverished women in the Global South – face pressures to engage in paid employment, no matter their culture or custom. Further, different cultural, religious, and national norms place greater or lesser value on the male breadwinner and female homemaker ideal. Such variation exists even within otherwise similar regions. Take Europe. Scholars often highlight the German idea of the *Rabenmutter* ('raven mother') – a pejorative term for working mothers with young children. They argue that Germany's cultural prioritization of the at-home mother explains the country's paucity of public childcare options. By contrast, no such term circulates in Scandinavia, where countries' generous provision of public daycare explicitly facilitates women's workforce participation.

Keeping such variation in mind, this chapter focuses on women and the public sphere, with an emphasis on workforce participation. In this chapter, 'work' is understood as labour in exchange for wages (whereas Chapter 6 examines women and the private sphere and takes 'work' to mean unremunerated work done in the home). Exchanging labour for wages may seem simple, but the transaction – as well as the policy demands that emerge from it – is complex. On the one hand, women activists share a clear goal: women should have equal rights to participate and receive fair treatment in waged work. On the other hand, turning this right into reality raises myriad questions of gender, class, opportunity, and occupation. What 'equal rights to participate' means for garment workers when compared with women lawyers is sometimes the same, but sometimes different. All want fair wages and protection from sexual harassment, but lawyers might not worry about how flammable garments, unsafe conditions, and factories' lack of emergency exits increase the likelihood of injury or death. Women's working conditions are profoundly shaped by their individual circumstances and by their country's location in the global economy.

To sketch the terrain of women and work, this chapter begins by discussing the concept of economic empowerment and why women's movements have prioritized women's access to the public sphere. In some ways, the division between public and private spheres is artificial: as noted, cultural and religious ideals about family operate alongside socioeconomic necessity to shape *which* women exit the private sphere and enter the public one. These ideals also shape how easy or difficult countries may make women's employment, as norms about gender roles shape policies from maternity leave (covered in this chapter) to childcare provision (covered in the next chapter). Cultural and religious ideals also shape how easy or difficult it is for women to access education, with education in turn influencing the level at which women enter the labour market. After reviewing the concept of economic empowerment, this chapter will briefly turn to education before examining three specific feminist blueprints that shape women's experiences in paid employment.

Selecting which feminist blueprints to emphasize, however, proves a daunting task. In the policy area of women's employment, the United Nations operates alongside other important international governance organizations. That is because women's employment does not just matter for individual women's economic wellbeing: it matters for countries' gross domestic product, their total wealth, and their position within the global economy. Generally speaking, the more individuals work, the more money circulates in the economy; the more money circulates, the greater the countries' economic growth. Consequently, every international organization engaged in economic development – such as the World Bank, all the regional development banks, the OECD, and the International Monetary Fund – offers blueprints for addressing women and work. This chapter focuses on the United Nations' International Labour Organization (ILO) as one leading voice in norm setting around women and work. Founded in 1919, the ILO has a unique tripartite design that gives equal voice to workers, employers, and governments. Fourteen ILO conventions on international labour standards speak directly to women's workforce equality, on matters ranging from night work to harassment and violence.[9] This chapter examines three conventions representing key policy areas in which women's rights advocates mobilized: the 2000 Maternity Protection Convention; the 1996 Home Work Convention; and the 2011 Domestic Workers Convention.

The public sphere as a site of economic empowerment

Feminist blueprints tie women's access to employment to *economic empowerment.* 'Women and the economy' constitutes one of the 12 priority areas in the Beijing PfA. The document stresses that women's economic participation is vital for poverty alleviation in general and for alleviating women's and children's poverty in particular. The PfA calls for ending gendered inequalities in family and in society that prevent women from exerting power over economic decision-making, both within households and at a policy level. The desired actions include legislation mandating equal pay for equal work and non-discrimination against women in the labour market and facilitating women's access to financial resources and labour force opportunities.

Consequently, just as with political empowerment (Chapter 3), the presumption is that women's economic empowerment is a desirable good. Some might contest this assumption. Just as some might argue that politics is fundamentally corrupt and hierarchical and that having women enter broken systems does not advance equality, some might argue that the workforce is fundamentally transactional and exploitative and that having women become cogs in capitalism's wheels makes neither women nor society better off. These critiques illuminate how political and economic structures perpetuate unfairness and injustice. They underscore how reforms equalizing men's and women's opportunities can close gender gaps and move women closer to equality while still producing suboptimal outcomes. For example, securing equal pay between the men and the women who work on the factory floor does not change the fact that such wages are substandard and workers (men and women alike) still have unmet basic needs. Similarly, when women become executive officers of corporations long maligned for labour violations or environmental damage, their leadership does not necessarily undo the harm such companies generate in the world (though the tantalizing prospect that women in business, like women in politics, will lead corporations differently is often used by advocates campaigning for more women in business).

Some feminists may thus prefer to not legitimize capitalist systems by selling their labour (just as some may prefer to not legitimize certain regimes by entering their political institutions). Nonetheless, many women *have* demanded rights to work, including the rights to work in morally questionable occupations or in ethically dubious sectors or companies. Demands for equal access to paid employment have shaped the women's rights era and are enshrined in the era's feminist blueprints. When women cannot be in the workforce on the same terms as men, they are unequal in terms of their resources, status, and authority. Individuals can have different preferences over whether such resources, status, or authority should be desired, but the women's rights era's protagonists were determined that equal access should exist for those who seek it.

Where are women working?

Employment can take place in what scholars call the 'formal sector', meaning the regulated labour market, where companies and businesses are legal entities that follow countries' laws around how businesses form and operate (including how they treat their employees). Formal sector workers pay taxes on their income and benefit from protections afforded by national labour laws – though such benefits vary depending on how worker-friendly and gender-equal these laws are and how easily workers can access official channels of redress. The formal sector includes entrepreneurs or sole proprietors (e.g. an artist who sells her paintings directly to clients) when these sole traders register their businesses and report their wages. A central struggle within the realm of women and work relates to revising countries' labour laws to ensure women's equal access to formal sector benefits and protections. The US salary history bans constitute one example of how policy reforms level the playing field for men and women in the formal sector.

However, women's work also takes place in the informal sector, meaning the unregulated labour market where workers do not benefit from state protection. In the informal sector, individuals' work arrangements lie outside the state's gaze. Some women, for instance, might receive money in exchange for domestic work or for selling food in street markets. They usually collect their wages as cash and do not register with the state, meaning that they operate without licenses and may not pay required fees and taxes. Other women might enter informal – and often illicit – work schemes in bars, factories, or other spaces. Some women could even be trafficked, pressed into horrific conditions against their will.

Importantly, engaging in informal work and thus failing to follow existing laws does not make women criminals. For marginalized women, the informal sector may be the best or only option. Informal work tied to skills women learn in the domestic sphere – such as cleaning, baking, or sewing – requires little to no schooling. Informality also offers women flexibility over working hours, allowing them to fit waged work around domestic responsibilities. Registering with the state can also be difficult for myriad reasons related to literacy and required fees. Informal work is thus not a purely free choice, but one influenced by the structural and material conditions shaping women's lives. Women enter the informal sector out of necessity, but then are vulnerable to exploitation and abuse, since informal workers cannot benefit from labour protections. Another central struggle within the realm of women and work is formalizing women's work, such that informal workers gain rights and protections.

The ILO Home Work Convention and the Domestic Workers Convention discussed below offer two examples wherein women informal workers organized themselves into labour unions and sought legal changes that would transform informal jobs into formal ones. Such efforts have mattered especially in the Global South, where a much larger share of total employment occurs within the informal economy. The ILO estimates that less than 20 per cent of employment in the United States, Canada, Europe, Australia, and New Zealand occurs in the informal sector, by comparison with more than 50 per cent in some parts of Latin America and Central Asia and over 75 per cent in sub-Saharan Africa, Southeast Asia, and the Pacific Islands.[10] Globally, about 55 per cent of women work informally, by comparison with 60 per cent of men.[11] These numbers might seem quite large to those accustomed to the primarily formal labour markets in the Americas and Europe – but in Africa and Asia-Pacific most women and most men work informally. Women are concentrated in the informal sectors associated with traditionally feminized activities like preparing food, cooking and cleaning, sewing, and selling handicrafts.

Why working for wages matters for gender equality

The separate spheres ideology provides insight into why women's access to employment generates economic empowerment and thus remains important for gender equality. At the most fundamental level, employment, whether in the formal or in the informal sector, means having money, and money means having purchasing power. People trade money for goods, services, and opportunities. The separate spheres associate productive work with economic value, because it earns money, and reproductive work with moral value, because it cares for families and children. And while feminists have criticized gender hierarchies that place productive work above reproductive work and purchasing power above moral power, no society has fully divested itself of this basic structure.

Economic men are ranked above domestic women, even in communist societies (see Chapter 3).

Since money enables choices, money also confers individual autonomy and freedom. When women have money, their options increase. Consider the opposite scenario, where a woman in a heterosexual relationship in a patriarchal society has no money of her own, relying solely on a male breadwinner for household income. Of course, this relationship could be emotionally healthy and benefit both partners. Yet if the male partner takes advantage of the head-of-household status that both patriarchy and breadwinning give him, women become disadvantaged, dependent, and disempowered. By controlling the purse strings, the male partner decides everything, from where the family lives to where they eat and what clothes they wear. And if the male partner is violent or abusive, women have few exit options.

This stylized presentation of within-household gender equality shapes how feminists have approached economic development and economic growth. In the early decades of the women's rights era, feminists challenged standard models of economic development (as they still do today). Then as now, countries emerging from colonialism and conflict needed to tackle poverty. Of course, poverty is not only a problem in the Global South, but countries on the periphery face pressure to reduce poverty through development, which means producing goods, ideally via industrialization, to sell and trade on international markets. Feminists pointed out, however, that development models from the 1960s onward did more than just impose capitalist models of production and consumption across the globe. They were also gender-blind.

First, the standard development models assumed that households were unitary and overlooked the power dynamics within them. Development experts focused on ending poverty wanted to boost employment, which would inject more money into households. With more money, households could then move beyond subsistence, meaning beyond activities focused on day-to-day survival. A supposedly virtuous circle would then follow, where more goods being purchased for a higher standard of living (consumption) would fuel markets for these goods, leading to more businesses producing them (production). Yet feminist economists countered that households are not unitary: within households, those members who earn money have bargaining power, and those with bargaining power can ignore the needs of those without it. As Indian economist Bina Agrawal wrote in a 1997 landmark essay, women lacked within-household bargaining power and thus found their survival needs deprioritized.[12] Men would go to work in the formal economy, but their earnings would prioritize feeding, clothing, and educating the household's men and boys. Development would not necessarily benefit women.

Second, when the development models did account for women, they focused on launching women into the supposedly virtuous circle of consumption and production without accounting for gender inequality. For women to become consumers, they would need to become formal sector workers. The standard development models did recognize that women existed, insofar as women represented an untapped labour pool. If women were pushed out of the home and into the factory, then more household income would accrue and women, too, could become consumers. The traditional development experts were sanguine, however, about what women's jump from private to public looked like. Since their perspective was gender-blind, they overlooked that many women already were engaged in income-generating tasks, albeit in the informal economy (e.g. selling extra food in markets). They also overlooked how, when women entered the formal economy, their entry was shaped by persistent wage discrimination and occupational segregation. Further, women were often regarded as the household's supplementary worker: a man's wages belong to him, to distribute as he wishes, but a woman's wages add to the family income, supporting children and other dependents.

On the one hand, when women earn money – even a little – their household bargaining status improves, because their own income gives them voice and influence over choices. Even small amounts of autonomy can boost women's economic empowerment: when women leave (even if briefly) the household to go to work, they gain mobility and earn money, opening more opportunity for themselves and other women. On the other hand, women still face barriers to taking advantage of their newly improved status. Feminist development experts argued that wages alone would not make women economically equal to men. Women would still earn less than men and households would still invest in men and boys first. Putting the pieces together, Agrawal wrote: 'Incorrect perceptions [about women's value] can thus reduce a woman's bargaining power in relation to family subsistence not only by leading to an underestimation of her needs and an undervaluation of her waged contributions, but also by affecting her "worth" in the labour market, thus limiting the mentioned potential advantage of her seeking waged work.'[13]

Feminist perspectives on women, money, and work

These feminist critiques had numerous significant consequences. Theoretically, they identify how the public and private spheres are tightly bound, and how tackling women's economic empowerment requires addressing the intertwined forces of household inequality and labour market discrimination. Practically they reshaped global understandings of development models, shifting international discourses away from an approach called Women and Development (which characterized the first decades of the women's rights era) and towards an approach called Gender and Development (which came to dominate the era's later part). Gender and Development would, in theory, not just 'add women and stir' to classic development models, but account for how gender inequality shapes women's entry into and benefit from development programmes. This shift occurred thanks to the four world conferences on women and other international convenings. As Global North and Global South women debated their perspectives on women and work, feminist blueprints began reflecting more sophisticated understandings of how gender shapes households' ability to exit from poverty, of women's labour force participation, and of countries' overall prospects for economic growth. A key achievement of the women's rights era was the formal recognition that simply pushing women out of the kitchen and into the factories would not produce the desired results.

For example, the Beijing PfA tackled women's economic empowerment not just in the section 'Women and the Economy', but also in the sections 'Women and Poverty' and 'Education and Training of Women'. In 'Women and Poverty', the PfA follows feminist economists in linking employment, education, and even political participation together and in emphasizing structural changes: 'Women's poverty is directly related to the absence of economic opportunities and autonomy, lack of access to economic resources, including credit, land ownership and inheritance, lack of access to education and support services and their minimal participation in the decision-making process. Poverty can also force women into situations in which they are vulnerable to sexual exploitation.'[14] The PfA also recognizes the differentially situated positions of women both within and across countries. The document discusses the barriers faced by low-income women and migrant women in the informal economy, for example, while also noting gender discrimination in the formal economy: 'in the private sector, including transnational and national enterprises, women are largely absent from management and policy levels, denoting discriminatory hiring and promotion policies and practices.'[15]

That individuals' socioeconomic status and their countries' position in the global economy affect women's prospects for employment highlights one element that makes women's economic empowerment distinctive: some women may gain economic empowerment at the expense of other women. To understand, first consider a truism in every country across the globe: while women's time spent on waged work has increased dramatically during the women's rights era, their time spent on household chores has not decreased proportionally. On average, men have not increased their contributions to unpaid household work at the same pace at which women have increased their participation in waged labour. This pattern holds as much in Sweden and Germany as it does in Bolivia and in Bangladesh. Consequently, middle- and upper-class women often enter the labour force by relying on domestic servants such as Casimira Rodríguez. Middle- and upper-class women have greater purchasing power, which means that they can purchase the labour of lower-class women, offloading domestic work.

These dynamics happen within countries and between countries. Labour migration occurs internally, when women like Casimira Rodríguez migrate from rural areas to urban areas to become domestic workers. Labour migration also occurs across borders, when women domestic workers migrate from Anglophone Caribbean to the United States, Canada, or Europe or from Southeast Asia to the Gulf states. In many cases, domestic work happens as part of the unregulated informal economy. Labour migrants face particular precarity: in addition to working informally, they often lack legal documents to prove their identity or their status. Migrants may even pay unscrupulous or criminal brokers for help with accessing employment in the receiving city or country. Brokers may force them to surrender their passports and other personal documents until they earn enough to repay the money for their journey. Such migrants thus become victims of human trafficking, a form of modern slavery that subjects victims to severe abuse and exploitation.

This intersectional perspective underscores that women's rights reforms affect women in varied ways, depending on their other identities. In the case of women and work, labour market gains for certain groups of women happen because of economic inequality *among women.* Many privileged women gain economic autonomy because they can pay for minoritized women to complete their domestic chores. They can hire a domestic worker such as Casimira or send dependants (including children, people with disabilities, and elders) to daycare centres or care homes. Yet since work in what feminists call the 'care economy' – the sector encompassing nurseries, early education, care centres, and care homes – is feminized and also racialized, these jobs are underpaid. Thus, as some (usually upper status and privileged) women achieve higher status jobs and make more money, they increase the demand for other (usually lower status and minoritized) women to enter lower status jobs and make less money. Labour market structures prevent the benefits of employment from accruing equally to women.

There are many potential solutions to the conundrum wherein women's greater labour force participation depends on and exacerbates inequality among women. The first entails shifting gender norms about domestic work and women's work. Since the start of the women's rights era, feminists have talked about 'co-responsibility' in the domestic sphere, meaning that man must share reproductive tasks. The 1975 Mexico City conference report mentions the need to 'bring about the acceptance of shared responsibilities for home and children by both men and women'.[16] The second solution constitutes raising wages within the care economy, especially for the predominantly female workers who occupy the lower rungs of the education and healthcare sectors. The naturalization of women as carers leads care economy jobs to be perceived as less skilled, and higher wages would grant these jobs more earning power, dignity, and status. A third and related solution is for governments to provide care services directly, on the assumption that governments are better positioned to distribute care equally and to ensure that care workers receive living wages. Though care economy workers labour within the public sphere, the association of these jobs with traditionally private household tasks means that policy demands related to care work and care workers are tackled in the next chapter (Chapter 6). The present chapter highlights instances where women conducting paid domestic work in other women's homes fought to have this remunerated work recognized as formal sector employment.

Education as a right – and a precursor to employment

So far, this chapter has emphasized how socioeconomic status, race and ethnicity, and their multiple intersections affect whether, where, and how women might expect to enter the labour market. Another important dimension affecting where women (and men) can enter the labour market is education. Of course, women's equal access to education is a policy area of its own. Education allows individuals to develop their full potential, to understand their world, and to chart a life course on their own terms. The major feminist blueprints of the women's rights era all included education – and this policy area shows enormous progress. World Economic Forum data show that the closing of gender gaps in educational attainment constitutes a major achievement of the women's right era. Examining four indicators – the literacy rate and women's enrolment in primary, secondary, and tertiary (university) education – the World Economic Forum's 'Global Gender Gap 2024' report found that 143 countries had collectively closed 94.9 per cent of the education gap between women and men.[17]

This near gender parity in education did not exist 50 years ago. Take sub-Saharan Africa, one of three regions the United Nations identifies as having among the largest gender gaps in education (the other two are Northern Africa–Western Asia and South Asia). According to UN data, in 1970, 80 per cent of women in sub-Saharan Africa aged 20–24 could not read. By 1990, only 50 per cent of women aged 20–24 could not read, by comparison with 30 per cent of men in the same age bracket – a gender gap of 20 percentage points.[18] Women's literacy rates thus improved between 1970 and 1990, and the trend continued in the next decades. By 2023, the World Bank found a gender gap in literacy of just 12.4 percentage points for the sub-Saharan population aged 15 and above.[19] While the UN and World Bank numbers examine different age cohorts and are thus not perfectly comparable, they nonetheless show these education gaps narrowing.

Similarly, the United Nations found that in 1985, in sub-Saharan Africa, about 60 girls were enrolled in secondary school for every 100 boys – a gender gap of 40 percentage points.[20] By 2021, the World Bank estimated the gender gap in secondary school completion to be just three percentage points. Importantly, however, this gap exists within low rates of lower secondary enrolment overall for sub-Saharan Africa: 43.5 per cent for girls and 45.3 per cent for boys in 2025.[21]

Small or vanishing gender gaps thus do not mean that countries are succeeding at raising *everyone*'s standard of living. The data suggest that, in sub-Saharan Africa, boys and girls are pushed out of secondary school at similar rates, though the factors shaping boys' and girls' exit vary by gender (e.g. girls may leave to shoulder domestic chores while boys leave to undertake informal work). Other regions have nearly no gender gaps on key metrics related to educational attainment. Gaps of less than 1 per cent appear for literacy in Latin America, the Caribbean, Europe, and Central Asia, and gaps of less than 1 per cent appear for secondary school completion in Europe and Central Asia.[22] In Latin America and the Caribbean in 2025, 84 per cent of girls and 79.2 per cent of boys complete lower secondary school, and in Europe and Central Asia, the completion rate climbs to 92 per cent for girls and 91.7 per cent for boys.[23] At higher levels of education, gender gaps have even reversed in some regions, with more women than men attending university in the Global North, as in the United States, Canada, the United Kingdom, and Australia.

Key policy changes from the women's rights era accelerated women's literacy and educational attainment. Since the 1970s and even earlier, large proportions of development aid earmarked for education flowed into the Global South, funding initiatives that ranged from infrastructure improvements to the elimination of school fees for enrolment and supplies. The latter matters for girls' access to education, as families with fewer resources prioritize school attendance for boys. Three sub-Saharan African countries that eliminated their school fees overnight – Ethiopia, Kenya, and Malawi – subsequently approached gender parity in primary and secondary school enrolment.[24] While governments did not eliminate school fees with gender equality in mind (these policies were considered general anti-poverty measures), the reforms had important gendered effects. Non-profit organizations and women activists continue tackling other gendered barriers to girls' schooling, obstacles that range from social norms that undervalue girls' education to structural barriers that interfere with girls' school attendance, such as adolescent pregnancy and child marriage.

One important effort has centred on ensuring that pregnant students can remain in school. Most sub-Saharan African countries have 'continuation' or 're-entry' policies preventing pregnant students' expulsions, thanks to women's activists' efforts. For instance, Equality Now Africa and national partner organizations filed international court cases against Sierra Leone and Tanzania in 2018 and 2020, respectively. The cases challenged policies preventing pregnant girls from returning to school. In the Sierra Leone case, the court sided with the women activists.[25] In Tanzania, the government acted before the court decided. Tanzania issued Education Circular 2 in 2021, clarifying that pregnant students who dropped out of school could return. A year later, more specific re-entry guidelines for exiting students were established by Tanzania's Ministry of Education, Science and Technology.[26]

Several sub-Saharan African countries go further than continuation or re-entry policies: Mauritania, Benin, Nigeria, the Democratic Republic of Congo, South Sudan, and Zimbabwe all have laws asserting pregnant students' and mothers' rights to education.[27] In Zimbabwe's case, the 2019 reform clarified a vague 1999 continuation guideline by specifically stating that neither pregnancy nor marital status (among other characteristics) could be grounds for discrimination in school admission, suspension, exclusion, or expulsion. The Zimbabwe reform also mandated that the state must provide sanitary products and menstrual health facilities in all schools.[28] MP Priscilla Misihairabwi-Mushonga led the effort, alongside a consortium of international organizations.[29] Such laws are also not limited to the African continent. In Argentina, a 2002 law prevents schools and universities from denying pregnant students and parents school entry or continuation, and a 2006 reform mandates breastfeeding spaces, requires flexible attendance and absence policies for parents, and allows parents to bring their children to school.[30]

Both Zimbabwe and Argentina thus went beyond pregnancy-related discrimination to consider how matters related to women's health, such as menstruation and breastfeeding, inhibit school attendance. For many girls, the stigma of menstruation impedes school attendance, especially when poverty prevents them from affording menstrual products. Tackling period poverty thus constitutes yet another site of feminist struggle. In 2004, Kenya made news by becoming the first country in the world to eliminate the value-added tax (VAT) on menstrual products. In 2017, Kenya modified the Basic Education Act to provide 'free, sufficient, and quality' menstrual products to all girls in public education, alongside safe and environmentally responsible systems for disposing of used products. Two years later, when a young Kenyan girl committed suicide after being period-shamed by her teacher, women MPs charged down to the Ministry of Education and occupied a conference room in protest, demanding better implementation of the measure.[31] Such efforts are not limited to the Global South. In the mid-2010s in Scotland, Victoria Heaney from Women for Independence (WFI) started the online campaign #FreePeriodScotland.[32] Member of the Scottish Parliament Monica Lennon helped bring WFI's campaign to the government, and in 2020 Scotland became the first government to mandate the free provision of period products.[33] The Scottish law specifically names educational institutions as among those public institutions that must provide free products.

Tackling gender discrimination in tertiary (university) education has been equally important. The 1972 amendment to the US Higher Education Act predates the women's rights era, but created an important legal foundation that women's rights advocates would refine in the ensuing decades. Known as 'Title IX', the non-discrimination amendment was authored by congresswoman Patsy Mink of Hawai'i, the first woman of colour elected to the US Congress and a key women's rights leader. Title IX established that women must have equal access to all educational opportunities, including participation in university sport – a big business in the United States, where university sport provides pipelines into professional leagues. About the same time, other countries also included higher education in their general anti-sex discrimination laws. For example, the UK Discrimination Act of 1975 and the Finnish Equality between Women and Men Act of 1986 both included higher education. These laws later expanded their definitions of what counts as discrimination. In response to student activism about sexual harassment and sexual assault on campus, the US Department of Education gradually interpreted Title IX to include sexual harassment and sexual assault as instances of gender discrimination, ordering universities to proactively combat sexual violence in higher education. The 2010 UK Equality Act, which replaced the 1975 Act, also prohibits sexual harassment and sexual violence and holds that public authorities such as universities are responsible for the prevention of both. The 2014 revisions to the Finnish Act likewise include comprehensive definitions and prohibitions of sexual harassment in educational institutions.

Some countries have gone even further. In Spain, the women's movement actively inserted education-specific considerations into many equality laws adopted in the 2000s.[34] Women's advocacy resulted in victories that included (1) updating the 2004 law on gender-based violence to require that universities promote gender equality and non-discrimination in training, teaching, and research and (2) stipulating in the 2007 general equality law that the federal, regional, and local governments must all incorporate gender equality between men and women into their curricula and create specific post-graduate courses on gender equality. The 2011 Spanish law on science, technology, and innovation establishes gender as a cross-cutting category in science. Addressing gender equality not merely in terms of women's access to and experience in universities but in terms of teaching, curricular, and research activities cements higher education as a place where women's lived experiences are addressed. Barriers remain, but women's literacy and educational status have improved steadily since 1975 – as has women's entry into the workforce.

Maternity protections

Just as women have fought to prevent pregnancy and motherhood from disrupting their education, they have fought to ensure that pregnancy does not impede their employment. In the 1970s, many of the anti-discrimination laws passed by countries such as the United States, the United Kingdom, and Finland prohibited pregnancy-related employment discrimination. Many of these laws define pregnancy-related discrimination broadly, including practices that reduce pregnant women's roles or wages, but at a minimum the laws prohibit pregnancy-related dismissals. The World Bank estimates that in 1971 less than half the countries in Europe, Central Asia, and Latin America explicitly prohibited pregnancy-related dismissals. By 2021, however, nearly all of them had established such laws.[35] Elsewhere in 1971, no sub-Saharan African countries prohibited pregnancy-related dismissals, and fewer than 10 per cent of countries in East Asia, the Pacific, the Middle East and North Africa did. By 2021, these regions too had made progress: 79 per cent of sub-Saharan African countries and 50 per cent of countries in the remaining regions had adopted pregnancy discrimination bans in employment.[36] Progress is not universal – about 38 countries still lack explicit prohibitions on pregnancy-related dismissals – and enforcement remains challenging, but the on-paper protections have advanced considerably.

Another important set of maternity protections allows women to take paid maternity leave. Across all occupations and incomes, paid maternity leave constitutes an essential employment protection – one that women from all countries and all backgrounds agree on seeking. The 1975 Mexico City Programme of Action stated: 'governments, employers, and trade unions should ensure all women workers the right to maternity protection, including maternity leave with a guarantee of returning to their formal employment . . . Provisions relating to maternity protection should not be regarded as unequal treatment of the sexes.'[37] The PfA established that 'maternity, motherhood, parenting and the role of women in procreation must not be a basis for discrimination nor restrict the full participation of women in society'.[38] The PfA further outlined the policy goals: 'Eliminate discriminatory practices by employers and take appropriate measures in consideration of women's reproductive role and functions [. . .] take effective measures to ensure that pregnant women, women on maternity leave or women re-entering the labour market after childbearing are not discriminated against.'[39]

This emphasis on preventing discrimination via potentially *unequal* treatment echoes how maternity protections raise the difference versus sameness debate discussed in Chapter 1. Many claims to gender equality are premised on giving women the same rights and entitlements as men, but pregnancy and maternity protections (like gender quota laws) require giving women *different* rights and entitlements from those given to men. Feminist blueprints attempt to reconcile the difference versus sameness debate by clarifying the importance of differential treatment in the instance of pregnancy and childbearing. Here, equality is attained by recognizing how biological difference creates unlevel playing fields between men and women and by using policy to mitigate the unequal effects.

Yet questions still remain about how far this differential treatment should go. Generally, feminist scholars take the legally mandated number of weeks of maternity leave as evidence of countries' commitment to women's employment rights. The more weeks available, the better the circumstances for women, as new mothers receive more time to recuperate and bond with their children. Critics argue, however, that very extensive periods of leave might tip towards pro-natal policies – policies that countries implement to encourage more births and, by extension, encourage women to prioritize family over work. Some feminists are therefore sceptical about overly generous periods of maternity leave, alongside ancillary policies that support at-home mothers, for example cash-for-care schemes in which governments pay family members for providing dependent care. By making staying at home to fulfil caregiving duties less financially burdensome, these policies could well encourage women *not* to return to the workforce, thus reifying rather than transforming their private sphere roles. At the same time, many countries are facing demographic crunches, where declining birth rates leave the population below replacement rate. Demographic crunches are becoming particularly pronounced in industrialized countries in the Global North, where the rapid change in women's public roles, the glacial change in their domestic responsibilities, and the high costs of outsourcing childcare make work and family life very difficult for women to reconcile. As ideals about co-responsibility struggle to take root among men and as governments fail to increase public funding for childcare, women simply opt to have fewer children.

Insofar as declining birth rates signal women's preference for earning wages over raising children, policies that help women combine work and family – while protecting women's access to paid employment – can be equality promoting. However, such policies can become equality eroding when they encourage women to abandon economic empowerment and rededicate themselves to traditional gender roles. To understand the difference, contrast two approaches within Europe. In Scandinavia, policies emphasize *parental leave* over maternity leave, allowing leave to be shared between parents and thus facilitating co-responsibility in caregiving and domestic tasks. In Denmark, for instance, the birth parent may take four weeks of leave prior to birth, and each parent is entitled to a 24-week leave after birth, for 52 weeks in total. In Sweden, where new parents can share up to 480 days of leave, social norms have evolved such that fathers are expected to claim a portion.[40] Such shared parental leave policies are more aligned with the feminist objective of encouraging men to undertake caregiving and ultimately eroding the binary economic man versus domestic woman. In Croatia, by contrast, pro-natalist reformers have, since the 1990s, routinely tried to introduce a compulsory three-year maternity leave (alongside removing abortion rights and instituting a state-paid profession of mother-caregiver for women with more than four children). Pushback, including lobbying and lawsuits from the Croatian feminist organization Budi aktivna, Budi emancipirana (B.a.B.e.: Be Active, Be Emancipated) has halted the reforms each time.[41]

When it comes to maternity protection and other work–family reconciliation policies, the devil really lies in the details. Researchers need to understand which set of actors seek the reform and the kinds of incentives around work and family life the reform creates. Generally speaking, however, a generous maternity leave remains central to women's employment equality.

Maternity protections and the International Labour Organization

The ILO's recommended maternity protections date to its founding, emerging from a lobbying process that mirrored how women activists would work at later UN conferences (see Chapter 2). The ILO's inaugural conference took place in Washington, DC in late autumn 1919. Women labour activists from the United States, France, and Britain organized a simultaneous First International Congress of Working Women, convened by the National Women's Trade Union League of America. Two hundred labour feminists representing not just Europe and the United States but also Asia and South America attended the women's congress. Over at the official ILO venue, the delegates were all men, but 23 non-voting women advisors participated – many of whom also participated in the women's congress. Four women played key roles in bridging the two events: Jeanne Bouvier (France), Margaret Bondfield (Britain), Mary Macarthur (Britain), and Tanaka Taka (Japan). Mona Siegel notes that, despite the geographical divides separating the feminist labour activists of the era, women's congress participants found common ground on paid maternity leave. Thanks to Bouvier's, Bondfield's, Macarthur's, and Tanaka's back-and-forth diplomacy between the ILO conference and the women's congress, paid maternity leave constituted the third convention adopted at the ILO's inaugural meeting. The all-male delegates initially balked at imposing such expenses on employers, but Siegel recounts that Bouvier and Macarthur refused to stand down.[42] The ILO Maternity Convention of 1919 (Convention 0003 or C0003) established that women were to receive six weeks of paid leave before birth, six weeks of paid leave after birth, and two daily 30-minute nursing breaks upon returning to work.

The ILO would then update this recommendation twice. In 1952, the ILO issued Convention 103 (C103), a revised Maternity Protection Convention that expanded the guidelines for maternity leave benefits and nursing accommodations. In 1998, midway through the women's rights era, the ILO announced its intentions to once again revise its maternity standards. After all, women's labour force participation had increased dramatically since the 1950s. This announcement prompted advocacy organizations to regroup and influence the new convention. For instance, a consortium of international women's health NGOs wanted to strengthen the ILO's recommendations around nursing and breastfeeding protections.[43] In Convention 183 (C183) of 2000, the ILO extended the required leave period from 12 to 14 weeks and added that employers could not discriminate against or terminate women for nursing (whereas C003 and C103 had only mandated remunerated breastfeeding periods during the workday).

Since the passage of C183, women's labour unions have lobbied their governments for its ratification, as well as invoked the convention in their broader advocacy efforts. These efforts have especially resonated in the Global South. As Keonhi Son finds, both C003 and C103 led to notable national-level reforms in maternity leave protections, but C183 did not. When C003 and C103 were respectively adopted in 1919 and 1952, most countries had yet to adopt maternity leave. By C183's adoption in 2000, however, most Global North countries already had achieved or exceeded the ILO standard, as seen in the Scandinavian examples above. (Notoriously, the United States remains the only industrialized country without a national paid maternity leave mandate).[44]

C183 thus matters most in Global South countries where maternity leave provisions lag. For instance, the IndustriALL Global Union, which represents workers in the mining, energy, and manufacturing sectors of 140 countries, has led C183 ratification campaigns in places such as Cambodia, Indonesia, Thailand, and the Philippines.[45] Women workers in all four countries have rallied outside parliaments and marched on government buildings, demanding C183 protections.[46] In the Philippines, lobbying succeeded in 2018, when Senator Risa Hontiveros worked with IndustriALL's Philippines Women's Committee to introduce and pass the 105-Day Expanded Maternity Leave Law in 2018. The new law grants 15 weeks of maternity leave alongside 60 days of paid leave for women workers who suffer from miscarriage or medically approved pregnancy termination.[47] In Indonesia in 2024, the parliament responded to women's mobilization, expanding its paid maternity leave provisions from 1.5 months to three months (with an additional three months in circumstances related to the woman's or the infant's health).[48] As a feminist blueprint, C183 especially offers women working on the global assembly line in Southeast Asia and the Pacific greater labour protections.

Homeworkers' rights

Global South women also mobilized for ILO Convention 177 (C177), on homeworkers' rights. *Homework* is not to be confused with reproductive labour, meaning the household and caregiving tasks performed by women 'for free'. Nor is homework to be confused with domestic work, meaning the work performed by paid in-home caregivers or cleaners like Casimira Rodríguez. 'Homework' describes situations in which workers complete tasks for their employers in their home, as specified by the employer. Homeworkers typically prepare garments, handicrafts, and electronics for large companies that export and sell these goods abroad. They put the finishing touches on products in their home rather than on the factory floor. Approximately 260 million people worldwide are homeworkers. Of these, 65 per cent live in Asia and the Pacific and 88 per cent are women.[49] Homeworkers cannot set their own wages or bargain with employers, and they have no contract guaranteeing them hours, work, or pay. These conditions mean that most homeworkers are informal workers, so they also cannot collect benefits such as disability compensation and severance pay.

To understand homework, consider the description offered by the WINGO Women in Informal Employment: Globalizing and Organizing (WIEGO). This transnational organization lobbies for women's labour rights, focusing on informal women workers in the Global South. WIEGO describes a typical scenario in Tirupur, India, the 'T-shirt factory of the world', where over 40,000 homeworkers perform tasks such as stitching and embroidering, cutting loose threads, and inserting ties into hoodies. In Tirupur, the factories hire contractors, who serve as intermediaries. The contractor visits the homeworker two to three times a week, to drop off unfinished pieces and collect the finished ones. The factories just provide the pieces; the homeworkers supply their own thread, needles, and equipment (e.g. scissors or sewing machines). Sometimes factories outsource to small workshops, which then subcontract to the homeworkers via informal arrangements that further separate homeworkers from factories. The more distant the homeworkers are from the factory, the harder it is for them to organize and make collective demands. The factory and the contractor pay cutthroat wages: for example, WIEGO interviews Tirupur resident Sridevi, who in 2018 received US$1.43 per day for inserting ties into 100 trackpants, a wage that barely covered her rent of US$20.89 per month.[50]

Sridevi is clearly exchanging her labour for money. However, governments and employers do not necessarily see homeworkers as workers. Traditionally, labour unions did not represent homeworkers: since the work takes place in the home, and since tasks like sewing resemble women's 'regular' domestic chores, workers such as Sridevi remain outside the formal economy. Further complicating the picture is that homeworkers may accept work from multiple contractors who represent different factories, or simultaneously undertake other income-generating activities, such as selling food in markets. From the governments' and the trade unions' perspective, the fact that homeworkers have no single employer and have multiple income streams further distinguishes them from formal sector workers.

Conceptualizing and treating homeworkers as *workers* with labour rights constituted the major reason why Indian activist Ela Bhatt founded the Self-Employed Women's Association (SEWA) in Gujarat, India in

1972. Bhatt wanted all informal sector workers, including homeworkers such as Sridevi, to be seen as workers. She recounted:

> The hard-working *chindi* workers [i.e. textile weavers working with scraps], embroiderers, cart-pullers, rag pickers, and forest produce gatherers can contribute to the nation's gross domestic product, but heaven forbid that they be acknowledged as workers. Without an employer, you cannot be classified as a worker, and since you are not a worker, you cannot form a trade union.[51]

SEWA sought to remedy this gap. Rather than helping its members collectively bargain with a single employer, SEWA helps women to form their own labour cooperatives. Women are then employed by the cooperative, and the cooperative provides labour benefits and protections, including childcare, loans to support entrepreneurial schemes, and pensions.[52]

SEWA would lead the campaign for ILO C177. In the 1990s, Bhatt and other SEWA leaders such as Renana Jhabvala travelled to Geneva to campaign for a homeworkers' convention. In 1995 Martha 'Marty' Chen, a Harvard academic and experienced development practitioner, went to meet them. Over breakfast, Bhatt asked Chen if her Harvard team would assemble statistics about the prevalence and plight of homeworkers. Bhatt recalls:

> I wanted a Harvard "stamp" on the statement of SEWA for the ILO session on home-based workers being workers and needing the lawful protection of basic labour standards . . . so that we would not be ridiculed or discarded to a dustbin by the Employer Group . . . that is why we needed the Harvard stamp, and [Chen] did so and we won our ILO Convention 177 on Home Work.[53]

When C177 passed in 1996 – the first international convention to recognize informal workers as having rights to equal and fair treatment – Bhatt and Jhabvala sent Chen a postcard from Geneva that read: 'The employers had their ideology. The workers had their statistics. The Convention was passed!'[54] The following year, Bhatt, Jhabvala, Chen, and seven other labour activists founded WIEGO.[55] Other WIEGO founders included representatives from UNIFEM, the World Bank, and Homenet, a global support network for homeworkers.

SEWA has inspired homeworkers across the globe and C177 has underscored their demands. C177 clarifies that homeworkers are workers deserving equal treatment. C177 states that homeworkers have the right to organize and to receive labour protections related to non-discrimination, maternity leave, minimum wages, health and safety standards, and dispute resolution mechanisms. To date, 13 countries have ratified C177, primarily in Central and Eastern Europe and the Caribbean. Elsewhere, countries have passed laws matching C177's vision, even as they have not yet ratified the convention. Take Pakistan, where homework constitutes a major source of women's employment. In 2009, Pakistani women homeworkers established their first trade union: the Home-Based Women Workers Federation (HBWWF).[56] In Pakistan, labour laws are set by the provinces, so the HBWWF operates at the subnational level. In 2018 in Sindh province, which includes the capital Karachi, the HBWWF secured the Sindh Home-Based Workers Bill, which allows homeworkers to register with a provincial council. The registration gives homeworkers access to social, medical, maternity, marriage, and death benefits that all formal sector employees also receive. The approximately 5 million Sindh homeworkers also gain access to arbitration in labour disputes.[57] The homeworkers' movement, with C177 as a feminist blueprint, demonstrates how Global South women workers mobilize politically and win labour rights protections.

Domestic workers' rights

Domestic work constitutes another form of remunerated work that women perform in the home. Here, women enter others' homes to complete household chores and care work, including cooking, cleaning, and caring for dependents. Domestic workers may work in several homes, visiting them on a schedule, or they may work exclusively for a single household, even living in the household. Live-in domestic workers are especially vulnerable to exploitation and abuse, particularly when they are labour migrants who lack knowledge of and access to the outside world (and might not even speak the language of their host family, city, or country). Yet domestic workers, like homeworkers, have found each other and have organized collectively.

Fighting for national laws

In Bolivia, Casimira Rodríguez was not alone.[58] She founded the Cochabamba Domestic Workers Union in 1985. About the same time, women activists founded similar unions in other Bolivian cities, including La Paz and Santa Cruz. In 1993, union leaders and members convened in Cochabamba for the First National Congress of Household Workers, where they founded the National Federation of Paid Workers in the Home (FENATRAHOB from its Spanish name). FENATRAHOB then joined the main Bolivian labour union, which facilitated members' access to policymakers. Since its founding year, FENATRAHOB began presenting lawmakers with a draft law that would protect domestic workers' rights. In 1997, a consortium of NGOs representing labour groups, women's rights groups, and Catholic organizations united to form the Committee to Promote the Law, creating a broad-based advocacy coalition that propelled FENATRAHOB's activism forward.

In 2003 the Bolivian assembly passed Law 2450, which regulates paid household work. The statute grants domestic workers the same legal rights as the country's existing labour force, including the legal minimum salary, yearly holidays, free time, health insurance, and disability and retirement pensions. Beyond these formal rights, the law addresses the racist practices that Bolivian domestic workers, most of whom are Indigenous, face from their non-Indigenous employers: the law prohibits employers from seizing domestic workers' belongings and affirms that domestic workers' cultural identities must receive respect. Without FENATRAHOB, the law would never have passed, as Bolivian researcher Pablo Castaño notes that 'domestic workers' rights were almost wholly absent from the political agenda before the creation of the federation'.[59]

Like homeworkers, domestic workers create their own movements, with notable parallels between how the movements intertwine their countries' class and racial politics. In Latin America, many Indigenous or Afro-descendant women migrate internally to become domestic workers in the homes of families of Hispanic descent. Similarly, in South Africa, Black women become domestic workers in the homes of white families. These legacies date to the colonial and apartheid eras. Under apartheid, a system of racial segregation that concentrated power in the hands of the country's white minority of European descent, Black women and men had few formal-sector opportunities and were relegated by law to undesirable and low-paying jobs. During the apartheid period, Black South African Myrtle Witbooi migrated internally as a teenager, going to work for a family in Cape Town. Witbooi would later form the South African Domestic Workers' Union (SADWU) in 1984, while also joining the anti-apartheid resistance movement led by the African National Congress (ANC). After apartheid fell, Witbooi became the general secretary of SADWU's successor, the South African Domestic and Allied Workers Union (SADSAWU), founded in 2000.

Two years later, SADSAWU successfully campaigned to include domestic workers in South Africa's Basic Conditions of Employment Act and the Labour Relations Act. Incorporating domestic workers into the existing labour regulations means that domestic workers are entitled to a minimum wage, annual wage increases, written contracts, regulated working hours (including rest periods, meal intervals, and Sunday and public holidays), and overtime.[60] Employers became prohibited from wage deductions for tools, work clothing, and break time.[61] Yet one measure remained elusive – the inclusion of domestic workers in the unemployment insurance fund. In 2003, Witbooi and four other domestic workers chained themselves to the gates of parliament.[62] Two weeks later, South African domestic workers became eligible for unemployment insurance.

Forging transnational ties and winning an international convention

Witbooi later became a leading figure in the international campaign for ILO Convention 189 (C189) on domestic workers' rights.[63] At the 1995 Beijing conference, domestic worker organizations from Latin America, South Africa, and the Caribbean met with the Wages for Housework campaigners (see Chapter 6), creating the International Network of Workers in Domestic Service (INWDS). The organization would struggle to take flight, confronting the headwinds that, during the 1990s, still viewed domestic workers as maids or servants. Despite this obstacle, domestic workers' national organizations continued to forge important ties. These groups included FENATRAHOB and SADWU/SADSAWU alongside groups founded in Brazil, Costa Rica, Peru, Trinidad and Tobago, Jamaica, Tanzania, Kenya, India, and Hong Kong. Regional organizations also formed in the 1980s and 1990s, for example the Latin America and Caribbean Confederation of Domestic Workers (CONLACTRAHO from its Spanish name).

In 2006, movement leaders hosted the first ever global conference of domestic workers' organizations in Amsterdam. The conference attracted participants from 60 different domestic worker organizations, alongside representatives from WIEGO and from mainstream global labour unions, including the International Union of Food, Agricultural, Hotel, Restaurant, Catering, Tobacco and Allied Workers' Associations (IUF). The conference consolidated the demand for an ILO convention. Dutch activist Anneke van Luijken agreed to coordinate the ILO lobbying campaign in collaboration with WIEGO and IUF. In 2008, the ILO responded, announcing plans to draft a convention. In 2009, activists formed the International Domestic Workers' Network (IDWN), led by Witbooi. IDWN installed a steering committee that represented regional organizations such as CONLACTRAHO and the Asian Domestic Workers Network (ADWN) alongside national groups such as SADSAWU and groups from Peru, Indonesia, and Trinidad and Tobago.[64]

All told, between 2008 and 2011, IDWN, WIEGO, the IUF, and even organizations like SEWA joined forces to shape the ILO convention. They formed a transnational movement and they followed a central guiding principle: mobilize domestic workers and keep their voices central. Globally, IDWN rallied local workers' associations around the prospect of a convention, conducted research, and drafted policy statements. In Geneva, IDWN insisted that delegates in the ILO's Workers Group contain actual domestic workers rather than the usual representatives from mainstream labour unions. IDWN succeeded in naming domestic worker organization leaders as delegates and installing them in the draft meetings. Before the meetings, IDWN distributed talking points to all delegates, including those representing the ILO's two other arms, the Employers Group and the Government Group. At the 2010 drafting meeting, all delegates received IDWN's 'Platform of Demands'. At the 2011 meeting, delegates were given IDWN's publication 'Myths and Realities about Domestic Workers: What THEY Say and What WE Say' – designed precisely to counter the employer and government objections raised the previous year. Delegates also heard impassioned speeches from domestic workers' union representatives authorized to speak before the convening, including Witbooi, Ida le Blanc (Trinidad and Tobago), Evaline Mulo (Kenya), and Shirley Pryce (Jamaica). Out in the streets, IDWN leaders such as Nepal's Sonu Danuwar organized marches and demonstrations to support the conversations happening inside.

In 2011, the ILO voted affirmatively for C189, which starts by recognizing the 'significant contribution of domestic workers to the global economy' and adds that domestic work is 'undervalued and invisible, and is mainly carried out by women and girls, many of whom are migrants or members of disadvantaged communities'.[65] C189 affirms that domestic workers have the same rights as all workers and that governments must take measures to ensure these rights. The convention prohibits forced labour and child labour and seeks particular safeguards against abuse for workers, especially migrant workers, who find employment via private agencies. C189 was accompanied by Recommendation 201 (R201), which provides further guidance on domestic workers' protections, including their freedom to organize and form unions and their rights to equal treatment and to workplace safety.

Like C177, C189 represents a profound victory for women workers, especially marginalized women and Global South women, who united to author this feminist blueprint. Though countries such as Bolivia and South Africa, alongside others such as Nicaragua and Uruguay, passed laws protecting domestic workers' rights before C189, a number of countries did so after, including Argentina, Bahrain, Brazil, the Philippines, Singapore, Spain, Thailand, Vietnam, and Venezuela.[66] Like C177, C189 legitimates domestic workers organizations' advocacy and envisions just and equal treatment for some of the world's most disadvantaged women workers. Commenting on the historic vote, Kenya's Evaline Mulo said: 'The vote marked the beginning of social justice for domestic workers internationally . . . I joined a big group of domestic workers at the conference and started singing in jubilation as we danced to celebrate the moment.'[67] CONLACTRAHO's general secretary at the time, María del Carmen Cruz, captured how C189's passage reflected women's transnational organizing and solidarity: 'What serves us most is making networks, uniting forces . . . to unite in one cause, and plan with the same target in mind.'[68]

The collective struggle for women's economic empowerment

When Casimira Rodríguez organized Cochabamba's domestic workers in the early 1990s, she probably never anticipated that she would become Bolivia's first Indigenous woman to serve in the cabinet, as minister of justice from 2006 to 2007. When Witbooi joined the anti-apartheid struggle and formed South Africa's first domestic workers' union, she perhaps did not anticipate that she would become the first president of IDWN's successor organization, the International Domestic Workers Federation, formed in 2013. Neither might have imagined ILO C189. And when cafeteria workers in Massachusetts unsuccessfully sued for equal pay in 1991, they perhaps did not envision how their lawsuit would inspire salary history bans 15 years later.

These stories capture the piece-by-piece nature of policy change. Women protagonists identify problems and raise awareness; they build solidarity and found organizations in order to raise their voices collectively; they mobilize to change international norms and domestic statutes; they seek and attain political positions that grant them more decision-making power within the policy process; and they use the newly created feminist blueprints to advocate for yet more changes. The international frameworks and domestic laws cannot change women's economic autonomy overnight – but Mulo's recounting of domestic workers' celebrations following the C189 vote indicates the importance women activists place on using the international system to secure formal recognition for their rights. When C189 passed, Indonesian organizer Suyati from the Tunas Mulia trade union reflected on women's accomplishments: 'We got it because we worked for it. We gathered our strength, and urged others to get involved. No-one else gave it to us. It is the result of our efforts.'[69]

Women continue to face profound challenges in their quest for economic empowerment, both within and across national borders. The global economy knits countries and women together in complex ways, often working against equality among women. Yet women have found ways to bridge these differences, as when Harvard professors provide the research that legitimizes homeworkers' demands, or when women form multisectoral coalitions to win maternity leave. The COVID-19 pandemic, which ground the world's economy to a halt in 2020, also accelerated conversations and connections among women on the shared priority of tackling the sexual division of labour and the longstanding assumption that women – and not men – are responsible for unpaid work in the home. The next chapter discusses how women have challenged inequalities not only in the workplace but in families and in the home.

SIX

Family Law and Care Work

In March 2020, the COVID-19 pandemic ground the world to a halt. The pandemic's initial months meant lockdowns or shutdowns – periods where all but the essential industries closed, workers who could not work remotely lost income, and universities and schools ended in-person instruction and moved online. Economies retracted, generating a 3 per cent drop of the world's gross domestic product in 2020 (by comparison with a 2.8 per cent rise in 2019).[1] Amid stay-at-home orders, domestic responsibilities ballooned. School, nursery, daycare, and other health and community centre closures meant that young children, elders, and family members with disabilities were now at home, requiring minding. Places for socializing also closed, so all family members needed more meals and entertainment in the home. And even as economies slowly reopened and lockdowns slowly lifted, any persons experiencing COVID-19 symptoms or contracting COVID-19 needed to quarantine at home, again requiring care.

COVID-19 thus dramatically affected women's lives. The women's rights era saw closed gender gaps in education and narrowed gender gaps in workforce participation, but without any noticeable shifts in unpaid care work, meaning the domestic responsibilities traditionally assigned to women as custodians of the private sphere. Take data compiled by the OECD, which examined time use surveys conducted between 1998 and 2015 for its 30 member countries plus China, India, and South Africa. In every single country, women spend more minutes per day than men on unpaid domestic chores. Women's greater care burden appears in countries with generous parental leaves, such as Sweden and Denmark, where each day women spend respectively 49 and 57 minutes more than men on unpaid care. The care gap also appears in countries marked by more traditional gender roles, such as Mexico and Italy, where each day women spend respectively 200 and 219 more minutes than men on unpaid care. In the United Kingdom, women's daily domestic load amounts to 109 minutes more than men's.[2] The pandemic exacerbated these gaps. In every global region, women reported an increase in their unpaid domestic activities following COVID-19 lockdowns.[3] Women spent more time cooking and serving meals, cleaning, caring for children, caring for pets, teaching, and playing with children.

Other forces affected women's work and family lives during the pandemic. Women more than men exited the workforce. In some cases, rising care needs compelled women to reduce their working hours in order to perform more unpaid tasks, such as childcare and homeschooling supervision. In other cases, women were forced out of the workforce, as many women work in sectors unable to adapt to remote work, especially the retail and service sectors. In the healthcare sector, women remained employed but vulnerable. Women in healthcare are overrepresented among lower wage earners, such as nurses and hospital assistants – the very occupations with the most patient contact. Further, many frontline healthcare workers are ethnic and racial minority women, including immigrant women. Given their marginalization as lower paid or minoritized women or both, frontline women in healthcare received scant economic compensation or physical protection. They rarely received hazard pay or bonuses. Personal protective equipment had been manufactured to fit the average male body, poorly fitting women's smaller frames and faces. During the COVID-19 pandemic, women frontline workers experienced high risks of infection while still earning the low wages that characterize the care economy's bottom rungs.

In addition to increased care burdens and diminished economic opportunities, COVID-19 increased violence against women. Feminist activists named this problem 'the shadow pandemic'. Across the globe, shutdowns trapped women and girls at home with their abusers. Heightened family stress also meant heightened abuse. Women in countries with gender-discriminatory family laws or personal status laws – laws governing everything from their mobility to their rights in marriage, divorce, child custody, property and inheritance – especially had few options for exiting the home or seeking legal redress. In July 2020, Musawah – a transnational NGO dedicated to equality within Muslim families – surveyed women's rights activists and lawyers in 12 countries in the Middle East and North Africa (MENA).[4] Musawah's researchers found that the pandemic exacerbated MENA women's unequal treatment within the family and that marital rape increased. Many MENA countries closed their family and civil courts, suspending any in-progress divorce and child custody cases and leaving women vulnerable. Law enforcement's attention shifted away from abuses in the home, allowing many formally banned practices to resurge, as families turned to child marriage and forced marriage to resolve economic difficulties. Though women in Global North countries were less likely to experience early or forced marriage and more likely to benefit from judiciaries in their countries going remote, domestic violence still increased by about 8 per cent in countries such as the United States.[5]

COVID-19 thus affected women across the globe. The striking commonalities between women's experiences had a mobilizing effect, uniting women activists, scholars, policymakers, and healthcare practitioners on shared problems. The Gender and COVID-19 working group, founded by feminist health scholars, rapidly evolved to incorporate 300 members from countries in every global region. Collectively, members shared research and best practices; applied for and received grants; wrote policy reports and manifestos; and convened an international conference.[6] Feminist collectives in places as diverse as Hawai'i, the Philippines, Canada, and Northern Ireland crafted what they called 'feminist COVID-19 recovery plans' – advocacy documents that summarized their policy demands relative to recognizing and remunerating women's unpaid care work, among other priorities. Their efforts received international attention and informed UN Women's own feminist recovery plan, a new feminist blueprint published in late 2020. The pandemic seemingly opened a new chapter in the international and national policy conversations about women, family roles, and unpaid care work. Women's rights advocates hoped the pandemic would push forward their long-sought reforms in two intertwined policy areas: family law and care work.

Women, the family, and the private sphere

In all societies, culture and religion establish expectations for how families should form and how men, women, and other family members should behave within them. Many societies then encode these expectations into law – hence the term 'customary law', referring to governance by societies' cultural and religious traditions. In many countries, especially those in Europe and the Americas, rules eventually consolidated into either common law systems or civil law systems. Both systems draw on customary practices, but both fashioned a single set of rules for all members of the polity, essentially choosing one set of customs to govern everyone. European colonizers then imported their legal systems to the colonies, overlaying European civil or common law systems with the customary laws of the different ethnic, religious, and ethnic-religious groups already living in there. This process created a profound tension that still resonates today: either all members of the polity are governed by one universal legal code or the polity recognizes multiple legal codes. If the polity recognizes multiple legal codes, some usually are the customary laws corresponding to distinctive tribal, ethnic, or religious groups. Even societies not subject to European colonization have faced this state-building dilemma: unite the nation under one legal system or allow the distinctive groups that form the nation to follow their own customs.

Legal systems that encode patriarchy

The debate between civil and common law on the one hand and customary law on the other has profoundly shaped women's rights. In the Global South, many customary laws encode traditions regarded as harmful to women – such as child marriage and female genital mutilation. Further, as discussed in Chapter 8, these harmful practices have no equivalent among men. Young girls are married at the age of 15 and below, to men old enough to be their fathers or grandfathers, but young boys are not married to women old enough to be their mothers or grandmothers. Boys may undergo circumcision, but not one designed to constrain their sexuality and that has lifelong, negative consequences for their mental, sexual, and reproductive health. Women cannot inherit property, but men can. Feminist activists and scholars often perceive a tension between civil law or common law, one the one hand, and customary law, on the other, often contending that the latter offers women better protection. Civil law or common law systems are typically based on western, Enlightenment-era ideas about individuals as rights bearers, whereas customary laws typically treat the family, not the individual, as the constitutive unit of society. A rights-based system more easily accommodates claims that choices over marriage or entitlements to own property belong to women as individuals, not to men as family heads.

This contrast between civil law or common law and customary law shapes the battles over family law that took place during the women's rights era, particularly in the Global South and outside the West, where customary law remains more common. In these contexts, women's rights activists seeking to eliminate harmful practices are perceived as fighting culture and tradition. Yet Global North women fought these battles as well, mostly (though not exclusively) before the women's right's era. Historically, common law and civil law also encoded patriarchal norms and treated women as second-class citizens.

Early European and anglophone common law systems followed the doctrine of 'coverture', which subsumed married women's legal status under that of their husbands. Until the late nineteenth century, married women could not own property, represent themselves in courts, or retain custody of children upon divorce (if divorce was allowed). Granting fathers custodial rights may seem surprising in societies assigning primary childrearing responsibility to women, but the rationale entailed locking women within marriage: even if the law permitted divorce on grounds of neglect or violence (and it usually did not), women would not leave abusive spouses if divorce meant forfeiting custody of their children. Coverture therefore gave husbands complete dominion over their wives, creating the legal edifice that explains why married women could not vote; why no concept of domestic violence existed; and why the work women performed in the home bore no economic value. Under coverture, married women were simply not legal persons. Many of these inequalities persisted well into the twentieth century. Women in Ireland could not own their own homes until 1976. The German family code stating that the wife's responsibility was to run the household remained unaltered until 1977.[7] UK courts did not declare marital rape a crime until 1991.

At the four world conferences on women, Global South feminists were therefore not impressed by Global North feminists' critiques of 'backward' customary practices such as child marriage – especially when Global North women failed to see the parallels with wife abuse in their own societies.[8] Gradually, however, feminists found common ground, especially related to discrimination within the family and domestic violence. Together, they launched the transnational campaign Women's Rights Are Human Rights in the early 1990s (see Chapter 2). The feminist blueprints from the Mexico City, Copenhagen, Nairobi, and Beijing conferences all recognized inequalities in the family and called for the elimination of discriminatory national laws. CEDAW's Article 16 explicitly states that countries 'shall take all appropriate measures to eliminate discrimination against women in all matters relating to marriage and family relations'.[9]

Still, by the start of the women's rights era, family laws were equalizing far more rapidly in the Americas, Europe, Australia, and New Zealand than in MENA, sub-Saharan Africa, and Southeast Asia. In the former, coverture disappeared with the introduction of married women's property acts in the late nineteenth and early twentieth centuries, and many remaining discriminatory family laws fell before or around 1975.[10] Where European countries' legal systems also applied to then colonized countries, clashes ensued, as the evolving common law or civil law systems became more gender-equitable than local customary law. These conflicts informed the tension between common law or civil law and customary law described above: though common law or civil law systems also encoded patriarchal gender roles, common law or civil law systems reformed their discriminatory family codes faster. As colonization ended, many newly independent countries kept multiple and overlapping civil law or common law and customary legal systems intact.[11] Other countries not subject to colonization remained governed by customary law, often permitting different ethnic groups or religious sects to follow their own rules. In the Global South, discriminatory family laws remained largely undisturbed as the women's rights era gained steam.

Homegrown contestations over religion and tradition

Mala Htun and Laurel Weldon identify the political institutionalization of religious authority as the major factor explaining where family laws discriminate against women. They write: 'In the context of a separation between secular and religious institutions, family law tends to be more egalitarian. When religion is institutionalized, patriarchal interpretations – and interpreters – of family law gain greater authority and more immunity to contestation.'[12] This contrast helps to explain why, during the women's rights era, women's movements centred on eroding discriminatory family law predominate in regions where religious authorities on average hold greater influence over political institutions, including legal systems.

That does not mean, however, that religion existentially harms women. Htun and Weldon wrote that *patriarchal interpretations and interpreters* of religion matter, not the fact of religion itself. Musawah agrees, explaining:

> In almost all instances, whether in majority Muslim countries or countries with Muslim minorities, those formulating or interpreting Muslim family laws claim that these laws are 'divine' and therefore unchangeable. In reality, these laws are based on interpretations of religious texts made by primarily male Islamic scholars and based on a legal framework developed by Muslim jurists centuries ago.[13]

Since family law reflects religious interpretation, feminist activists can contest these interpretations, reinterpreting religious texts. For example, Rachel Rinaldo analyses how Indonesian Islamic feminists use a contextual – rather than textual – understanding of Islam to challenge doctrinal practices such as polygamy, which remains legal in Indonesia.[14] The activists critically engage with religious texts in order to argue for women's rights and equality. For example, feminist leaders argue that the Quran's discussion of polygamy 'needs to be understood with regard to the historical context of Arabia in the sixth century'.[15] Rinaldo further explains how Islamist feminists' rights-based critique of polygamy takes transnational feminist ideas about women's autonomy, dignity, and safety and combines them with Islamist texts that emphasize women's well-being. Since polygamy tends to result in husbands being unable to materially and emotionally support all wives equally, Indonesia's Islamic feminists conclude: 'it makes sense that polygamy should not be allowed in contemporary society'.[16] Indonesian feminist groups would ban polygamy entirely.[17]

Religion, then, constitutes a site of political and feminist struggle over meaning, interpretation, and application. Not all women will agree, of course. Rinaldo also analyses Indonesian women who adhere to more textual interpretations of Islam and therefore do not share Indonesian feminists' advocacy for a legal prohibition on polygamy (some of these more traditional women remain uneasy about the practice, but do not wish to see a law that would, in their view, contravene the Quran).[18] Yet as Chapter 1 points out, women's rights emerge objectively from patriarchal structures, not from universal agreement among women.

The point here is that, during the women's rights era, challenges to discriminatory family laws – often called 'personal status laws' – come from the women who themselves live under such patriarchal laws. As Chapter 2 describes, African feminists took 'women's rights are human rights' forward, crafting their own regional women's rights charter. The 2003 Protocol to the African Charter on Human and Peoples' Rights on the Rights of Women in Africa (the Maputo Protocol) addresses concerns especially relevant to the continent's women and girls. The protocol contains an entire article on the 'elimination of harmful practices', described as those 'which negatively affect the human rights of women and which are contrary to recognised international standards'.[19] The Maputo Protocol calls upon governments 'to achiev[e] the elimination of harmful cultural and traditional practices and all other practices which are based on the idea of the inferiority or superiority of either of the sexes, or on stereotyped roles for men and women'.[20]

Notably, however, the Maputo Protocol refers only to 'harmful cultural practices' and not explicitly to customary law. Women face intense opposition when directly challenging discriminatory family laws. The private sphere is where culture and tradition, including doctrinal beliefs, are enacted and maintained. The very word – 'private' – sets the household beyond the state: in giving husbands dominion over their wives, family law in every legal tradition asserted that male household heads' authority was absolute and free from state interference. Women's demands for family law reform therefore defy legalized patriarchy. When religious doctrines underlie family law, women's demands *also* defy spiritual authorities, challenging the religious foundations of government itself. Seeking women's rights in the family, then, provokes existential conflicts among citizens and among political elites.[21] Patriarchy, especially when perceived to be religiously ordained, has profound consequences for women's lives – but is also the foundation on which many governments rest their legitimacy. Thus, battles over changing the culture and the legal norms that govern private sphere relationships become high-stakes battles fought over, about, and on women's bodies. These battles include those over familial and domestic roles (this chapter) and also over reproductive rights (Chapter 7) and violence against women (Chapter 8). The pandemic so frightened women activists precisely because it threatened their hard-fought gains, which had worked towards, not against, liberating women from patriarchal domination within the private sphere.

Eroding discriminatory family laws

Family laws, also called personal status laws, are complex bundles of legislation covering diverse matters related to family formation, residence, and income. They encompass property ownership and inheritance, including marital property ownership and inheritance following a male relative's death; spousal rights and duties, including whether women can work without their husbands' permission; marriage regulations, such as minimum marriage ages, permissions around polygamy and marriage between close relations, and requirements for women's affirmative consent; and regulations about divorce and adultery. Women's rights campaigners fight complex multi-front battles, as reforming family laws requires dozens or hundreds of changes. Different campaigns will tackle different issues, depending on the window of opportunity and political elites' reformist moods (see Chapter 3).

Morocco illustrates the long road to revisit family laws in one Muslim-majority country.[22] The landmark 2004 reform to the Moudawana (family code) required decades of activism, including initial wins, setbacks, and later victories. The Union of Women's Action (UAF from its French name) and the Moroccan Women's Democratic Association (ADFM from its French name) launched their 'one million signature' campaign on 8 March 1992. At the time, UAF and ADFM sought prohibitions on polygamy and on the principle that husbands retain ultimate authority over wives. After receiving UAF's petition with more than one million signatures, then King Hassan II formed a commission that implemented some changes. Notably, the 1993 reform required women's verbal consent to marriage, repealing fathers' right to force marriages upon daughters. The UAF's main demands, however, were not met: polygamy and husbands' dominion remained, though husbands seeking to practice polygamy would now need judicial authorization. The reform also did not change husbands' unilateral and unconditional right to divorce (whereas women could only seek divorce on certain grounds). Still, the tepid reforms were symbolically important: they showed that, contrary to arguments made by some traditionalists and Islamists, the Moudawana's religious grounding did not make it immutable.

Moroccan women's groups built on this proof of concept that family law could evolve. ADFM carried the momentum forward in the 1990s. With women from Tunisia and Algeria and using the Beijing PfA, they formed the Maghreb Equality Collective and published the *Guide to Equality in the Family in the Maghreb*. The guide detailed the necessary family law reforms and outlined the religious arguments to confront conservative groups advocating an Islamist approach. In 1999, ADFM published the 'Plan of Action for the Integration of Women in Development' (PANIFD), which focused on women's desired revisions to the Moudawana. Parallel shifts in Moroccan politics temporarily gave the ADFM an advantage. First, King Hassan died and his son, Mohammed VI, ascended to the throne, promising modernizing reforms. Second, left-wing parties won more seats in the Moroccan legislature, installing a socialist prime minister who proclaimed his support for PANIFD.

Backlash proved swift, however. Conservative groups mobilized against PANIFD. Opponents began preaching about PANIFD's alleged anti-Islamic views in marketplaces, mosques, and the media. Feeling pressure, the prime minister retracted his support. Undaunted, ADFM organized over 250 women's groups into two new networks: the Network of Support for PANIFD and the Front for the Defence of Moroccan Women's Rights. Tens of thousands of men and women demonstrated to support PANIFD, marching through the capital Rabat on 12 March 2001. King Mohammed responded, forming a Royal Consultative Commission to analyse the Moudawana. Women's groups, however, did not rest. They monitored and pressured the commission. They publicized stories of women hurt by Morocco's discriminatory family laws. They held a sit-in outside parliament. They led teach-ins and family law literacy campaigns. They argued that 'building a democratic Moroccan society depends on the respect of women's rights'.[23] Yet the true window of opportunity opened in 2003, when suicide bombers from a fundamentalist Islamist organization attacked several locations in Casablanca, killing 33 people. With public opinion temporarily turned against conservatives, the Moroccan parliament passed a revised Moudawana in 2004.

The revisions included over 100 amendments. Key changes included eliminating the principle that wives must obey their husbands and stipulating that women and men are joint household heads; raising the minimum marital age for girls from fifteen to eighteen; and granting women equal rights in initiating divorce. Polygamy was not banned, but became heavily regulated: women gained the right to require a monogamy clause in their marriage contracts, and men seeking judicial authorization to take additional wives needed to prove that they could financially support all wives and children. The first wife also must be present when men seek judicial approval for a second wife. The reforms also improved protections from domestic violence, such as allowing women with abuse allegations access to courts without first securing their husbands' approval. Altogether, the 2004 Moudawana reform created what Moroccan American lawyer Leila Hanafi called an 'undoubtedly progressive piece of legislation for women in Morocco'.[24] Still, the 2004 reform left key discriminatory areas intact, including inheritance rights, where a principle of double shares for males applies, and marital rape, which remains uncriminalized. Women's groups continued pressing these points, with the pandemic opening a new window of opportunity: faced with economic challenges, 'improving women's status is a promise the government can deliver'.[25] The king opened another family code reform in 2023 (ongoing as of 2025).

The Moroccan account illustrates how family law reform happens neither overnight nor in a single instance. Women's rights activists and their modernizing allies continuously confront conservative forces among religious and political elites. The resultant reforms rarely ever meet the expectations of feminists, who must settle for incremental change. A similar story unfolds in Jordan, where the Arab Women's Association (AWO), the Jordanian Women's Union (JWU), and other groups have long contested Jordan's discriminatory personal status law.

Like their Moroccan colleagues, Jordanian women have won change in phases. In 2001, amendments raised the minimum marriage age to 18 from 15 (though judges may still permit marriage at younger ages) and required that, for polygamous marriages, courts inform each wife of the others' existence.[26] Further reforms occurred in 2011, focusing on property and inheritance, and specifically on the practice wherein families pressure women into renouncing their inheritance rights. The 2011 amendments (1) require judges to inform all heirs of their inheritance and of the legal consequences of self-exclusion and (2) install a three-month waiting period between time of death and any heir's renouncement of their inheritance rights.[27] Further reforms in 2019 allowed DNA evidence in family courts to prove paternity (which would assist women rape victims in seeking financial support); extended maternal custody until children turn 15 years old or complete their studies; and gave daughters' grandchildren inheritance rights equal to those of sons' grandchildren. Still, many reforms remain pending.[28] AWO continues campaigning against provisions that prevent mothers from transmitting their citizenship to their children, for example.[29] In Jordan as in about 24 other countries in 2025, women who marry foreigners cannot pass their citizenship on to their children.[30]

Morocco and Jordan are both Muslim-majority countries, but Muslim-majority countries are not alone in encoding custom into discriminatory personal status laws. In South Korea, where the family law follows Confucian ethics, discriminatory provisions persisted until a 1989 reform. The All Women's Federation to Revise the Family Law formed in 1973, but reform did not occur until after South Korea's 1987 democratic transition, as the transition suddenly 'made the women's vote count'.[31] The 1989 reforms removed the default marital residence as the husband's family home and permitted married couples to jointly determine their residence; entitled a woman to an equal share of property upon divorce; established maternal custody following divorce; and abolished daughters' receipt of one-fourth of sons' inheritance, allowing daughters and sons to inherit equally.[32] In predominantly Christian Ethiopia, the Ethiopian Women's Lawyers' Association helped to coordinate the campaign to revise the country's discriminatory family law. In 2000, Ethiopia eliminated the provision allowing spouses to prevent each other from working outside the home (a gender-neutral provision that, in practice, only ever applied to husbands' preventing wives' employment) and gave women equal rights to administer common marital property, to initiate divorce, and to receive an equal division of property upon separation.[33]

In India, the Hindu majority follows Hindu law (while the Muslim minority follows Muslim personal law). Hindu law also historically discriminated against women.[34] The 1956 Hindu Succession Act (applying to Hindus and also to Buddhists, Jains, and Sikhs) gave women full property ownership, but left some areas untouched. The 1956 Act did not, for example, discuss inheritance of agricultural land or make women coparceners (persons who by birth can claim ancestral land). The 1956 Act also did not specify how jointly inherited land could be disposed of, meaning that male heirs can make decisions without consulting female heirs. A campaign to update the 1956 Act dated back to at least the 1980s, steered by committed feminists such as economist Bina Agarwal. In 2004, a proposed amendment introduced in India's lower house would have eliminated the gender discriminatory clauses related to agricultural land inheritance, but did not go far enough to make women coparceners – the proposal stated that only unmarried daughters could become coparceners. Frustrated, Agarwal, the Human Rights Law Network, and the Housing and Land Rights Network prepared a memorandum eventually signed by 50 organizations. Their lobbying efforts worked, and the 2005 amendment to the Hindu Succession Act made women coparceners regardless of their marital status, ended formal inequalities in inheriting agricultural land, and established that women and men heirs must jointly agree on property disposition.

Granting women greater control over their inheritances matters for women's autonomy. As some Indian states modified their state-level Hindu Succession Acts before 2005, economists Minali Grover and Ajay Sharma could compare the amendments' effects over time.[35] They found that women who gain inheritance rights also gained increased choice of husbands and increased ability to access income-generating opportunities outside the home, including through participation in microlending groups. The amendments further decreased expressed acceptability of interpersonal violence. Family law reforms can thus move cultural norms, eroding women's treatment as second-class citizens.

Wages for housework and the burden of unpaid care

Among their many targets, family law reforms take aim at family codes' explicit statements that assign women responsibility for household management and domestic chores. Even when not written down, the division between a public economic sphere and a private domestic one assigns women primary responsibility for household chores and childrearing. Ideas about gender naturalize women's domestic role: since women are perceived as essentially caring and maternal, their reproductive tasks are seen as extensions of their nature and thus regarded as expressions of love, not products of labour. This question of unpaid care long has been on women's movements agendas. Feminists dispute the idea that care work – the reproductive work that women perform within the home – is natural and costless for women.

All four documents from the world conferences on women discuss how unpaid care perpetuates gender inequality. These feminist blueprints all agree: unpaid care is *work*. Unpaid care does not emerge from any essential, biological predisposition that women possess. Rather, unpaid care requires women to sacrifice time and opportunity that could be spent on other pursuits. It requires effort and skill. Most significantly, feminist economists point out, it bolsters economic production. The domestic sphere provides workers with rest, shelter, food, and clean clothes, a respite and recovery that enables their return to the workforce each day. The domestic sphere is also the place where children are raised to become the next generation of workers.

To make this point, feminist groups in Italy, England, the United States, anglophone Canada, Switzerland, and Germany formed the international Wages for Housework campaign in the 1970s. Their efforts were not without controversy – some feminists felt then (as they do today) that monetizing domestic work would lock women into domestic roles, reifying rather than undoing the relationship between women and home. Louise Toupin explains, however, that Wages for Housework allowed women to conceive of themselves as economic and political subjects who had rights and thus agency to make policy demands.[36] As Toupin describes, positioning oneself as a worker meant 'destroying the idea that doing housework was an integral part of women's nature'.[37] This self-conception 'was also to discover other possibilities, such as struggling against the conditions of this work, defining the duration and extent of the workday, and, as the case may be, refusing to work'.[38] The idea that women need not accept domesticity as their natural and inevitable condition, but could bargain over household responsibilities and conditions the same way labour unions could bargain with employers, informed women's activism around economic inequality.

Further, Toupin points out that the Black women leaders of the Wages for Housework campaign anticipated women of colour's contemporary critiques about interlocking forms of degradation and oppression.[39] The international campaign contained internal groups that organized autonomously alongside the main group, including Wages Due Lesbians and Black Women for Wages for Housework. The latter drew connections between women's unwaged work in the home, the underpayment of women workers in the care economy, and ongoing struggles against colonialism and legacies of enslavement.[40]

For Black women, wages for housework constituted not just remuneration but reparation. As descendants of formerly enslaved persons, Black women argued that they had provided reproductive work for white families *and* productive work on plantations not just for free, but *by force.* Black Women for Wages for Housework published their own magazine, *Safire.* One edition describes how their formation in 1975, International Women's Year, actually had roots in their 1950s-era struggles for civil rights and welfare reform: 'But two decades before, Black Women of all ages the world over – from Soweto [South Africa] to New York – had come out of our homes claiming our right to a standard of living equal to the wealth in money and technology that our unpaid work building the world's richest and most developed nations had produced.'[41] Black Women for Wages for Housework further argued that racism made their *own* unpaid domestic chores more burdensome than those of white women. US activist Willamette Brown, co-founder of Black Women for Wages for Housework, linked the group's demands to the harms of environmental racism. In a 1983 essay entitled 'Roots: Black Ghetto Ecology', Brown identifies how Black communities live in much closer proximity to environmental hazards like polluting factories, which means that Black women's housework includes protecting their families from and caring for those sickened by polluted air, water, and soil.[42] Black women also must protect their families from interpersonal and structural racism, including police violence.

Four decades later, the feminist blueprints aiming to guide COVID-19 recovery would reiterate how valuing women's care work matters for both gender and racial justice. The first plan appeared in the United States, written by the Hawai'i State Commission on the Status of Women in collaboration with grassroots groups representing Black, Native, and immigrant women.[43] Hawai'i has the largest non-white population of all US states and high levels of social need. During the pandemic, shutdowns in tourism disproportionately affected women of colour, who fill the lower tiers of Hawai'i's service-dependent economy and work in care-adjacent roles (e.g. as hotel cleaners, restaurant servers, and nannies). Hawai'i's collectively redacted intersectional feminist recovery plan reflected this reality. The plan's authors wrote:

> The cheap value of caregiving is not natural, but has political origins. Caregiving, associated with and expected of women, is necessary for economic production to take place and yet it is split off from economic production, thereby structurally subordinating women in society. This is why even within their own racial, indigenous status, and economic groups, women are the most marginalized.[44]

The plan further documented women's gendered and racialized care burdens during the pandemic, from how environmental racism meant that non-white communities endured more illness and death to the absence of public funding for frontline workers' childcare and eldercare.

Farther north, in British Columbia, Canada, the feminist COVD-19 recovery plan written by Feminists Deliver – who describe themselves as an organization that 'centres intersectional feminism, anti-oppression, and decolonization' – makes the same point about women's unremunerated work: the plan is titled 'This economic labour hurts the arch of our backs'.[45] The sentence echoes the title from a famous anthology produced by US feminists of colour in 1981, *This Bridge Called My Back* – a path-breaking literary collection regarded as among the first texts to elevate women of colour's voices. The question of unpaid care links women and women of colour across generations, connecting gender inequality within the household to critiques of capitalism, colonialism, and racism.

Reforms valuing and providing care

Women's movements seek policies that place an economic value on care – but what kinds of reforms realize this goal, exactly? As feminist theorist Corinna Dengler points out, Wages for Housework did not argue that housewives should receive salaries merely to monetize the private sphere.[46] Rather, Wages for Housework wanted domestic work to hold economic value so that women would gain choices about where, when, and how to work. To achieve this goal, movement leaders offered two distinct proposals: a care income, meaning care wages provided by the state, and a reproductive commons, meaning the collective provisioning of care from within self-organized communities.[47] To achieve the first would also require calculating the exact economic value of unpaid care.

Compensating for care

The first proposal, for care income, falls within a broader class of social protection policies that scholars call cash transfers or cash allowances. In these instances, governments simply transfer money directly to parents or households. Countries across the globe pay annual or monthly child allowances or reduce parents' tax burdens via reductions or credits. Such policies do not actually pay women for providing care, but they do offset children's costs by contributing towards nursery fees or compensating for household expenditures on other consumables, such as food and clothing. In many cases, cash transfers or cash allowances are means-tested, so parents or families must fall below a certain income to qualify. In other cases, the policies are universal, like Argentina's monthly child allowance, in place since 2009 (similar schemes exist across Latin America and Europe). Either means-tested or universal policies can be conditional, imposing requirements such as children's school attendance or parents' employment. Some countries also pay women one-off 'baby bonuses', which also vary by whether the benefit is means-tested (as in Italy, France, or the Czech Republic) or universal (as in Singapore and Lithuania). Other countries offer more comprehensive cash-for-care or carer allowance schemes, where family members receive monthly or even hourly payments for care (the vast majority of recipients are women). Such schemes have existed since about the 1980s in many European countries, including the United Kingdom, Norway, Finland, Sweden, the Netherlands, Germany, Italy, and Austria. They cover children or dependent adults (or both). These policies are not mutually exclusive, with many countries offering combinations of baby bonuses, cash allowances, and other forms of social assistance.

As noted earlier and in Chapter 5, such policies are not uniformly embraced by women's rights activists. On the one hand, cash transfers – especially unconditional or universal ones – play important anti-poverty roles and overwhelmingly benefit women (who are more likely than men to be poor). Typically, payments are made to the mother, even when she cohabits with a male partner. Cash allowances can empower women to make choices: if women want to remain in paid employment, for instance, cash transfers can offset the costs of daycare. Women receiving Argentina's universal child allowance, for example, report greater economic autonomy alongside pride in having their own income and not needing to ask their husbands for money.[48] In Europe, carers' non-profit groups – many of them led and staffed by primarily women – advocate for expanded carers' benefits, including allowances.

On the other hand, such reforms can have pronatalist aims; they can impose a burdensome conditionality on women, especially poor women; and they still undervalue care and leave slack that gender norms see women (rather than men) taking up. The money distributed in most cash-for-care schemes is far below what a paid carer would need to earn a living wage. In Ireland, for instance, the 2025 carers' allowance for those under 66 was €260 a week (about €1,170 per month). The allowance is means-tested: eligible carers cannot be engaged in employment, self-employment, training, or education courses for more than 18.5 hours per week, meaning that at least half their working week must be spent on care.[49] However, €1,170 Euro per month would not even cover the estimated €1,700 per month rent for a one-bedroom flat in Dublin – let alone other expenses.[50] Irish carers will struggle to make ends meet even when combining the carers' allowance with wages from a half-time work week. Overall, policies resembling care incomes offset households' operating costs, but they do not place a dollar value on care akin to a formal-sector wage.

Similar challenges appear with policies such as maternity credits – schemes wherein governments top up women's pensions in recognition that the gendered division of household labour diminishes women's lifetime earnings. Such reforms are popular in Latin America. In Chile, beginning in 2008, women receive a per-child deposit into their pension account worth 10 per cent of 18 months' minimum wage.[51] In Uruguay, also since 2008, women receive a per-child pension top-up equivalent to one year's contribution, up to a five-year maximum for children either born or adopted.[52] In Bolivia, as of 2010, women receive a per-child social security credit equivalent to one year's pension contribution.[53] Argentina's 2021 policy follows Bolivia's (one year per child), but the credit is equivalent to two years for adopted or disabled children and three years for women previously receiving low-income child subsidies. These policies, generally applauded by women's groups, acknowledge the trade-off women make between work and family – but they also imply that the lifetime hours spent on childrearing are equivalent to one or two years of full-time employment. Wages for Housework might say that maternity pension credits are an initial but insufficient step towards an actual care income.

Calculating the costs of care

The documents emerging from the second and third world conferences on women wanted the economic value of care not just recognized, but calculated. The 1980 Copenhagen Programme of Action instructs governments that 'a system should be devised for placing a monetary value on unpaid work, in order to facilitate its reflection in the gross national product'.[54] The 1985 Nairobi conference report states: 'The remunerated and, in particular, the unremunerated contributions of women to all aspects and sectors of development should be recognized, and appropriate efforts should be made to measure and reflect these contributions in national accounts and economic statistics and in the gross national product.'[55]

Women's organizations, often women's budget monitoring groups consisting of feminist academics and policymakers, have long pressed this point. To make visible but also measure care's economic value, they lobby for time use surveys to be conducted by government research agencies or statistical bureaus. Some countries do follow Copenhagen's and Nairobi's exhortations, requiring that government time use surveys include care work in satellite accounts. These include Finland since the 1970s, Canada, Australia, and the Netherlands since the 1990s, Mexico since 2003, Costa Rica since 2015, and Georgia since 2020.

Satellite accounts, however, are supplemental macroeconomic measures. They are not countries' *main* national accounts, the figures that report countries' official production, income, consumption, and wealth.

The 2009 Bolivian Constitution stipulates that 'the state recognizes the economic value of work in the home as a source of wealth and ought to quantify this work in national accounts'.[56] In 2010, Colombia adopted an even firmer mandate. Two feminist legislators introduced a bill that would mandate the calculation and inclusion of unpaid household work into the country's national accounts (including via the use of time use surveys). Congresswomen worked together to ensure passage. As one woman legislator explained, they seized the opportunity to 'do a little teaching' for other legislators about the effort and value of unpaid care.[57] The law passed, making Colombia a pioneer in factoring unpaid care work into central economic measures. In Colombia and elsewhere, time use surveys have become key lobbying tools for women's movements and other movements, such as disability movements, that work with governments to adopt universal care systems. These policies integrate childcare, eldercare, and disability care with respite, education, and economic empowerment programs for caregivers, and have proved particularly popular in Latin America (discussed more below).

In countries not yet implementing time use surveys, women's organizations create these lobbying tools themselves. ActionAid Bangladesh began its Time Diary campaign in 2013, encouraging women to log their daily activities.[58] The organization used the Time Diary to spark household and community conversations, where – as the group explained – the diaries meant that 'men were confronted with the real weight of their partners' daily labour'.[59] In 2014, Action Aid received a boost from an external study, which estimated that, if women's unpaid care work were monetized, it would account for nearly 77 per cent of Bangladesh's GDP. That same year, the Manusher Jonno Foundation alongside 122 other women's organizations launched the Equality with Dignity campaign, which also raised awareness about women's economic contribution.[60] In 2021, Bangladesh's Bureau of Statistics conducted its first official time use survey, finding that women performed 6.8 hours of unpaid care daily, whereas men performed 1.2 hours daily.[61] These efforts culminated in 2025, when Bangladesh's interim government announced that, beginning in 2025–2026, women's unpaid care work would be factored into the country's gross domestic product.[62] This policy makes Bangladesh the first country in South Asia, and perhaps the world, to include unpaid care work in the most important economic measure of all: GDP.

Improving the care economy

The idea of providing care via self-organized collectives looks beyond the market and beyond the state. Silvia Federici, the Italian co-founder of Wages for Housework, envisions a 'reproductive commons', an approach emerging from real-world instances wherein social movements' members have coordinated among themselves to provide public goods, often during crisis. For instance, women faced with economic crises, natural disasters, and even pandemics have combined their time, labour, and other resources to collectively deliver essential services – like Chile's 'communal pots', urban soup kitchens that women formed during the 1973–1990 dictatorship and revitalized during the COVID-19 pandemic.[63] Another example comes from the Poble Sec neighbourhood of Barcelona. Faced with few nursery spaces and an inability to pay fees when spaces did exist, Poble Sec women formed groups of shared caring where parents and educators pool their time and money to rent shopfronts and run nurseries.[64] The groups began during the mid-2000s global financial crisis, but continue to the present day. For many feminist theorists, including Federici, collective provision offers a transformative path, one that brings the private into the public – but without the market's capitalist logic and the government's regulatory apparatus.

Other feminists acknowledge that capitalism devalues care work, but see the solution as increased government investment in care provision. Rather than retreat from the state, these feminists would have the state do more than offer meagre carers' allowances or baby bonuses; they would have the state fund universal care services and ensure that workers delivering the services enjoy a living wage. This idea may not seem radical in Europe, where countries in Scandinavia and other regions have provided universal childcare for many decades (alongside guaranteeing their residents and citizens higher standards of living). Sweden's universal childcare policy began in 1975, for example. Outside Europe, however, publicly funded care, especially childcare, has constituted a core women's movement demand, one elevated by the COVID-19 pandemic.

There is no shortage of feminist blueprints for achieving universal care provision. International frameworks call for greater public funding of care services, alongside universal care systems attending to the cared for and the carers. The latter treat care holistically, ending the siloing of care policies into different ministries and installing cooperation across government branches, levels, and agencies. Importantly, these feminist blueprints adopt expanded visions of care, where care is a right, a public good, an economic asset, and essential for people and planet.

For example, UN Women's 2021 document *Beyond COVID-19: Feminist Plan for Sustainability and Social Justice* advocates a new economic paradigm. This new approach 'would ensure sustainable livelihoods for all and would stop treating unpaid care work and the environment as limitless resources that can be used for free and depleted without cost or consequence'.[65] The document envisions a care-led future and is worth quoting at length:

> A care-led recovery would prioritize investments in the expansion of quality care services to create jobs and increase support for unpaid caregivers, including through paid family leave and universal child allowances, to address long-standing care deficits . . . Instead of a commodity, a personal choice or family obligation, care would be treated as a collective good that is adequately resourced and regulated to ensure continued supply and quality as well as decent pay and working conditions for paid care workers. The critical role that women-led cooperatives, workers' organizations and other civil society organizations can play in the articulation of community-based health, child and elder care networks would be recognized, and sustainable partnerships would be forged with national and local governments to enable these networks to deliver quality care that is affordable for the families they serve while ensuring living wages and social protection for all care workers.[66]

Here UN Women's plan acknowledges the kinds of reproductive commons that Federici envisioned and that grassroots women in places such as Chile and Spain created. These frameworks also expand the idea of co-responsibility in care provision from shared responsibility between men and women in the home to shared responsibility across state and society. Similarly, UN Women coordinated the 2024 policy paper *Transforming Care Systems*, which lays out the principles of and a template for universal care systems.[67] As UN Women's Executive Director Sima Bahous writes in her introduction, 'Investing in care systems on a large scale is not just necessary – it is transformative. Such investments have undeniable benefits for women, care recipients, communities and entire nations. It is imperative that states, civil society, the private sector and communities share the responsibility of framing care as a public good and as a fundamental right that benefits all'.[68] In 2022, the OAS released its template model law for universal care systems.

In fact, Latin America had advanced in care provision even before the pandemic revitalized conversations about care policy. In Uruguay, the first country to adopt an integrated, universal care system, time use surveys also played a starring role. Feminist academics from the National University of the Republic and feminist policymakers from the women's ministry and the national statistical office together carried out three time use surveys in 2003, 2007, and 2013.[69] The surveys were among the 'political tools' leveraged by the Gender and Family Network, which formed in 2008 to further advocate for care policy.[70] In 2010 a left-wing government came to power and formed a care policy working group, which included academics and activists working on the time use surveys.[71] The survey data supported advocates' quest for a universal care system. For instance, the 2013 survey revealed that Uruguayan women performed on average twice as much care work as men and that Uruguayan women's care of dependants increased as family incomes decreased, suggesting that women bore the trade-off between unwaged and waged labour more than men.[72] In 2015, Uruguay created the National Integrated Care System, a milestone law that defined care as a universal right and covering services for both the cared for and the carers. Colombia followed in 2023, as did Venezuela in 2021 and Chile in 2024. Mexico, Costa Rica, Ecuador, and Peru are pending.

Feminists outside Latin America also seek greater government investment in care provision. In 2020, the South African parliament presented a Children Amendment Bill that, in activists' view, did not adequately fund early childhood development (ECD).[73] Advocates responded by founding the group the Real Reform for ECD, which launched the #MakeTheBillBetter Campaign.[74] Two hundred organizations joined, including Ilifa Labantwana, a non-profit organization focusing on care and early learning.[75] In 2025, Real Reform for ECD claimed an initial victory, when the national budget increased the daily means-tested child subsidies and child support grants and invested in building and improving ECD centres. Ilifa Labantwana celebrated the advance, noting that 'investment in children and the women-led care economy addresses our greatest challenges of unemployment, poverty, and inequality'.[76]

South Africa's budget reform falls short of universal childcare and ECD coverage, but constitutes what Ilifa Labantwana recognizes as a critical step. Farther north, the pandemic helped Canada achieve feminist activists' and policymakers' long-sought goal: establishing a permanent, federally funded Canada-wide early learning and childcare program (CWELCC). Feminist economists drafted Canada's feminist COVID-19 recovery plan, presenting the plan to then Prime Minister Justin Trudeau and Deputy Prime Minister and Finance Minister Chrystia Freeland. In November 2020, Freeland's autumn economic statement described childcare as 'a vital part of our social infrastructure that has been weakened by COVID-19' and announced the then largest ever investment in federal childcare provision, staffing, and infrastructure.[77] In 2021, Freeland's budget created the CWELCC. The program creates a 50–50 cost-sharing model between the federal government and each province or territory, where the combined contributions from each government level amount to no family paying more than 10 Canadian dollars a day for childcare by 2025–2026. Freeland wrote: 'Early learning and childcare has long been a feminist issue; COVID has shown us all that it is an urgent economic issue, too.'[78] Though childcare in Canada will not be 100 per cent free, the cost cap exists alongside other child benefits (cash allowances) that make childcare dramatically more available and affordable.

A new care agenda

The global women's movement has forged common ground on addressing inequality within the family. The women's rights era has sought to undo discriminatory family laws, especially where customs and traditions give women fewer rights than men. Women's rights activists have sought and won reforms to laws governing marriage and divorce, child custody, inheritance and disposal of property, decision-making in the home, and access to legal systems. Yet even as discriminatory laws fall, discriminatory norms do not. Rituals and traditions change more slowly than codes and statutes, especially relative to women's familial and domestic roles. Women enter the workforce faster than they shed their caregiver status. Relative to the public sphere, then, the private sphere remains a stickier sphere to transform, a place where the adoption–implementation gap is larger. The question of unpaid care animates women's movements, with feminist academics and activists linking the undervaluing of unpaid care work in the home to the undervaluing of paid care work in the economy.

This connection fosters several intertwined movement claims around care: for factoring care work into national accounts; for more public investment in making care services universal and affordable; and for higher wages and better working conditions for labourers in the care economy. For minoritized women especially, these claims intertwine gender and racial justice, as gendered and racial hierarchies mean that women of colour, migrant women, and Global South women are concentrated in the care economy's bottom rungs.

As Wages for Housework campaigner Selma James said in 1975, '[o]ur experiences as exploited women, urban or rural, Third World or metropolitan, are unique in each case. Our needs and our desires are international and universal: to be free, to be free of the labour that has worn us down over centuries, to be free of domination and dependence on men.'[79] James's call for an economic value on care that would contribute to women's liberation still shapes women's movements. Contemporary feminist blueprints on care identify how women occupy the home's and the economy's most undervalued spaces, moving beyond women's degradation by men to focus on their degradation by unjust and exploitative capitalist systems. They articulate feminist visions that would transform the social and economic structures that make care burdensome. They seek to recognize and redistribute unpaid care by increasing government investment in the care economy. They continue to challenge the longstanding separation of production from reproduction, arguing that public and collective models of care will create more just, more sustainable, and even more wealthy societies.

SEVEN

Reproductive Rights

In October 2012, Savita Halappanavar was 17 weeks pregnant with her first child when she visited Ireland's University Hospital Galway for back pain.[1] Medical staff concluded that Halappanavar would miscarry, but since they detected a foetal heartbeat, they could not perform an abortion to hasten the pregnancy's end. The Irish constitution's Eighth Amendment, adopted in 1983, guaranteed 'the right to life of the unborn . . . as far as practicable' with respect to the right of life of the mother.[2] By placing what an investigation later determined was undue emphasis on the foetal heartbeat, the University Hospital Galway medical staff let Halappanavar miscarry naturally. When she miscarried three days later, she died of septic shock. Halappanavar's death became a focusing event, fuelling vigils, protests, and calls to reform Ireland's strict abortion ban. In 2013, the Irish parliament passed the Protection of Life during Pregnancy Act, which permitted medically necessary abortions but only to save women's lives.

Two other developments would spur further action. First came a 2016 UN ruling that Ireland's abortion ban violated women's human rights.[3] Informed that her foetus would not survive the birth, Amanda Mellet had become one of the thousands of Irish women who each year travel to England or Scotland for an abortion. Mellet and two other Irish women brought their cases to the UN Human Rights Committee, which ruled that Ireland must compensate them for the trauma of seeking abortions abroad. The Irish government accepted the ruling and compensated Mellet, a move that galvanized Ireland's legal abortion campaigners: in their view, the ruling and the government's acquiescence acknowledged that Ireland's constitution needed to change. After the Mellet case came the 2017 decision of the Irish Citizens' Assembly, which recommended unrestricted abortion access during the early phase of pregnancy.[4] Convened to evaluate proposed constitutional reforms, the Citizens' Assembly voted to overturn the Eighth Amendment, a decision that laid the groundwork for the abortion referendum. Over 70 organizations formed the Together for Yes campaign to persuade voters that – as organizer Karen Hand said – '[a]ccess to abortion for women is more than a rights issue and will contribute to overall societal health and well-being'.[5] They succeeded, with an overwhelming 66.4 per cent of Irish voters choosing 'yes' in 2018. The call for change came across the country, not just from progressive, young, and urban voters: the 'yes' vote won every Irish constituency save County Donegal.[6]

The 2018 referendum replaced the Eighth Amendment with the Thirty-Sixth Amendment, which states that 'provision may be made by law for regulation of the termination of pregnancy'.[7] The Irish parliament then passed the 2018 Regulation of Termination of Pregnancy Act, which allows voluntary abortion up to 12 weeks and medically necessary abortions thereafter. Ireland's abortion reform drew international attention, given the country's reputation as deeply Catholic and the Catholic Church's official position against abortion. (The 2016 Irish census found that 78.3 per cent of the country identified as Roman Catholic.[8]) The #HomeToVote campaign proved especially newsworthy, as the London-Irish Abortion Rights Campaign looked to mobilize an estimated 40,000 Irish emigrants living in the United Kingdom and elsewhere to return to Ireland for voting day.[9] Irish men and women on both sides tagged themselves 'Going #HomeToVote', but the #HomeToVote campaign focused on those who would vote 'yes'. In Dublin Airport, abortion rights activists greeted arriving 'yes' voters with cheers, banners, and applause.[10]

Elsewhere, abortion reform also progressed through many stages. Women's movements in Latin America spent decades marching and introducing abortion rights legislation that failed again and again, until finally succeeding in Uruguay, Argentina, and Chile.[11] Each victory depended on the alignment between movement activists, feminist legislators, and a supportive president. In Urugay, an abortion liberalization bill failed in 2002 and 2008, but a bill allowing voluntary abortion within 12 weeks of pregnancy succeeded in 2012. In Chile, during President Michelle Bachelet's second term, a bill liberalizing abortion for three causes – danger to the women's life, foetal malformation incompatible with extrauterine life, and rape – passed in 2017. In Argentina, feminist legislators introduced abortion bills in 2008, 2010, 2012, 2014, 2016, and

2018. These never advanced, but with the election of left-wing President Alberto Fernández in 2019 the women's movement succeeded. In 2020, the Argentine Congress passed – and Fernández signed – a law that allows voluntary abortion up to 14 weeks.

Abortion activists worldwide have celebrated Latin America's 'green wave', referring to the colour donned by Argentine women – and now adopted by abortion campaigners worldwide as well.[12] While Uruguay, Chile, and Argentina liberalized abortion access via the legislature and Ireland via a referendum, other countries have expanded access via executive branch orders or rulings from constitutional or supreme courts. According to research by Katy Mayall, Laurenne Ajayi, and Caitlin Gruer, over 60 countries have substantially or wholly liberalized abortion access since the 1994 International Conference on Population and Development (the Cairo conference).[13] These expansions to abortion rights have occurred in all global regions, in countries as diverse as Benin, Ethiopia, Iran, Nepal, New Zealand, Spain, Thailand, and Togo.

Legal abortion is not, however, the only policy objective associated with realizing women's reproductive rights. Ensuring women's full autonomy to decide whether and when to have children encompasses the rights to sexual health, sexual health education, protection from and treatment for sexually transmitted diseases, including HIV/AIDS, and high-quality sexual and reproductive healthcare. Sexual and reproductive rights further include the right to information about and access to family planning methods, including all forms of contraception. Exercising this larger package of sexual and reproductive rights, in turn, depends upon other women's rights, such as their rights to education, health, and to live free from discrimination, coercion, and violence. Further, sexual and reproductive rights encompass women's rights to choose their gender identity, sexual preference, sexual and romantic partners, and preferred family formations.

The diverse reforms that count as advancing sexual and reproductive rights mean that, even when liberalizing abortion remains politically impossible, countries can still adopt policies that expand women's sexual and reproductive choice and autonomy. Attaining none of these reforms is easy: sexuality and reproduction touch on deeply rooted moral and religious views. Even as countries adopt other reforms, such as expanding access to contraception, liberalizing abortion remains the most difficult: the question of whether the foetus constitutes a life, and how this life may or may not have rights that are independent of the pregnant woman, has vexed philosophers, activists, and politicians for decades. Even women's rights advocates can reasonably disagree on how unrestricted abortion should be. For example, feminists in Uruguay, Chile, and Argentina wrote legislation that incorporated at least some exceptions for doctors and healthcare providers who wish to exercise conscientious objection.[14] The 2018 Irish law also exempts practitioners expressing conscientious objection.

Further, as recent high-profile reversions to abortion access have demonstrated – such as the US Supreme Court's repeal of a federal right to abortion in 2022 – abortion access and other reproductive rights are never safe. Expansions to reproductive rights galvanize opposition forces, who organize before and during reform efforts in order to block passage, and afterwards in order to mute the reforms' effects or halt implementation. In Uruguay, for instance, conservative groups attempted to call a referendum to repeal the reform (but failed to gain sufficient signatures). In Latin America, Ireland, and elsewhere, countermovements deploy various obstructionist tactics, including blockades outside clinics and campaigns urging providers to exercise conscientious objection. The latter create service gaps, resulting in areas where nearly all providers are objectors – some because they do object in principle and others who do not necessarily object but fear censure or even attacks from anti-abortion supervisors, colleagues, and community members.[15]

The advancement of reproductive rights is therefore notable because these gains provoke organized and mobilized resistance from countermovements and conservative actors. Women's rights reforms always trigger opposition, but this resistance does not always spur opponents to seek reversals. True, opponents may take to the airwaves and complain about the death of traditional values, and conservative forces may lobby as vigorously against a women's rights reform as feminist advocates lobby for it. After women's rights reforms are passed, conservative politicians may also underfund and underimplement progressive measures they find distasteful. Yet rarely do entire social movements form to prevent or rollback expansions to women's political rights or economic rights. Countermovements do not generally organize nationwide marches to stop gender quota laws from being adopted or to prevent maternity leave from being expanded. They do, however, lead nationwide protests and efforts to obstruct reproductive rights, as seen with the Marches for Life that happen annually around the world. They further commit violence, as evidenced by the threats to and assassinations of abortion providers and the harassment experienced by women seeking abortions and by abortion rights activists. In the calendar years of 2023 and 2024, the US National Abortion Federation counted 671 acts of vandalism, 621 acts of trespassing, 38 assaults on staff, and 297 death threats aimed at staff.[16] In fact, anti-abortion activists are the top perpetrators of terrorist attacks in the United States.[17] Their violence is not limited to the Global North: in 2023, Amnesty International documented threats and attacks faced by abortion providers and activists from Colombia to Ghana.[18]

Protagonists seeking reproductive rights thus face a uniquely hostile environment. Advocates are harassed and threatened in person and on social media. Their policy victories are distinctly fragile, exacerbating political violence and inspiring opponents to mobilize and counterattack. Like personal status laws governing marriage and family (Chapter 6), reproductive rights target deep-seated doctrinal issues. For this reason, reproductive rights fall on the more transformative end of the policy spectrum. The gulf between feminist visions and daily reality remains large, and bridging this distance depends not just on designing better policies and electing progressive politicians committed to effective implementation. Closing the gap also depends on securing citizens' agreement about how to ensure women's autonomy and freedom, with consensus being difficult to achieve precisely because women's autonomy and freedom is bound up with their capacity to conceive, gestate, and birth another human. This chapter examines how these principles about reproductive autonomy and freedom evolved and shaped policy during the women's rights era.

Feminist blueprints on reproductive rights

Cultures and communities have strong, enduring customs about appropriate expressions of sexuality and appropriate family formations, including appropriate forms of pregnancy and childbearing. Feminists seeking sexual and reproductive rights often challenge the values and assumptions underlying these customs. Like the activists seeking family law reform and sanctions for violence against women, activists looking to expand sexual and reproductive choice and autonomy are often accused of betraying their societies' religious and ethical values. Opponents may make specious and outrageous claims about feminists' disrespect for the moral order, like US politicians suggesting (in these very words) that doctors 'abort' babies upon birth or that teachers instruct children how to be gay.[19] Of course, these statements are hyperbolic exaggerations of feminists' policy demands for compassionate and medically appropriate miscarriage care and inclusive sexual health education. Still, feminists fighting for reproductive rights share several principles that inevitably do challenge some foundational ideas about sexuality and family: feminists view patriarchal family formations that limit and control women's sexuality and reproduction to be unjust, and they want laws and policies revised to guarantee women autonomy over their sexual and reproductive lives. The idea of autonomy means that each woman has the ability to choose for herself, even as every individual woman will make different choices, each according to her values.

Reproductive rights and the UN Decade for Women

Voluntary abortion – what some activists call voluntary interruption of pregnancy or voluntary termination of pregnancy – constitutes the 'ultimate' sexual and reproductive right. Allowing voluntary abortion prioritizes women's rights to life, healthy, and safety over the rights of a foetus or a baby. Nonetheless, enduring doctrinal controversy over abortion means that the specific right to abortion does not appear in the core feminist blueprints of the women's rights era. Neither the CEDAW Convention nor the declarations from the world conferences on women mention voluntary pregnancy termination. The issue proved too polemical for earlier generations of feminists – but not only because they disagreed on abortion's morality. As noted in Chapter 1, feminists travelling to the Mexico City, Copenhagen, and Nairobi conferences had different experiences with pregnancy and childbirth and thus different orientations towards policies affecting fertility.

US and European feminists wanted the right to choose *not* to have children, and therefore the right to access the means necessary for preventing and terminating pregnancies. For them, this choice could only benefit women – including women in the developing world, whom they initially viewed as equally poised to be as 'liberated' by reproductive choice as they were.[20]

Many non-white and non-western feminists did not perceive birth control and abortion as liberating, however. In the post-Second World War era and in the decades after the United Nations' founding, development policies had linked poverty to overpopulation. As feminist activists and scholars argued, population control policies relied on blind spots and assumptions, themselves informed by racist and colonial ideas about 'third-world women'. Development planners approached fertility as something that needed reining in, ignoring that high birth rates reflected not women's ignorance or licentiousness but their lack of control over marriage and sexual intercourse. Development policies pushed or even forced long-term birth control and sterilization on women, especially marginalized and minority women. This coercion occurred not just in the Global South but in Indigenous territories, communities of colour, and poor communities in the Global North. For example, women seeking caesareans would have hysterectomies performed without their consent.[21] Consequently, western women prioritized policies that would allow them *not* to have children, whereas non-western women and non-white women prioritized reforms that would allow them to *have* them – but under conditions where patriarchy, racism, and imperialism did not place impossible constraints on this choice. Being coerced into family planning was not liberating, but neither was childbearing in situations of poverty, underdevelopment, abuse, and discrimination. Global South feminists and feminists of colour understood reproductive choice as freedom from coercive population control policies and they sought better conditions for pregnancy and childrearing, such that marginalized women would not see illegal abortions as a solution.

On this latter point, activists did agree: illegal abortions pose grave dangers to women's lives, as black market providers have few reasons to follow health and safety measures. The Mexico City Programme of Action reflects this consensus, referencing abortion twice in relation to the dangerous conditions of pregnancy and childrearing that place women in untenable situations. The first reference indirectly refers to women's inability to control sexual intercourse and their recourse to illegal abortions: 'The hazards of child-bearing, characterized by too many pregnancies, pregnancies at too early or too late an age and at too close intervals, inadequate pre-natal delivery, and [poor] postnatal care and resort to illegal induced abortions, result in high rates of maternal mortality.'[22] The second reference describes the peril of illegal abortions: 'The high rate of illegal abortions performed by non-qualified persons is a serious maternal health problem in several developing countries.'[23]

One way to end unsafe abortions is to eliminate their necessity. While neither activists nor member-state delegates agreed on calling for voluntary abortion, they agreed on designing family planning policies that would enhance women's ability to freely make sexual and reproductive choices. The Mexico City Programme of Action asks for 'the development of means of contraception and birth control that will be both efficient and compatible with cultural values prevailing in different societies'.[24] The 1985 Nairobi conference report states that 'the ability of women to control their fertility forms an important basis for the enjoyment of other rights . . . All couples and individuals have the basic human right to decide freely and informedly the number and spacing of their children.'[25] The Nairobi report also emphasizes the relationship between 'voluntary and free choice' over the desired number of children and information about 'all medically approved and appropriate methods of family planning' that should be 'widely available to both men and women'.[26]

The 1994 Cairo conference and its aftermath

This endorsement of reproductive autonomy attained via education, information, and choice over childbearing would be as far as the feminist blueprints would go, until the 1994 Cairo conference. Researchers and practitioners today often remember Cairo for the controversy over abortion, itself generated by a then emergent (but now well-established) alliance of conservative governments against women's rights. At Cairo, the Vatican led this coalition together with some Islamic and some Latin American countries. Still, the Vatican's campaign did not fully carry the day: the Cairo Programme of Action did not endorse abortion rights, but did constitute a remarkable paradigm shift relative to population policy.

It was at Cairo that women activists successfully installed their critiques of development policies' emphasis on demography and population control. They introduced a new paradigm prioritizing women's sexual, reproductive, and maternal health and emphasizing women's autonomous and empowered choices.[27] The international women's health movement led this push. The movement began as a loose network of US feminists but, over the UN Decade for Women, grew into what Amy Higer describes as 'a global movement of women around the world sharing strategies, analyses, and information'.[28] Still, like in all women's movements, the participants did not always agree on priorities and strategies, and did not initially approach Cairo with a unified voice.[29] As Higer recounts, the more radical feminists found Cairo's focus on population inherently problematic, seeing no room to manoeuvre within an international system committed to thinking of development in terms of lowering third-world births (rather than addressing the structural inequalities within the global economy). Other activists, however, embraced the opportunity to promote a development viewpoint that would prioritize respect for women's rights rather than control over their sexuality and reproduction. Pursuing what Higer calls the pragmatist strategy, these activists aligned with UK activist Marge Berer's advice that the movement either articulate and promote a 'feminist population strategy' or risk being ignored entirely.[30]

The international women's health movement would navigate this tension between radicalism and pragmatism in the run-up to Cairo.[31] They prepared for the Cairo conference as women activists prepared for all other international conferences: they held pre-event networking events, formed alliances and coalitions, and circulated collectively authored manifestos. In 1993, 218 women met at the Reproductive Health and Justice Conference in Rio de Janeiro, with organizers ensuring the representation of women of colour and Global South women. The 21-point Rio Statement expressed points of unity between the radicals and the pragmatists, opening with an indictment of current development approaches to women's fertility. The Rio Statement then formed the basis of the Women's Caucus's demands at Cairo (see Chapter 2), as the Women's Caucus members lobbied member-state representatives to adopt a population perspective centred on health and choice. Though ultimately this perspective was more pragmatic than radical – emphasizing women's empowerment *within* policies aimed at reducing fertility and, thus, population growth – Cairo marked the first time governments at an international convening openly discussed subjects like abortion, female circumcision, and women's sexuality.

Women's lobbying around a feminist population strategy worked. Cairo's 177-page Programme of Action describes how sexual, reproductive, and maternal health matter for women's well-being and dedicates an entire chapter to empowering women and recognizing their human rights. The programme departs from taboos and victim-blaming approaches to sexually transmitted infections, stressing the prevention and treatment of diseases such as HIV/AIDS. Relative to abortion, the programme exhorts governments to avoid abortion by providing complete and comprehensive sexual, reproductive, and maternal health care, including family planning, and to provide humane treatment and medical attention to women who have 'had recourse to abortion'.[32] Ultimately, advocates viewed Cairo as a milestone achievement, one in which transnational feminists succeeded in shifting the focus from demographic targets (which are not mentioned) to sustainable development and humanitarian approaches to sexuality and reproduction.[33] In her closing speech, Nafis Sadik of Pakistan, conference secretary-general and then executive director of the UN Population Fund, called the Cairo consensus a 'quantum leap forward'.[34]

This vision reappeared one year later in the Beijing PfA. The PfA frames women's reproductive health, autonomy, and choice in broad, rights-related ways. For instance, the PfA notes that reproductive and sexual health is 'the enhancement of life and personal relations, and not merely counselling and care related to reproductive and sexually transmitted disease' and that 'reproductive rights embrace certain human rights'.[35] These rights include women's 'right to freely and responsibly decide the number, spacing and timing of their children' and 'the right to make decisions concerning reproduction free of discrimination, coercion and violence'.[36] The PfA discusses abortion relative to preventing unwanted pregnancies in the first instance, and also relative to eliminating unsafe abortions and providing humanitarian and therapeutic abortion care (no matter how abortions are obtained). The PfA also invites governments to 'consider reviewing laws containing punitive measures against women who have undergone illegal abortions'.[37]

The PfA did miss some activist targets, however. The emphasis on unsafe and illegal abortions falls short of endorsing voluntary abortion. Nor did the PfA mention sexual orientation or gay rights. Even so, member-state delegates at least discussed including a line that would have disallowed discrimination on the basis of sexual orientation – an unprecedented debate among governments at the time.[38] Lesbian activists had lobbied delegates to include sexual orientation, and they did receive support from many corners. South African delegate and Health Minister Nkosazana Zuma delivered an especially noteworthy speech in support, asserting that South Africa's traumatic experience under apartheid made the newly democratic country committed to ending discrimination against all groups. Ultimately, however, the Vatican-led alliance resisted and the reference to sexual orientation was removed in order to obtain consensus on the PfA as a whole. Supporters had to settle for an implied protection for non-heterosexual women, which appears in the PfA's endorsement of women's right to make sexual and reproductive decisions free from coercion and violence. These gaps notwithstanding, Beijing confirmed and expanded Cairo's vision of sexual and reproductive rights as women's rights and thus human rights.

This rights-based understanding would inform later UN affirmations. In 2016, the UN Committee on Economic, Social, and Cultural Rights would issue General Comment 22, which reinterpreted the 'right to health' in the 1976 International Covenant on Economic, Social, and Cultural Rights as including the right to sexual and reproductive health. General Comment 22 further clarifies that the 1976 Covenant's non-discrimination injunction applies to reproductive health and 'encompasses the right of all persons, including lesbian, gay, bisexual, transgender and intersex persons, to be fully respected for their sexual orientation, gender identity, and intersex status'.[39] At the regional level, the 2003 AU Maputo Protocol enumerated several reproductive rights, including the right to family-planning education, the right to any method of contraception, and the right to medically necessary abortions.[40] The 2013 Montevideo Consensus, adopted by Latin American and Caribbean countries at their first regional population and development conference, lists similar rights and goes further by reaffirming that a secular state is fundamental to the full exercise of these rights.[41] These regional affirmations of the feminist blueprints matter, offering activists further ammunition against conservative governments' claims that reproductive rights are 'western' imports at odds with 'non-western' traditions and values.

Family planning, contraception, and sexual health

The Cairo conference restructured normative understandings of and policy approaches to population. Yet as the more radical activists within the international women's health movement feared, Cairo did not completely sever questions of sexual and reproductive health from questions of development and population. At the UN level, family planning, contraception, and sexual health fall under the purview of the UN Population Fund (originally the UN Fund for Population Activities: UNFPA). Founded in 1967, UNFPA emerged from this earlier, problematic approach to fertility: its own origin story explains its creation in response to 'rapid population change and hope in new family planning technologies'.[42] UNFPA operates as a voluntary fund similar to the original UNIFEM. Its activities are not supported by the United Nations' regular budget but by donations from public and private donors, including governments, foundations, and individuals. UNFPA then designs and implements projects across the globe, in collaboration with international and national NGOs and national and local governments. UNFPA reports directly to the UN General Assembly.

UNFPA today follows Cairo's emphasis on women's empowerment rather than population control. Three goals – the 'three zeroes' – form its mission: attaining zero unmet need for family planning; zero preventable maternal deaths; and zero gender-based harmful practices.[43] Each corresponds to targets set by the SDGs on health and well-being (area 3) and on gender equality (area 5). These SDGs include: reducing maternal mortality to 70 per 100,000 live births by 2030 (3.1); achieving universal access to sexual and reproductive care, family planning, and education (3.7); and realizing reproductive health and rights (5.6), including eliminating forced marriage and female genital mutilation (5.3) and ending violence against and exploitation of women and girls (5.2). In this way, the SDGs similarly reflect more updated thinking about development, focusing on human flourishing rather than economic growth, thanks largely to women's NGOs' participation in the drafting process (see Chapter 2). Still, those feminists holding the radical perspective might argue that colonial development thinking endures in both UNFPA's mission and the SDGs: neither challenge the underlying wealth disparities among or within countries, leaving unaddressed structural inequalities that fuel unmet contraceptive need, maternal mortality, and gender discrimination in the first place.

Those pursuing the feminist population policy approach might accept this critique, but point out that UNFPA-funded projects bring much needed financial and technical resources to countries and NGOs that genuinely wish to improve women's access to sexual and reproductive healthcare. Such support especially matters in countries where health coverage and health infrastructure are weak and under-resourced. Without UNFPA funding, low- and middle-income countries might be unable to pay for and distribute contraception even where contraception is legal. UNFPA pools resources with other UN agencies, such as the UN Children's Fund (UNICEF) and the World Health Organization (WHO), to distribute condoms and pharmaceutical contraception in over 50 countries.[44] In 2023, UNFPA reported that 85 per cent of these countries were able to make at least three modern contraceptive methods available in at least 85 per cent of healthcare places.[45] These countries include Cambodia, where UNFPA and partners have ensured that contraceptive methods are supplied in all public hospitals.

UNFPA-funded initiatives also go beyond contraception distribution and encompass training, education, and norm shifting about reproduction and sexuality. For instance, the Sahel Women's Empowerment and Demographic Dividend (SWEDD) operates in Burkina Faso, Chad, the Ivory Coast, Mali, Mauritania, and Niger. UNFPA leads SWEDD, with participation and funding from other international organizations. SWEDD encompasses myriad different projects, including midwifery training, public health workshops, and radio programmes aimed at disseminating information about sexuality and sexually transmitted diseases.[46] In all six countries, SWEDD offers a 'safe spaces' educational curriculum, where young girls attend 'life skills courses' about sexual and reproductive health, women's rights, and economic empowerment.[47] UNFPA underscores that 'life skills' is a culturally appropriate name and explains that all courses are led by community mentors who, on the basis of their own experiences, can identify with the girls.[48] In its use of workshops and courses SWEDD is not unique, but leverages the standard intervention of development practice: educational activities that disseminate information and encourage cultural change.

This project-based approach to family planning, contraception, and sexual health emerges for several reasons. First, unlike abortion, the main barriers to family planning, contraception, and sexual health services are often not outright statutory bans. Rather, the main barriers are practical questions of knowledge, funding, supplies, delivery, coverage, and usage. Having money to pay for contraception is only the beginning. Governments still need to negotiate contracts with multinational pharmaceutical companies; to import and distribute the products without damage or spoiling; to embed information and availability about contraception within a larger suite of respectfully delivered reproductive and sexual healthcare; to guarantee that providers offer these services; and to ensure that women and men feel safe and empowered to discuss their options with medical providers. Attaining these latter objectives is where UNFPA's and other NGOs' emphasis on training, education, and norm shifting especially matters. Overall, delivering comprehensive and high-quality sexual and reproductive healthcare remains difficult even in wealthy countries where contraception is legal, promoted, and provided by government health services, and not overtly stigmatized. Take the United Kingdom, for instance: women of colour and women living in economically disadvantaged areas have more difficulty accessing contraception than white women and women living in wealthy areas. Reasons for these gaps include ongoing stigma from providers and from the women's and the girls' own communities, alongside under-resourcing of health services in marginal areas.[49]

Second and relatedly, questions of funding, supplies, delivery, coverage and usage become highly technical questions, hammered out by policymakers within government ministries and agencies – and not necessarily fought about in parliaments or demanded in protest marches. Cairo especially encouraged governments to develop and release national population policies, which are usually worked on by small numbers of ministers and bureaucrats. The policy planning typically occurs in ministries of health, or in multistakeholder fora convened by international organizations such as UNFPA, which bring government representatives together with academics, experts, activists, and local organizations. All these advocates are committed to improving women's and girls' lives, but their work occurs in expert meetings and without the mobilization or fanfare accompanying other women's rights reforms.

That said, some countries have changed their statutes, setting new mandates for the more technical work that government ministries and non-governmental stakeholders will then carry out. Argentina illustrates this process.[50] In the 1980s, contraception became legal not via a lengthy parliamentary process, but via an executive branch rule change. Feminist doctors and activists appointed to head a Women, Health, and Development programme within the Ministry of Health successfully pressured then President Raúl Alfonsín to issue a decree on couples' rights to decide the number and birth spacing of their children. This decision legalized contraception, but did not address availability and coverage. Legislators then introduced a bill to create a nationwide mandatory family planning program – but did not succeed, as the Catholic Church mounted significant opposition. The prospect of a nationwide programme diminished even further in the 1990s, when Alfonsín's successor, Carlos Menem, allied with the Vatican at the 1994 Cairo conference and 1995 Beijing conference. In fact, Menem fought openly with feminists during the Cairo and Beijing preparatory processes. Menem blocked prominent feminists from travelling to and serving as delegates in Beijing, including some who had led the original Women, Health, and Development team.

Undaunted, Argentine feminists regrouped. They had founded organizations such as the Foundation for Studies and Research on Women (FEIM from the Spanish name) and the Center for the Study of State and Society (CEDES from the Spanish name). FEIM, CEDES, Catholics for the Right Choose, and other organizations continued to seek a national programme. Legislators introduced 22 additional proposals between 1990 and 2000. In 2003, Argentina elected Néstor Kirchner, who held more secular views than previous presidents and who appointed a progressive health minister. Women legislators, FEIM, CEDES, Catholics for the Right to Choose, and the new health minister launched a vigorous lobbying campaign, persuading legislators to pass the 2003 National Law on Sexual Health and Responsible Procreation, which made contraception universal and free.

In subsequent years, Argentina further expanded its legislative scaffolding for reproductive health, passing two laws in 2006: the law on surgical contraception, which allows voluntary tubal ligation and vasectomies in all public and private health centres, and the law on comprehensive sexual education, which recognizes sexual and reproductive health education as a right and mandates that all schools enact a curriculum grounded in principles of gender equality. The latter remains unevenly implemented but constitutes an important reference for public health interest groups. Though statutory reform in the area of sexual health education remains under-researched, other countries passing laws mandating school programs include Colombia, Liberia, and Zambia.[51]

Abortion reform

In 2022, the US Supreme Court repealed a federal right to abortion in the United States. Feminists found the *Dobbs v Jackson* decision devastating but not surprising: since the 1973 *Roe v Wade* decision granting a federal right to abortion, conservative opponents had sought to undermine abortion access. The United States' abortion reversion – like Turkey's 2012 withdrawal from the Council of Europe Convention on Preventing and Combating Violence against Women and Domestic Violence (Chapter 8) – receives considerable attention. Abortion supporters fear that reversions in large, powerful, and wealthy countries imply a broader trend of global backsliding on women's reproductive rights.

Comparing the number of advances to the number of rollbacks offers more context. Between the year of the 1994 Cairo conference and the calendar year 2023, abortion laws progressed in over 60 countries and regressed in just five (the United States, Poland, El Salvador, Nicaragua, and Turkmenistan).[52] Progressions include complete decriminalization or legalization, meaning reforms that allow voluntary abortion, and partial decriminalization or legalization, meaning that abortion becomes allowed in some circumstances but not all. Since Cairo, countries have moved away from total bans and towards voluntary abortion without restrictions.[53] In 1994, abortion was banned entirely in 40 countries, but by 2023, complete abortion bans existed in just 18 countries. In 1994, only 47 countries allowed abortion on request within some number of weeks, but by 2023, 75 countries did.

Liberalizing abortion access

Feminist mobilization plays a significant role in liberalizing abortion access, as the chapter's opening stories show. In Latin America, feminists marched for years if not decades to secure abortion reform in Argentina, Uruguay, Chile, Mexico, and Colombia. In the latter two countries, feminists engaged in strategic litigation, bringing cases to court that challenged prohibitions on human rights and constitutional grounds. In the former three, feminists worked with legislators to introduce bills and then to craft the legislative coalitions that would vote 'yes'.[54] Negotiating abortion reform in parliaments proves tricky, however. Feminists typically do not have sufficient votes from left or centre-left legislators to pass their ideal version of the law. Instead, they must negotiate with moderate legislators, who extract concessions in exchange for their support.[55]

All legislative processes require negotiation and sacrifices, though abortion reform invokes especially high emotions. Grassroots activists often prefer more permissive legislation than elites can achieve, provoking disagreement within the reproductive rights movement between protagonists who are willing to compromise and those who are not.[56] In Chile in 2017, for instance, feminist elites within President Michelle Bachelet's governing coalition pursued abortion only on 'three grounds': danger to the woman's life, foetal malformation incompatible with extrauterine life, and rape. The women ministers and legislators knew that winning abortion on demand was not possible; even securing liberalization for the three grounds was not guaranteed. They negotiated the legislative votes behind closed doors, without involving the larger feminist movement, fearing that any insistence on a more expansive reform would destabilize an already fragile effort. In the end, the three grounds reform passed, but some feminist activists resented what, in their view, was a secretive process leading to a tepid reform.

The women's movement in Uruguay felt similarly betrayed when feminist legislators negotiating the voluntary abortion reform introduced two restrictions during the legislative debates. In 2012, the abortion bill had passed the Senate but was two votes shy in the lower house. To secure moderate legislators' votes, the bill's proponents agreed to a waiting period and to a requirement that women first consult a multidisciplinary healthcare team made up of a doctor, a social worker, and a psychologist. The feminist movement rightly viewed the multidisciplinary team and waiting period as constituting access barriers. One legislator eloquently described the decision he faced in trading a perfect bill for an actual one, saying: 'I cannot remain rigidly loyal to the original bill while criminalization and women putting their lives at risk continue. I can either raise that flag and die with it in my hands, or I can be more flexible.'[57] Another woman legislator conceded that activists were disappointed, but reflected: 'In politics, you always reach the same point: either everything stays as it is, or we move forward. For some, moving forward was a lot; for others, it was a betrayal of fundamental principles.'[58] In other words, the elected officials chose to fulfil their mandate to make policy, viewing any liberalization as preferable to no liberalization.

These agonizing trade-offs illustrate the complexity of abortion reform, which entails not just removing the criminal penalties associated with abortion but making complex determinations about under what conditions and through what legal procedures women can access the service. They demonstrate the tension between idealism and pragmatism. Abortion campaigns also make these trade-offs in the very way they frame the issue, in order to gather public support. Guyana, one of the few Caribbean countries to liberalize abortion and the only one allowing voluntary abortion, demonstrates that discourses reifying traditional gender roles, while normatively problematic, can craft the coalitions necessary for reform.[59] In this case, the window of opportunity opened as part of the country's transition to multiparty democracy. The People's National Congress party, which had ruled since 1966, lost the 1992 elections to the People's Progressive Party (PPP). As with other cases, the movement to liberalize abortion predated this political shift. A self-described Pro-Reform Group organized in the 1980s, working with PPP parliamentarians (who were then in the opposition) to draft various versions of a liberalization bill. Once the PPP entered government and the prospect for a vote became real, the Pro-Reform Group mounted a vigorous public relations campaign. The group branded itself as 'pro-life, pro-choice, and pro-reform'.

Though abortion opponents elsewhere style themselves pro-life and abortion proponents call themselves pro-choice, the Pro-Reform Group argued that these positions need not be at odds. The group's members argued that they, too, were pro-life: they were against abortions, but they were especially against *unsafe* abortions and against women having children beyond their capacity to love and care for them. The Pro-Reform Group used data from surveys, personal stories, cartoons, and television ads to communicate their message that voluntary abortion would allow for safe motherhood and therefore strengthen families. Though these frames do not challenge patriarchal assumptions about women's natural roles, the messaging worked. Guyana's 1995 Medical Termination of Pregnancy Act allows voluntary abortion up to eight weeks, and then adds constraining conditions for after that.

South Africa offers another example where abortion reform occurred as part of a democratic transition, though with a more explicit focus on women's rights. Previously, the 1975 Abortion and Sterilization Act limited abortion to cases of threats to the woman's life or mental and physical health, rape or incest (which had to be proved), and handicap to the child. The Act had been adopted by South Africa's apartheid government. As Black South Africans fought and eventually triumphed against apartheid, women's rights – including the right to abortion – formed part of that struggle.

Women played an outsized role in the African National Congress (ANC), which organized Black South Africans against apartheid. Women's advocacy linked Black South Africans' quest for political equality to South African women's quest for gender equality.[60] In 1984, for example, the ANC's National Women's Coalition introduced the Women's Charter for Effective Equality, which included 'the right to control over their bodies which includes the right to reproductive decisions'.[61] In 1994, as the ANC prepared for the first post-apartheid elections, women's efforts ensured the ANC included abortion in their platform. The ANC's Reconstruction and Development Programme stated that 'every woman must have the right to choose whether or not to have an early termination of pregnancy'.[62]

The ANC won the April 1994 elections and then faced the massive task of completely transforming the country. Notwithstanding the ANC's formal commitment to women's rights generally and abortion rights specifically, women needed to lobby vigorously to keep their demands on the busy government agenda.[63] On the question of abortion, women activists convened a Women's Health Conference in December 1994. Attendees included representatives from women's organizations, health professionals, trade unions, and the ANC, all of whom underscored the importance of enshrining women's right to an early termination of pregnancy.[64]

However, this priority was not necessarily shared by all ANC members. Key protagonists helped convey the message to the party leaders.

Figures included Nkosazana Zuma, who attended the conference while sitting on the ANC Women's Health Commission.[65] (Zuma would later become the South African minister of health who supported the doomed effort to incorporate gay rights into the 1995 PfA.) Ultimately, the advocates' pressure succeeded. The ANC passed the Choice on Termination of Pregnancy Act in 1996, allowing voluntary abortion up to 12 weeks, with further restrictions thereafter.

Fighting the worst-case scenarios

Even where abortion reversions have occurred, feminists continue to mount significant resistance – often forestalling the worst outcome. This pattern reflects the longstanding interplay between feminists and conservatives in the quest for abortion reform: victory by one side provokes response from the other, each looking to shift momentum in their favour.

The US case illustrates abortion reform's never-safe character particularly well. In the 1973 Supreme Court decision *Roe v Wade*, abortion became allowed within the first trimester, with regulations left to the states. Feminists and conservatives then waged fierce state-by-state battles. Feminists lobbied state legislatures for permissive laws and conservatives lobbied for restrictive ones; whichever side lost then challenged the state law in court. In 1988, the question of whether states could impose restrictions such as waiting periods or parental consent for minors reached the federal Supreme Court in the case of *Planned Parenthood v Casey*. The US Supreme Court determined that such restrictions did not impose an 'undue burden' on women's abortion access. This decision emboldened states with conservative governments to add even more restrictions, furthering the United States' patchwork landscape of abortion access. The steady march of restrictive state laws culminated in the 2022 *Dobbs v Jackson* decision that overturned *Roe v Wade*. Yet the *Dobbs* decision only removed the federal guarantee for abortion. Individual states can still allow abortions. In the aftermath of *Dobbs* and as of September 2025, 12 US states have banned abortion entirely, but 28 states allow abortion at least prior to foetal viability and the remaining 10 allow abortions somewhere between six and 22 weeks (though many other access barriers, such as waiting periods, remain in permitting states).[66]

The US case thus illustrates how reproductive rights always face the threat of reversion – but also how outraged and mobilized groups of feminists can make their voices heard when faced with backsliding on abortion rights. In three US election years since *Dobbs* – 2022, 2023, and 2024 – 26 states have held abortion referendums, usually over amendments to the state constitution that would either guarantee or prohibit abortions. The abortion rights camp has won 22 of these votes, with women mobilizing extensively to campaign for abortion in all states where abortion appeared on the ballot.[67] Their efforts did not undo *Dobbs*, but did prevent abortion bans from being written into state constitutions. They even attained victories in states with conservative voting majorities, such as Kansas, Kentucky, and Missouri.

An even larger and more successful mobilization occurred in another notable case of abortion backsliding that has drawn significant attention: Poland. Apart from a brief period towards the end of the Second World War, Poland never allowed voluntary abortion. The communist and postcommunist governments allowed abortion only in limited circumstances, most commonly risk to the woman's health or life, rape, and foetal impairment.[68] In 2016, the conservative government introduced a bill that sought to ban abortion entirely, sparking widespread protests. Women activists marched dressed in black, earning the movement the name of Black Protests. The movement included a series of strikes. On 3 October 2016, an estimated 250,000 women and men refused to work and attend school across the country.[69] This coordinated opposition forced the government to abandon the bill, though in 2020 the Polish Constitutional Court would strike down the ground of foetal impairment, sparking another round of strikes and protests. Though these latter efforts did not prompt parliament to reverse the court's decision, Polish women's mobilization has avoided the complete ban that conservative political elites would prefer.

Feminists in El Salvador and Nicaragua also protested their countries' introduction of total abortion bans in 1998 and 2006 respectively. They additionally have pursued strategic litigation, with recent successes. One is the Beatriz case. In 2013, a Salvadoran woman known as Beatriz appealed to Salvadoran courts for an abortion. Beatriz was poor, suffering from severe chronic health conditions such as lupus and arthritis, and her foetus had acephaly and would not survive. She was denied. Eventually,

Beatriz became gravely ill and received an emergency caesarean, but her baby lived only a few hours. Activists carried Beatriz's case all the way to the Inter-American Court of Human Rights (IACHR), which ruled in 2024 that El Salvador violated her human rights. The court ordered El Salvador to pass legislation that would authorize doctors to terminate pregnancies that pose risks to women's health or life. The court further recommended a broader liberalization on other grounds, including foetal impairment.

Another case is that of Susana and Lucia, Nicaraguan minors who became pregnant as the result of rape. In 2025, the UN Human Rights Committee ruled that Nicaragua's abortion ban violated Susana's and Lucia's human rights.[70] The committee concluded that forced pregnancy and forced motherhood disrupted girls' lives, imposing physical and psychological suffering, and that the criminalization of abortion disproportionately affected marginalized girls living in poor areas, rural areas, or both. As a remedy, the committee ordered Nicaragua to modify its laws to allow abortion in cases of incest and rape and when sexual violence means that the victims' health is at risk. The UN Human Rights Committee issued similar rulings in similar cases from Ecuador and Guatemala, all brought by the global Girls Not Mothers movement.

Sceptics might point out that these decisions fall short of ordering countries to allow voluntary abortions and that countries often resist the required modifications even when, as in the Inter-American Human Rights System, the judgments are ostensibly binding. Activists, however, view these rulings as deeply significant for advancing their cause. In the Salvadoran case, abortion rights leader Mariana Moisa called the ruling 'hopeful', one that 'allows us to progress in countries where the laws are more restrictive'.[71]

Towards a feminist future of choice and autonomy

Reproductive rights are among the most challenging women's rights reforms to not just attain and implement, but protect. Dramatic repeals of abortion access, as in the United States and Poland, draw attention, but so do dramatic advances – which continue despite organized opposition. In 2024, France became the first country to enshrine the freedom to terminate pregnancy in its national constitution. In 2025, the United

Kingdom amended the Crime and Policing Bill to end the criminal investigation and prosecution of women who terminate their own pregnancies (e.g. by using at-home abortion medication). That same year, the IACHR and the UN Human Rights Committee grounded abortion access in human rights language, marking a noted shift away from an abortion reform premised on helping women to become good mothers and towards an abortion reform premised on women's autonomy and self-determination.

Beyond abortion, reproductive rights constitute a large policy arena. Activists and policymakers are keenly aware that effective interventions in the areas of sexual, reproductive, and maternal health must address the complexities of women's and men's lives and must attend to the intersecting forms of disadvantage that make access and choice particularly difficult for marginalized groups and underserved populations. These policy changes are often less visible: they are not necessarily demanded by protests and strikes, and they unfold in technical policy documents and development projects coordinated by international governance organizations and NGOs. They receive far less media coverage than abortion progressions and reversions. Still, the countless advocates who work behind the scenes on health and education policies also draw their inspiration from feminist blueprints on reproductive rights, looking to expand choice.

EIGHT

Violence Against Women

On 26 September 1999 in New York City, Gladys Ricart was getting married. Dressed in her wedding gown and about to depart for church, she was home taking some last-minute photos with her bridesmaids and family.[1] Then tragedy struck: her ex-boyfriend, who had been stalking her for weeks, barged in. He shot Gladys, killing her. At her funeral five days later, family members buried Gladys in her wedding dress.[2]

Gladys and her killer were immigrants from the Dominican Republic. The crime shook New York's Dominican community. In 2001, the Dominican Women's Development Center organized the Brides' March – a now annual event wherein protestors don wedding dresses to denounce domestic violence.[3] The imagery resonates not just locally but globally. In 2011, marchers in Istanbul, Turkey carried bloody wedding dresses and mock coffins to protest domestic violence.[4] In 2012, on Valentine's Day, commuters in Beijing's business district passed three women staging the city's first ever street performance to protest domestic violence; they, too, wore wedding dresses, which they splashed with red paint.[5] And in April 2017, in Beirut, Lebanon, 31 faceless dummies dressed in wedding gowns – representing the 31 days of the month – were hanged with nooses at the waterfront. The installation capped Lebanese activists' years-long campaign to repeal the penal code article granting a rapist exoneration if he marries his victim.[6] A bill overturning what activists call the marry-your-rapist exemption was pending in parliament. In August 2017, activists rejoiced when the repeal finally passed.[7]

Across very different national and cultural contexts, activists transform traditional wedding dresses and rituals into protests, demonstrating how violence against women (VAW) interrupts notions of romantic love. Other anti-VAW campaigns illustrate similar North–South convergences in activists' use of symbols, slogans, and performance. In another use of dress, women march in, carry, or exhibit the clothing they were wearing when assaulted. Indian activists staged I Never Asked for It walks.[8] Across the United States, Europe, and Australia, feminists organize What Were You Wearing art installations. In the Caribbean, the #LifeinLeggings campaign has organized marches in Barbados, Trinidad and Tobago, Dominica, the Bahamas, Guyana, Jamaica, and St Lucia.[9] Globally, activists use clothing to counter misogynistic beliefs that women invite assaults by dressing in certain ways.

Another global phenomenon is #MeToo. The name of the anti-sexual violence group founded by Black US activist Tarana Burke became a viral hashtag in 2017, when news broke about Hollywood mogul Harvey Weinstein's serial assaults. In two weeks from its first usage on 15 October 2017, women tweeted #MeToo from more than 85 countries, including in Africa, the Middle East, and Asia.[10] Many added hashtags to reflect their domestic contexts. South Korean women added #withyou to show solidarity and help overcome shame, and Ethiopian activists created #MeTooEthiopia to underscore the connection between sexual harassment and other abuses such as child marriage.[11] In subsequent months and years, #MeToo would bring down not just Weinstein, but prominent politicians, public figures, and entertainers across the globe. Leaders in countries as diverse as South Korea (including the mayors of Seoul and Busan and the governor of Chungnam Province) and Norway (including former ministers and members of parliament) left their positions in disgrace. Even where #MeToo did not change policy or generate more prosecutions, the hashtag raised consciousness, letting hundreds of thousands of women speak out.

Then there is the anthem 'The Rapist Is You' (also called 'The Rapist in Your Path'). The Chilean feminist group Las Tesis scripted and performed the song in 2019. Women chant lyrics such as 'and the fault wasn't mine / nor where I was / not how I was dressed' while wearing black blindfolds that symbolize the state's and society's blindness to VAW. Lyrics underscore how patriarchy and impunity for violence against women are intertwined: 'the rapist is you / it's the cops / the judges / the state / the president / the oppressive state is a male rapist'.[12] The song captured the world's imagination. GeoChicas, a Latin American women's organization that uses a gender lens to create digital maps of urban spaces, tracked all performances of 'The Rapist Is You' between 2019 and 2021. They found feminists singing the anthem in more than 200 cities, from New York to Tokyo and Vancouver to Nairobi.[13] In India, activists translated the song into Bengali.[14] In Tunisia, women performed the song when a viral video showed a newly elected lawmaker exposing himself outside a school.[15] In Turkey, women legislators sang 'The Rapist Is You' in parliament, before a convening of the majority-male cabinet.[16]

Combating VAW knits the global women's movement together. Symbols, slogans, and songs transcend their original contexts, resonating across national, cultural, and religious divides. During the first decades of the women's rights era, women conference-goers found much to divide them – but they united against the pervasive and universal prevalence of VAW. Even as harms differ from country to country and culture to culture, they share a common thread: women experience these violations as women, because they are women. Violence against women emerges from and reinforces the patriarchal structure of the state and society, and so it is more specific than gender-based violence. The latter captures how gendered hierarchies shape violence against those perceived as gender non-conforming, including heterosexual men and LGBTQIA+ individuals. While some activists and some feminist blueprints use 'gender-based violence' as the more inclusive term, others use VAW to underscore how only women experience violence for being women. Activists may also use the term 'violence against women and girls' (VAWG), emphasizing that girls also experience violence simply because they have female bodies. Indeed, many harmful practices that are forms of violence against women – such as child marriage or marry-your-rapist requirements – hurt girls. This book uses VAW, but considers victims and survivors to encompass all ages, as women and girls both experience violence due to patriarchal laws, structures, and norms. As Las Tesis so clearly articulates, '[t]he patriarchy is a judge / that judges us for being born / and our punishment / is the violence you don't see'. Women across the globe identify with these words.

Naming and acting on violence against women

Activists' performances and protests have proved critical for achieving the international normative frameworks defining and denouncing VAW. The 1993 Vienna conference and the 1995 Beijing conference invigorated women's efforts to tackle women's rights by appealing to human rights (see Chapters 1 and 2). Countries affected by armed conflict and authoritarianism were grappling with legacies of state violence, and women activists positioned VAW as requiring similar forms of redress. They argued that the private violence committed by (mostly) men against women was just as serious a human rights violation as public violence committed by the state.

For activists then and now, VAW covers the harassment, assault, and killing of women, whether in public or in private, and whether by non-state actors (e.g. a boss or a husband) or state actors (e.g. a police officer or a security official). VAW also covers practices that violate women's bodily integrity in order to maintain patriarchal gender roles. For activists, practices include child marriage, forced marriage and bride kidnapping, dowry deaths, virginity testing, female genital mutilation, and female infanticide, among others. Many practices have no equivalent that men experience. Young girls usually do not 'select' their husbands by kidnapping and raping young men, for example. Boy babies are not murdered because they have no value for their families.

Much VAW occurs in private, within families and within intimate relationships. Much of it is also informed by religious beliefs, cultural traditions, or both. These two features – VAW's often private character and its connection to custom – make tackling the problem especially difficult. Many abuses are normalized by decades if not centuries of regular practice, sustained by beliefs that these practices are essential for preserving cultural expressions, maintaining social cohesion, and adhering to religious tenets. For example, many cultures and religions value virginity and in-marriage childbearing, and so virginity testing and female genital cutting become seen as important for preserving these values. Women themselves may even normalize abusive practices, as they also internalize their community's and culture's norms – especially since women often bear the punishment for non-conformity. The separate spheres thus cast a long shadow: as seen in Chapters 6 and 7, norms about families are deeply rooted, heightening governments' reluctance to extend their regulatory power over the private sphere. Bringing private and often highly intimate practices into public light, and recoding these customs as abuses that cause harm and suffering, constitutes the core of feminists' struggle against VAW.

That feminists face uphill battles denouncing practices occurring within familial, cultural, and religious traditions helps explain anti-VAW activists' heightened reliance on artistic and symbolic forms of protest. Battles over defining VAW are not just limited to doctrinal practices and beliefs, however. Sexual harassment, for instance, is not expressly undergirded by most religions, but emerges from patriarchal structures all the same – like the idea of men's entitlement to women's bodies and men's use of sexual violence to keep women from occupying spaces associated with male status and privilege. VAW thus takes varied forms, but the abuses share the same origin in the gender hierarchies that give men power over women. Linking all forms of VAW together, feminist strategies – whether in the streets or at the United Nations – have defined VAW through its origins in patriarchal gender relations and through its resultant harms.

Yet narrating and demonstrating harm comes at great cost. Women's testimonials become activist strategies, as seen with the Global Tribunal on Violations of Women's Rights convened at the 1993 Vienna conference (Chapter 2). Whether offered at the international criminal court trials examining mass rape during war or in media interviews tracking the #MeToo movement, testimonials reveal how VAW causes physical wounds and internal suffering. Victim testimonies are important advocacy tools for raising awareness, sustaining calls to action, and motivating policy change – but they also force survivors to relive their suffering, often only to face continued doubt and disbelief. When practices are so normalized, it is difficult to convince others that these practices are unwanted, unwarranted, harmful, and forms of gender discrimination. Survivors continuously revisit and repackage their trauma for public consumption.

High costs notwithstanding, women's suffering often does mobilize action. Tragically, activists often benefit from focusing events – high-profile cases of VAW that mobilize large-scale protests. Horrific cases like Gladys Ricart's often push policymakers to action. In the United States, #MeToo generated nearly 300 new laws adopted by state legislatures between 2017 and 2021. These new statutes included a wide-range of measures, from establishing employer liability for employee behaviour to installing panic buttons for hotel workers.[17] In Italy in 2023, the country ignited when university student Giulia Cecchettin was murdered, stabbed over 70 times by her ex-boyfriend. Giulia's sister Elena denounced a 'patriarchal society steeped in rape culture' and, in a live television interview, called for action: 'Don't hold a minute of silence for Giulia – burn everything', she said.[18] Thousands took to the street, protesting Giulia's killing. In response, the Italian parliament in early 2024 strengthened the 2019 anti-VAW law, establishing (among other measures) priority processing for VAW cases and tougher restraining orders and surveillance measures for domestic abusers.[19] In Nepal in 2017, outrage over acid attacks on school girls helped the NGO Forum for Women, Law, and Development obtain a Supreme Court order mandating victim compensation and care.[20] Nepal later made acid attacks a specific crime in 2018.[21] And in Kazakhstan in 2024, widespread protests erupted when the former minister of economy killed his wife, leading the parliament to pass the first national law criminalizing domestic violence.[22]

As Mala Htun and Laurel Weldon assert, '[t]he concept of VAW is itself transformative: it did not exist before feminists proposed it. It is a feminist creation'.[23] Feminists have reshaped social and thus legal understandings of myriad forms of VAW. Examples include *marital rape* and *date rape*, which challenge ideas that preexisting relationships mean that women have consented to sexual activity within them. Breaking down the distinction between sex in marriage and rape helped overturn the marry-your-rapist laws found not just in Lebanon but also in Egypt, Morocco, Jordan, Tunisia, and Palestine. Similarly, Latin American women's movements helped introduce the term 'femicide' – the murder of women because they are women. As of 2023, several dozen countries have laws sanctioning femicide or considering homicide of women an aggravated crime if based on gender. These countries include those in Spanish- and Portuguese-speaking Latin America alongside Spain, Portugal, France, Cyprus, Malta, and Croatia.[24] In 2025, again in response to Giulia Cecchettin's death, Italy joined this list, declaring femicide a crime.

Most anti-VAW statutes explicitly reference the women's rights era's feminist blueprints. VAW further holds its own distinctive place in other international treaties and agreements. In 1998, the statute creating the International Criminal Court – the Rome Statute – recognized rape, sexual slavery, enforced prostitution, forced pregnancy, enforced sterilization, and 'any other form of sexual violence of comparable gravity' as crimes against humanity.[25] Combating VAW is further enshrined in three regional treaties: the OAS Belém do Pará Convention (1994), the AU Maputo Protocol (2003), and the EU Istanbul Convention (2012). These blueprints do not just name the specific crimes that constitute VAW; they establish mandates to protect women and girls, attain justice for victims, and end impunity for perpetrators. As such, international and regional feminist blueprints explicitly recognize the relationship between patriarchal and discriminatory social structures, VAW, and human rights violations, and they envision comprehensive, holistic policy actions.

The contrast between mobilization, norm setting, and legal advances, on the one hand, and the continued prevalence of VAW, on the other, represents the greatest paradox of the women's rights era. From the Beijing PfA to the regional treaties, countries do not lack guidance about the reforms necessary for combating and eliminating VAW. At the same time, on-the-ground progress remains stagnant. Femicide rates in Latin America and sub-Saharan Africa remain shockingly high. In Mexico, some estimates suggest that 10 or 11 women are murdered every day.[26] The enormous adoption–implementation gap also appears in the Global North. For example, a 2021 UK study found that only 5 per cent of rapes resulted in a criminal charge.[27] Sexual harassment also remains widespread: Harvey Weinstein may have been convicted, but millions of perpetrators remain unsanctioned. Even passing legislation to abolish customary practices such as marrying one's rapist does not change tradition overnight: many communities and families continue the practice, as maintaining social stability overrides the costs and stigma of pursuing justice through the courts. Families, abusers, and survivors all know that, laws notwithstanding, prosecutions and convictions remain rare.

This gulf explains why this book considers combating VAW to be the most transformative policy area. VAW presents the highest degree of complexity when moving from adoption to implementation. It contains manifold manifestations, many of which are normalized. It allows patriarchal societies to maintain control over women, often in the name of religion and tradition, making it difficult for individuals and communities to shift their attitudes and behaviour. Victims experience trauma and shame, which inhibit their ability to speak out; women's reticence, in turn, fuels a vicious cycle of silence and impunity. VAW's occurrence and harms are difficult to measure, document, substantiate, and quantify; and its policy response and solutions entail organized actions by countless public officials in the justice, security, healthcare, and welfare sectors, many of whom do not share feminists' understanding of the problem, let alone recognize that it *is* a problem.

Given these difficulties, that the women's rights era achieved *any* policy progress is remarkable. Translating on-paper reforms into on-the-ground reductions of VAW proves excruciatingly slow, but writing the international and regional feminist blueprints and changing the national laws matters. Treaties, agreements, and statutes encode the definitions of and necessary responses to VAW, giving activists clear and unequivocal statements. They help ongoing feminist mobilization to hold state actors accountable, whether for revising weak statutes or taking further action to strengthen or better implement progressive legislation.

The international normative framework

The women's rights era's early decades shifted the conversation on violence against women. The 1975 Mexico City conference report stated that 'women all over the world should unite to eliminate violations of human rights committed against women and girls such as: rape, prostitution, physical assault, mental cruelty, child marriage, forced marriage, and marriage as a commercial transaction'.[28] The conference's fifth resolution, on women and health, recommended that governments 'introduce effective measures for the prevention of all forms of discrimination and cruelty against the well-being of women, which keep them from participating actively in the political, economic, and social development of their community and which violate their human rights'.[29] Both passages connect VAW to human rights violations, a full two decades before 'women's rights are human rights' crystallized into a rallying cry at the 1993 Vienna conference and 1995 Beijing conference.

Falling between 1975 and 1993, the 1979 CEDAW Convention did not use the word 'violence'. CEDAW did, however, make allusions to the social and cultural foundations underpinning certain violent practices. Article 5, for instance, commits signatories 'to modify[ing] the social and cultural patterns of conduct of men and women, with a view to achieving the elimination of prejudices and customary and all other practices which are based on the idea of the inferiority or superiority of either of the sexes or on stereotyped roles for men and women'.[30] Article 16 affirms women's rights within marriage and family and requires state parties to specify minimum marriage ages (though did not say what this age should be). In 1992, the CEDAW Committee remedied the treaty's initial silence on VAW. General Recommendation 19 states that 'gender-based violence is a form of discrimination that seriously inhibits women's ability to enjoy rights and freedoms on a basis of equality with men'.[31]

Further shifts came in the 1990s. Following the 1993 Vienna Declaration's explicit recognition that VAW constituted a human rights violation, the UN General Assembly passed the Declaration on the Elimination of Violence against Women (DEVAW) in December that year. DEVAW bridges the gap between CEDAW and the international conference proceedings, recognizing that CEDAW's effective implementation depends on eliminating VAW. In addition to defining VAW as any act that 'results in, or is likely to result in, physical, sexual, or psychological harm or suffering to women . . . whether occurring in public or private life', DEVAW explicitly states that countries 'should not invoke any custom, tradition or religious consideration to avoid their obligations with respect to its elimination'.[32] Moreover, DEVAW itemizes how states 'should pursue by all appropriate means and without delay a policy of eliminating violence against women'.[33] The enumerated actions include: adopting statutes that sanction and punish VAW and adopting national action plans to prosecute VAW; providing resources to women victims and their children, such as by funding shelters, offering financial and psychological assistance, and designing recovery programs; training law enforcement authorities; and eradicating harmful stereotypes that perpetuate inequality.

As a feminist blueprint, DEVAW is short but comprehensive. DEVAW marks a holistic approach that would appear in later anti-VAW blueprints, establishing that addressing VAW is not just about criminal justice but about prevention, reparation, rehabilitation, and social assistance. The Beijing PfA reiterates but also expands DEVAW's definition and recommended actions. The PfA locates VAW in harmful stereotypes and beliefs about women; lists specific abuses (from dowry-related violence to sexual harassment to female infanticide); explains VAW's harmful effects; states that VAW 'is a manifestation of the historically unequal power relations between men and women'; and recommends victims' access to wide-ranging social services.[34] Both DEVAW and the

PfA further recognize how intersectionality exacerbates marginalized women's vulnerabilities.

Following the Vienna Declaration and DEVAW, the UN installed the Special Rapporteur on Violence against Women in 1994. The rapporteur reports directly to the Office of the High Commission for Human Rights. She undertakes country visits, prepares annual reports, and transmits urgent appeals regarding cases. Five women have served as rapporteurs, all from outside the West: Radhika Coomaraswamy of Sri Lanka; Yakin Ertürk of Turkey; Rashida Manjoo of South Africa; Dubravka Šimonović of Croatia; and (at the time of this writing) Reem Alsalem of Jordan. In other initiatives, the UN Trust Fund to End Violence against Women finances projects developed by local civil society organizations and women's rights organizations. The UN Peacebuilding Fund, established in 2006, does not focus solely on combating VAW but does support projects addressing VAW during and after armed conflict. For instance, the UN Peacebuilding Fund has financed 'one stop shop' anti-violence centres – offices where women victims can receive medical, psychological, and legal support all at once – in places such as Liberia and South Sudan.

Regional blueprints to combat VAW

For many activists, early feminist blueprints such as CEDAW had not gone far enough to name and sanction VAW, and the Vienna Declaration and Beijing PfA, while pathbreaking, did not bind countries to action. Transnational feminist activists thus turned to their regional governance organizations, hoping that treaties and agreements closer to home would pressure national governments into more rapid action. The regional level constitutes a distinctive place of anti-VAW activism, a significant arena in which activists have sought and won additional accords.

Latin America leads

The OAS adopted the first regional blueprint. In the late 1980s, Milagro Azcúnaga de Meléndez from El Salvador, then president of the Inter-American Commission on Women (CIM from the Spanish name), returned from UN CEDAW meetings frustrated with CEDAW's inattention to VAW.[35] She became the key protagonist in what became the 1994 Inter-American Convention on the Prevention, Punishment, and Eradication of Violence against Women (also known as the Belém do Pará Convention, after the Brazilian city where it was adopted). The CIM, composed of 33 delegates designated by member states and a small technical staff, steered the entire process. They convened a committee of experts representing Latin America's key feminist networks, such as the Latin American and Caribbean Committee for the Defense of Women's Rights.[36] In fact, when the UN adopted DEVAW in 1993, the CIM already had most of Belém do Pará drafted, an overlap that demonstrates how international and regional initiatives often unfold in parallel.[37]

Unlike DEVAW but like CEDAW, the Belém do Pará Convention is an international *treaty*, meaning that its provisions are legally binding on member states. In practice, the OAS's limited enforcement mechanisms mean that its treaties do not always induce compliance, but in the case of VAW, countries did reform their national laws after Belém do Pará's adoption (discussed below). In 2004, the OAS established the Mechanism to Follow Up on Implementation of the Inter-American Convention of the Prevention, Punishment, and Eradication of Violence against Women (MESCEVI), which provides further accountability by receiving and evaluating member-state reports on implementation.

The Bélem do Pará Convention informs human rights case law in the Americas. In 2009, the IACHR heard the case *González, Monreal, and Monarrez v Mexico.* Brought by mothers of three women whose bodies were found in a cotton field on 6 November 2001, *González* denounced the authorities' failure to appropriately investigate the young women's disappearance and murder. Though narrowly focused on the three victims, the case reflected the broader femicide epidemic in Ciudad Juárez, a factory zone along the US–Mexican border known throughout the 1990s for high rates of organized crime, generalized violence, and the widespread disappearance of women and girls. The *González* petitioners documented various investigative failures, including inadequate evidence gathering at the site, improper autopsies, botched DNA results, and threats against their own safety as the victims' advocates. The IACHR's judgment in what became known as the Cotton Field case marked its first invocation of the Belém do Pará Convention, its first comprehensive consideration of women's rights, and its first use of the term 'femicide'.[38]

The IACHR ruled that Mexico violated Belém do Pará's obligations for states to (1) exercise due diligence in preventing, investigating, and punishing VAW; (2) provide justice and judicial protection to the victims and their families; and (3) protect girls from VAW (two of three victims were minors). Importantly, the IACHR interpreted the Belém do Pará Convention's reparation requirement as extending beyond direct compensation to victims and requiring measures to 'identify and eliminate the factors that cause the discrimination'.[39] Reparations must – in the IACHR's words – 'be designed to change the situation, so that their effect is not only of restitution, but also rectification in this regard, the reestablishment of the same structural context of violence and discrimination is not acceptable'.[40] Put simply, the IACHR determined that authorities must not only identify, arrest, and punish perpetrators; countries must address the underlying, systemic causes of VAW and femicide.

The Cotton Field judgment required Mexico to pay US$200,000 in restitution to the victims' families, address and remedy investigative failures, and, as required in the IACHR's more expansive interpretation of reparations, end structural discrimination against women alongside violence against women.[41] The latter constitutes the most aspirational aspect of the ruling, hence the Cotton Field's jurisprudence matches what legal scholars call 'transformative reparations'. Countries such as Mexico will not achieve this objective overnight, but the ruling informed small and large changes alike. Mexico strengthened its Alba Protocol, the process followed when investigating women's disappearances; opened a community centre providing medical, psychological, and legal assistance for women victims in Ciudad Juárez; and strengthened its redaction of national and local action plans to fight VAW.[42] The IACHR would later expand its interpretation of transformative reparations, including case law and guidance notes emphasizing intersectionality and requiring states to end the interlocking discrimination and violence faced by Indigenous and other minoritized women.[43]

The Maputo Protocol

Unlike the Belém do Pará Convention, the Africa Union's 2003 Maputo Protocol is not a VAW-specific treaty, but addresses women's rights generally (see Chapters 2 and 6). The Maputo Protocol nonetheless holds a special place among the anti-VAW feminist blueprints: it is the first international treaty to specifically address customary practices as forms of VAW.

The Maputo Protocol, writes legal scholar Maame Efua Addadzi-Koom, 'distinguishes itself by framing the rights in a way that takes account of African cultural and pluralistic realities'.[44] The Maputo Protocol eschews the word 'custom' but directly names certain harmful practices.[45] For instance, Article 5 requires 'prohibition, through legislative measures backed by sanctions, of all forms of female genital mutilation, scarification, medicalisation, and para-medicalisation of female genital mutilation'.[46] The article also ties harmful practices to VAW, requiring the 'protection of women who are at risk of being subjected to harmful practices or all other forms of violence, abuse, and intolerance'. Article 6 prohibits forced marriage and child marriage. Article 17 states that 'women shall have the right to live in a positive cultural context'.[47] These articles provide activists with unambiguous statements that identify the harm caused by specific practices and that legitimize their efforts to transform the cultural contexts around these traditions.

The protocol also includes articles addressing concerns about women in armed conflicts, articles that further highlight the Maputo Protocol's responsiveness to the African context. Article 11 states that 'state parties undertake to protect asylum-seeking women, refugees, returnees, and internally displaced persons, against all forms of violence, rape, and other forms of sexual exploitation, and to ensure that such acts are considered war crimes'.[48] Other articles address sexual assault in general. Article 4 clearly states that violence against women includes 'unwanted or forced sex'.[49] Article 13, on economic and social welfare rights, outlines states' obligations to 'combat and punish' sexual harassment in the workplace. Articles about elderly women and women with disabilities further enumerate their rights to be from violence.

The Maputo Protocol is legally binding and, like the Belém do Pará Convention, contains a reporting mechanism wherein states and activists relate progress back to the regional body. Following the Maputo Protocol's adoption, 50 women's organizations founded the Solidarity for African Women's Rights (SOAWR) Coalition, which lobbies African governments to sign and ratify the protocol and to transform its mandates into domestic law and practice. SOAWR publishes research and guides and trains lawyers and judicial authorities to use the Maputo Protocol in litigation.[50]

Also like the Belém do Pará Convention, the Maputo Protocol shapes regional courts' rulings. Over 2017 and 2018, the Community Court of Justice for the Economic Community of West African States (ECOWAS) issued three rulings applying the Maputo Protocol. All cases addressed state negligence in responding to VAW, whether the perpetrators were state agents (as in *Dorothy Chioma Njemanze & 3 Others v Federal Republic of Nigeria*) or family members (as in *Mary Sunday v Federal Republic of Nigeria* and *Aminata Diantou Diana v Republic of Mali*).[51] The ECOWAS Community Court of Justice (ECCJ) used the Maputo Protocol to find countries responsible for failing their duty to protect women. Like the IACHR's Cotton Field judgment, the ECCJ determined that countries are responsible for eliminating the conditions that foment VAW in the first place. Regional feminist blueprints and resultant case law thus establish an important standard: VAW is not a private crime meriting individual remedy but a public offence that countries must proactively prevent. Feminist blueprints allowed courts to develop and assert this principle of due diligence.

The Istanbul Convention

Latin America and Africa pioneered the adoption of regional instruments to combat VAW, with Europe following later. As in other regions, advocates spent years building support for a Europe-wide anti-VAW treaty. The process launched in 2006, within the Council of Europe, a human rights organization with 47 member states and a 648-member parliament. A group of parliamentarians formed the Parliamentary Network Women Free from Violence, launching a 2006–2008 pan-Europe anti-domestic violence campaign.[52] The campaign drew participants' attention to European countries' varied anti-VAW laws and urged them to consider a Europe-wide framework that would harmonize standards. In 2008, the Network's task force led the Council of Europe's call to adopt a legally binding anti-VAW convention. The task force's final report bolstered its call by citing the Belém do Pará Convention's precedent within international law and the Maputo Protocol's framework protecting women in public and private.[53] The Council of Europe then created the Ad Hoc Committee on Preventing and Combating Violence against Women and Domestic Violence (CAHVIO) to lead the drafting process. CAHVIO included Council of Europe parliamentarians, and every Council of Europe member state sent between one and four of their representatives to drafting meetings. Other drafters included representatives from key NGOs, including the European Women's Lobby.[54]

CAHVIO Co-Chair Dubravka Šimonović would later become the UN Special Rapporteur on Violence against Women, but by 2008 she already counted on a storied international career. Her experience while on the CEDAW Committee – she was a member since 2002 and the 2007–2008 chair – informed her approach to the European treaty: she wanted a convention that would codify and extend CEDAW and its General Recommendation 19. She sought a feminist blueprint that would explicitly frame VAW as discrimination and a violation of human rights. She envisioned a synergy between CEDAW and the Istanbul Convention, wanting the CEDAW Committee to have a regional counterpart in the Istanbul Convention's monitoring body.

The Istanbul Convention – formally the Council of Europe Convention on Preventing and Combating Violence against Women and Domestic Violence – was adopted in 2011 and entered into force in 2014. The Istanbul Convention centres on four pillars: prevention, protection, prosecution, and coordinated policies. The document follows its predecessors in not just defining VAW but also insisting on eliminating all discrimination against women, promoting equality between men and women, and designing comprehensive criminal justice procedures alongside holistic social services. The Istanbul Convention adds that culture, custom, religion, tradition, and honour cannot justify VAW and that its anti-domestic violence provisions apply irrespective of countries' legal definitions or recognitions of what constitutes a family. In this way the Istanbul Convention realized Šimonović's and the drafters' vision and represents the state of the art in feminist understandings of VAW. The Istanbul Convention frames VAW as rooted in the unequal power relations between men and women and demands structural, comprehensive solutions. Legal scholar Gizem Guney describes the convention's 'dual character': the agreement is both an anti-violence and an anti-discrimination instrument.[55]

As of January 2024, all EU member states had signed the convention, as had Iceland, the United Kingdom, and Switzerland. In 2023 the European Union ratified the convention, transforming the Istanbul Convention into an anti-VAW framework for the European Union itself (insofar as the Istanbul Convention's mandates coincide with EU competencies). Countries report to the Group of Experts on Action against Violence against Women and Domestic Violence (GREVIO).[56]

The Istanbul Convention's normative advances notwithstanding, the document has sparked contestation. The backlash began in 2021, when Turkey withdrew from the Convention, citing the document's threat to traditional family roles and structures. The Convention now serves as a lightning rod, a cipher used by Europe's ever-growing number of right-wing anti-democratic and anti-gender politicians. These countermovement leaders denounce the global spread of multicultural and inclusive values, women's rights, and LGBTQIA+ rights. Poland, too, has threatened to withdraw. Armenia, alongside the EU member states Bulgaria, the Czech Republic, Hungary, Lithuania, and Slovakia, have signed but refused to ratify (meaning that they refuse to be bound by the treaty).

Resistance to the Istanbul Convention does not, however, render international instruments to combat VAW futile. First, the Istanbul Convention's sister instruments – the Belém do Pará Convention and the Maputo Protocol – also contain strong denouncements of patriarchal practices and gender discrimination but have not been similarly instrumentalized by anti-gender equality actors. Backlash is not inevitable (this point is revisited in Chapter 9).

Second, Turkey's withdrawal, Poland's blustering, and certain post-Soviet states' ratification delays notwithstanding, the Istanbul Convention *has* shaped domestic policy and practice, even in countries with significant right-wing movements. Turkey's Law 6284 on the Protection of Family and Prevention of Violence against Women, signed alongside its ratification of the Istanbul Convention back in 2012, remains in force. Turkish women's organizations continue to rely on Law 6284's provisions when accompanying women victims, insisting – for instance – that courts follow requirements to subpoena aggressors and to provide legal aid to victims.[57]

Similarly, Bulgaria has signed but not ratified the convention, but the document still shapes domestic activism and reform. Bulgarian women activists, and NGOs such as the Bulgarian Platform of the European Women's Lobby, appeal to the Istanbul Convention in their campaigns to improve anti-VAW legislation. In July 2023, Bulgaria broadened its anti-domestic violence law to include those in common law relationships and those experiencing abuse from a former spouse or parent's spouse.[58] Just days later, protests erupted when a court released a 26-year-old man for beating and stabbing his girlfriend, having judged her wounds as 'light'. In August 2023, the parliament responded by further broadening the law to include those in 'intimate relationships'.[59] These changes reflect the Istanbul Convention's standards. Echoing the common pattern, the feminist blueprint provided the legal grounding; feminist advocates' longstanding campaigns gained new meaning due to a focusing event; and governments felt compelled to act.

Third, like the Belém do Pará Convention and the Maputo Protocol, the Istanbul Convention shapes international human rights case law. The Council of Europe's European Court of Human Rights and the European Union's European Court of Justice (ECJ) have applied the Istanbul Convention to dozens of cases. In 2024, the ECJ's judgment in Case C-621/21 – known colloquially as the Women Victims case – held that migrant women facing domestic violence in their country of origin qualify as a 'protected social group' and can therefore access refugee status and protections under the Common European Asylum System.[60]

In the ruling, the ECJ used the Istanbul Convention to relax the usual standards on which refugees claim asylum. Traditionally, when refugees claim asylum on the basis of victimization by non-state actors, they must demonstrate that their aggressors intended to persecute them because of their social group membership. That would mean that women who are domestic violence victims need to prove that their abusers harmed them because they are women: they would need to prove their abuser's hatred of women as motivation. In Women Victims, the ECJ determined that, if the violence and the failure of state protection occurred for the same reason, then refugees could base their claims on state inaction rather than on aggressor motivation. Since the Istanbul Convention highlights discrimination against women as the underlying cause of VAW – and stipulates that countries have an affirmative obligation to eliminate both discrimination and VAW – the country's failure to protect becomes sufficient to demonstrate that women are persecuted for being women.[61]

Women no longer need to prove that their individual abusers hate women as a group; the fact of their abuse alone points to their country's failure to protect and allows them to claim asylum. This flexibilization dramatically improves women refugees' asylum claims.

Regional coordination and new frameworks

Women protagonists have made special efforts to coordinate the international and regional feminist blueprints that combat VAW. Dubravka Šimonović explicitly crafted the Istanbul Convention to codify and extend CEDAW. Upon becoming the third UN Special Rapporteur on Violence against Women, Šimonović established the group Ending Discrimination and Violence Against Women (EDVAW). Formally the Platform of Independent Expert Mechanisms on Discrimination and Violence against Women, EDVAW establishes links between the international and regional expert bodies that monitor countries' compliance with anti-VAW instruments. These expert bodies include MESECVI, GREVIO, the African Commission on Human and Peoples' Rights Special Rapporteur on the Rights of Women in Africa, and the CEDAW Committee.

In parallel, other regional organizations have created their own feminist blueprints. The League of Arab States launched the Arab Declaration on Combating All Forms of Violence against Women and Girls in 2022. The latter joins the Maputo Protocol in recognizing that VAW occurs in the private sphere, defining violence against women and girls as 'all acts of violence at the family and community level, which shall cause material or moral harm, including physical, sexual and psychological violence for women and girls, or the threat to perpetrate such acts, coercion or arbitrary deprivation of rights and freedoms'.[62]

The Arab Declaration emerged thanks to the drafting, advocacy, and lobbying efforts of the Coalition of Women MPs from Arab Countries to Combat Violence against Women, founded in 2014 by 12 women parliamentarians: Wafa' Bani Mustafa (Jordan), Magda Elnewishi (Egypt), Na'ayem Al Eadat (Jordan), Intisar Alkhutabi (Iraq), Hasnaa Marsit (Tunisia), Ebtisam Hejres Ahmed (Bahrain), Naima Rabbaa (Morocco), Sahar Alqawasmi (Palestine), Gilberte Zouein (Lebanon), Aicha Dabar Guelle (Dijbouti), Amira Elsir-Omer Babikir (Sudan), and Rola Dashti

(Kuwait).[63] In their founding statement, the women MPs ground their anti-VAW activism by intertwining international norms with religious doctrine. They write, 'Violence can infringe on women's dignity, demean their humanity, and deprive them from [*sic*] their basic rights, which were decreed by the divine laws, national constitutions, treaties, agreements, and international covenants.'[64] The Declaration repeats this sentiment, noting the compatibility between religion and women's rights and stating that women 'are on the same level as men in terms of honour, in light of the fairness established by Islamic law and other divine laws'.[65]

In every global region, women activists forged alliances around and authored feminist blueprints for combating VAW. This activism has even proceeded under non-democratic regimes with limited advocacy space, as in the Middle East. In all contexts, but particularly in the Middle East, anti-VAW activism places women in the difficult position of challenging longstanding doctrinal and cultural norms. For women parliamentarians, one way to mitigate backlash is by presenting themselves as engaging in feminine-coded political work: after all, in seeking to protect women from harm, they are talking about family matters and social issues. Authoritarian leaders may tolerate and even reward this activism because such challenges to tradition, while not necessarily desirable, are not as destabilizing to their regimes as are demands for democratic or electoral reforms.

Achievements in anti-VAW reform

This chapter already reviewed some instances wherein the anti-VAW feminist blueprints generated significant on-paper changes to laws and policies. Overall, dozens of changes occurred during the women's rights era. In the wake of Latin America's Belém do Pará Convention, all Portuguese- and Spanish-speaking countries made statutory changes in the 1990s and 2000s. They either revised their existing family codes or penal codes or adopted new, comprehensive statutes. Argentina, Bolivia, Brazil, Chile, Costa Rica, El Salvador, Guatemala, Mexico, Nicaragua, and Venezuela took the latter route, adopting 'general', 'universal', 'special', or 'integrated' anti-VAW laws. These terms describe laws that go beyond criminalization and cross various policy sectors to outline responsibilities for victim support alongside the prevention and elimination of VAW.

Latin America's comprehensive laws thus closely track the feminist blueprints. For instance, they define VAW as occurring in public and private spaces, including familial spaces and intimate relationships; they identify perpetrators as both private individuals and state agents (thus addressing many countries' troubling legacies of state security forces' perpetration of VAW); they recognize intersectionality, acknowledging the special vulnerability of and providing additional services for Indigenous women, migrant women, disabled women, and other marginalized women; and they envision significant and interconnected forms of medical, legal, financial, and psychological support. Since then, many Latin American countries continue to revise these comprehensive statutes in response to activists' articulation of and lobbying around diverse forms of VAW. For instance, recent reforms to countries' anti-VAW laws have added new articles codifying violence against women in politics (see Chapter 4).

In Europe, the Istanbul Convention contributes to activists' and policymakers' efforts to improve survivor services, legislate against psychological violence, and expand legal understandings of consent, among other initiatives. The United Kingdom's 2023 GREVIO report identifies the 2021 Domestic Abuse Act as a key advance, which included establishing a Domestic Abuse Commissioner.[66] The new commissioner subsequently worked to improve victims' experiences in family courts, prohibiting defendants from cross-examining victims and establishing independent advocates to accompany victims in family courts.[67] In Northern Ireland, the assembly cited the Istanbul Convention in its 2021 memorandum, which added the offence of coercive and controlling behaviour to the domestic violence statute.[68]

Similarly, after the passage of the Istanbul Convention, many European countries revised their national laws to update their definitions of rape. The Convention defines rape as the absence of freely given consent, a more expansive conception than defining rape as forced intercourse. Countries long considered beacons of gender equality – such as Sweden, Denmark, and Finland – did not drop the force requirement from their rape statutes until 2018, 2020, and 2022 respectively.[69] In all three countries, feminist activists translated this idea from the international to the national. They organized campaigns such as Denmark's #LetsTalkAboutYes; they met with ministers and gained public converts to their cause; and they raised public awareness. In Sweden, the feminist coalition Fatta did not just succeed in changing the legal code; its campaign shaped an entirely new sexual education curriculum in schools that now emphasizes the importance of affirmative consent.[70]

In Africa and Southeast Asia, many anti-VAW campaigns emerged from and remain linked to legacies of armed conflict. War exposes women to sexual violence from armed groups and state security forces, while exacerbating rates of domestic violence, family violence, and intimate partner violence. At the international level, women's mobilization against VAW in conflict settings shaped the Women's Rights Are Human Rights movement and influenced feminist blueprints such as UNSCR 1325 (see Chapter 2). At the country level, rather than follow the Latin American approach of adopting single, comprehensive anti-VAW statutes, other Global South countries follow Europe and take a step-by-step approach that reforms laws one by one, addressing different aspects of VAW each time. Examining the 1998–2018 period, Peace Medie finds that all 54 African countries amended or passed new rape laws, typically expanding the definition of rape and mandating harsher punishments for offenders. Only about half of these revised laws, however, included marital rape.[71]

Liberia illustrates feminists' quests to reform VAW laws in a post-conflict setting. During the 1989–1996 and 1999–2003 civil wars and after the 2003 peace process, widespread sexual violence fuelled considerable mobilization among Liberian women. Prior to the conflict, the penal code defined rape as intercourse with a woman younger than 16 under duress, by force or by penetration of the penis – suggesting that women over 16 could not be raped. Most Liberians adjudicated allegations of sexual assault via customary legal systems, which offered limited justice (for instance, custom allowed perpetrators to be absolved by paying restitution to victims' families).[72] These customary forms of dispute resolution eroded during the armed conflict, however: communities were uprooted, perpetrators were often not community members but combatants on the move, and family- and clan-based authority declined.[73] In the postwar environment, the women's movement identified ending impunity for rape as a shared priority, deciding to prioritize an anti-rape law over an anti-domestic violence statute.

Women activists wanted a law declaring rape illegal, no matter the victims' age. Among the protagonists was peace activist Ruth Caesar, founder of the Abused Women and Girls Project and member of the National Transitional Legislative Assembly (NTLA), the post-conflict lawmaking body that governed from 2003 until 2006. Caesar chaired the NTLA's Committee on Gender Equity, Women, and Child Development. She steered the rape reform through the NTLA, with support from the Association of Female Lawyers of Liberia (AFELL) and other women's NGOs. The Rape Amendment Act of 2005 makes rape illegal, forbids bail, defines rape as occurring via penetration of any bodily orifice, and names gang and marital rape as forms of rape. In her 2006 inaugural speech, Liberia's first woman president, Ellen Johnson Sirleaf, expressed her administration's commitment to enforcing the rape law.[74]

The women's movement also did not forget their promise to return to fight domestic violence. In 2013 the Liberian assembly passed the Domestic Violence Act, which defines and prohibits physical, sexual, and psychological domestic violence. Yet passing the law required advocates to make a strategic sacrifice: to secure its passage, Liberian feminists had to drop female genital mutilation. Upon leaving office in 2018, Johnson Sirleaf signed a one-year ban on the practice. The Liberian government extended the ban from 2022 to 2025, during which the National Council of Chiefs and Elders of Liberia declared a permanent ban.[75] While the chiefs and elders' statement is not a statutory prohibition, their call lends considerable weight to feminists' efforts, countering those who legitimize the practice by appealing to custom. As of 2025, AFELL, legislator Moima Briggs-Mensah, and other advocates are leading efforts towards a statutory ban.[76] They frame their current initiative around 'initiation without mutilation', a phrase that implies that the many rural centres inaugurating girls into womanhood would remain allowed so long as the centres replace cutting with alternative ceremonial celebrations.[77]

If successful, Liberia would join 28 other African countries with similar bans. These bans face threats but, in an important case of feminist resistance, the Gambia voted to uphold its ban in 2024. A male Gambian MP from a Muslim-majority state had initiated the repeal, backed by Muslim clerics. International and domestic women's rights advocates then lobbied intensely to protect the ban. Among the campaigners was Reem Alsalem, the UN Special Rapporteur on Violence against Women and Girls, and Mama Fatima Singhateh, the Gambian justice minister who signed the original 2015 ban. When the parliament voted to uphold the ban, women watching a screen outside the National Assembly erupted into cheering and fist bumps. Twenty-nine-year-old activist Absa Samba told reporters: 'There was a huge sense of relief. It felt really good.'[78]

The enduring feminist quest for women's safety and integrity

Eliminating violence against women is perhaps the most daunting transformation to achieve. The deeply rooted nature of the practice and its ties to culture, tradition, and religion mean that women's rights advocates fight uphill. The recent yet unsuccessful attempt by the Gambia to un-ban female genital mutilation indicates how – as seen with reproductive rights – reforms are never safe: they open new frontiers in the confrontation between conservatives and feminists, forcing women's rights advocates to remain vigilant, active, and mobilized.

The fact that reforms are never safe and that they face enormous implementation hurdles should not diminish their importance. A common critique levied against all women's rights reforms, but especially those to combat VAW, is that weak enforcement allows the cycle of abuse and impunity to continue while also undermining the relevance of the reform itself. This scepticism seems especially justified when groundbreaking treaties such as the Istanbul Convention become punching bags, leveraged by right-wing actors attempting to undermine the global consensus on women's human rights. At the same time, backlash often receives more publicity than does accomplishment: the number of scholarly articles, policy reports, and newspaper items covering Turkey's withdrawal from the Istanbul Convention far exceeds the amount of coverage received by reforms such as the expansive consent laws adopted in Sweden, Finland, and Denmark. The latter get their moment in the sun – newspapers cover the story and activists rejoice – but then fade from attention. By contrast, repeals indicate backsliding and become a drama that draws continuous attention.

Moreover, anti-VAW laws do generate positive changes, narrowing the gap between adoption and implementation in the long term. In the battle to preserve the Gambia's female genital mutilation ban, Rose Sarr, the country's UNFPA representative, noted a positive outcome: the fight to prevent the repeal generated an unprecedented public debate about female genital mutilation, with women breaking their silence and telling their stories. Estimates suggest that about three-quarters of Gambian girls and women undergo female genital mutilation, but support is waning. A 2011 study indicated that 77 per cent of Gambian women believed that the practice should continue, but Sarr reports that this proportion dropped to 47 per cent in 2024.[79] Similarly, in their analysis of Mexico's National Survey on the Dynamics of Household Relations, Mala Htun and Francesca Jensenius found that the 2007 General Law for Women's Access to a Life Free from Violence generated change. They found that the law led to increased rape reporting and increased victims' disclosure of violence to family or friends and decreased attitudes that condoned violence.[80] Women became more aware of their rights and more likely to speak out against assault.

Finally, the enormous complexity of anti-VAW laws explains why adoption does not produce results. Even the anti-VAW laws confined to one form of violence such as 'just' marital rape stipulate more than legal penalties. They also establish procedures for making complaints, investigating crimes, protecting and providing services to survivors, and prosecuting offenders. Implementing each of these measures requires coordination, willpower, resources, and enforcement. Analysing the #NiUnaMenos (Not One Less) protests that originated in Argentina in 2015 and then swept across Latin America, Stéphanie Rousseau, Debora Lopreite, and Eduardo Dargent Bocanegra found that women's movements can successfully pressure governments to step up implementation, for instance by getting policymakers to allocate more money to specialized prosecutors.[81] Similarly, in 2018, South African feminists organized the #TotalShutdown protests, forcing the government to articulate a new comprehensive plan to address femicide.[82] In Kenya, 2024 protests led to the creation of a government task force that feminists then accused of stalling – but from which they still demand accountability, urging the task force to adopt an intersectional approach and to declare femicide a crime.[83]

That women continue to mobilize against VAW is both disheartening, in that the problem persists, and inspiring, in that feminists have not given up. The protagonists of the women's rights era made concepts like human rights, designed to protect citizens from government abuse, apply to private abuses. They reconceptualized state responsibility for violence, arguing that states commit violence not only when security forces actually attack women but when government inertia, neglect, or complacency allows gender discrimination to unfold. Even as officials' and bureaucrats' everyday practice does not always reflect this understanding, feminists have insisted on international and regional treaties, statutes, and court rulings that make state responsibility plain. The feminist blueprints and resultant national reforms reflect powerful and important achievements that formally say 'no' to violence against women and girls and that make plain the conditions for its eradication.

NINE

After the Women's Rights Era?

The year 2025 marks 50 years since the First World Conference on Women in Mexico City and 30 years since the Fourth World Conference on Women in Beijing. Between 1975 and 2025, women across the globe advocated for – and won – significant women's rights reforms in the areas of political inclusion, education, work and family, sexual health and reproductive rights, and combating violence against women. In most countries across the globe, women in 2025 enjoy more formal rights and freedoms than they did in 1975.

Whether in the Global North or Global South, many basic rights now taken for granted were only awarded during the women's rights era. In the United Kingdom, women could legally be refused service in pubs until 1982, and rape within marriage was not named a crime until 1991. In the United States, pregnant women could be dismissed from their jobs until 1978, and no legal definition of sexual harassment existed until 1980. Women could not get divorced in Brazil until 1977, in Spain until 1981, in Argentina until 1987, and in Chile until 2004. Altogether, UN Women's flagship Beijing +30 report estimates that, since the 1995 Fourth World Conference on Women, countries passed 1,531 legal reforms to advance gender equality.[1] Nearly every country now bans discrimination in employment and counts on laws to sanction at least some forms of violence against women. Implementation and attitudinal and behavioural shifts may lag, but winning the constitutional, legal, and political guarantees of equal rights have constituted an essential first step.

Getting these rights on paper was not easy. When then First Lady Hillary Clinton took the stage in Beijing and helped immortalize the refrain 'women's rights are human rights', there was simply no global consensus that this statement was true. By 2025, however, every major international framework endorsed this premise. International organizations and political elites express allegiance to norms about gender equality – at least outwardly. True, government leaders in democracies and non-democracies alike initiate reforms to burnish their image, with little intention of actually transforming society. Nonetheless, the women's rights era's protagonists have leveraged windows of opportunity to win reforms, encoding into law their aspirations for future worlds with less patriarchy and more equality.

Still, in 2025, no country has achieved gender equality. UN Women's Beijing +30 Report finds that, thousands of legal reforms notwithstanding, women still have only 64 per cent of the legal rights that men have.[2] Persistent gaps remain, especially in family law. None of the SDGs will be met by the United Nations' target date of 2030, but progress on SDG 5 remains particularly off-track.[3] Some measures indicate that progress appears to be not just stagnating, but *falling*. In comparing 2023 to 2024, the World Economic Forum found that, in the space of just one year, the timeline for achieving gender equality in education and political participation lengthened. While in 2023 educational parity was predicted to take an additional 16 years and political parity an additional 161 years, in 2024 these estimates were extended to 20 years and 169 years respectively. The world now waits until 2044 for gender equality in educational attainment and until 2193 for parity in political participation.[4] Women's lives have worsened in other ways as well. Conflict-related sexual violence has been rising since 2022.[5] Access to abortion has reversed in countries once thought to be advanced, most notably the United States. In this context, the activists, practitioners, policymakers, and scholars first energized by the UN world conferences on women, and the subsequent generations that have followed in their footsteps, now express decidedly less hope for progress.

Does stalled or reversing progress mark the end of the women's rights era? This concluding chapter suggests that the answer depends on where you look. Democracy is indeed retreating, with the 2010s and 2020s marked by processes of democratic erosion, democratic backsliding, or de-democratization (scholars use all these terms to describe countries that begin abandoning democratic procedures, starting with making elections less free and less fair). The think tank Freedom House, which scores countries on the political and civil rights associated with democracy, reports more declines than improvements since the turn of the twentieth century. In 2023 alone, Freedom House estimated that one-fifth of the world's population in 52 countries experienced losses of rights, including enhanced restrictions on movement and freedom of expression and detention of activists without due process.[6] Countries also increasingly pass laws that restrict political competition and curtail NGO activity. Overall, since 2009, the proportion of people living in non-democracies has been higher than the proportion of people living in democracies.[7]

Increased state harassment, violence, and repression disproportionately affect women, both in their day-to-day lives and in their political organizing. Democratic backsliding creates grim and difficult environments for women and for women's rights activists and movements, eroding their safety and well-being. Politically, democratic erosion limits the space for civic organizing and closes windows of opportunity for women to win reforms. When leaders no longer care about democracy, advocates lose their ability to claim that governments ought to live up to democracy's promises of political equality and gender equality. De-democratization, then, makes women's advocacy more difficult and more costly.

Moreover, rolling back women's rights policies (and policies protecting other minority groups) now forms part of anti-democratic leaders' playbook. Both fragile and established democracies are unwinding. Afghanistan remained a flawed and struggling democracy in the aftermath of the 2001 US invasion, but between 2004 and 2021 the country succeeded in writing a new constitution, holding elections, and seating a parliament comprising nearly 30 per cent women. The Taliban's return in 2021 shattered any hope for democracy and for women. The Taliban reinstalled what Afghan women activists call 'gender apartheid', a severe form of gender segregation that excludes women from public and civic spaces. Afghan women cannot appear outside the home without being covered and cannot let their voices be heard in public. They cannot attend secondary school or university or be employed in workplaces or have jobs where they would work alongside men. Erasing women might be expected (though unwelcome) in countries with histories of excluding women from public life – but these manoeuvres are unexpected elsewhere. Upon taking office in 2024, US President Donald Trump rapidly undid all policies associated with what his team derisively terms 'diversity, equity, and inclusion'. Eliminating diversity has meant disproportionately firing women, especially women of colour, from federal agencies; removing portraits of women from government buildings; and removing information about women's historical achievements and legal rights from government websites.[8] Afghanistan's and the United States' expulsions of women from public life are dramatically different in degree, but rather similar in kind: both restore men's political dominance.

Democratic erosion thus threatens women's rights advocacy and reform. By 2025, the idea of backlash to gender equality came to dominate feminist academic and policy circles, as scholars and commentators attempted to explain stagnating or reversing progress. First popularized in the 1970s by US feminist Susan Faludi, backlash occurs, observers and scholars suggest, when conservatives respond viciously or violently to perceived or actual losses of power and prestige.[9] Faludi saw backlash in right-wing responses to the women's rights era's early gains, particularly in the United States and in European countries where reforms expanded women's access to universities and workplaces while legalizing contraception and abortion. With gender equality reforms subsequently spreading across the globe and into more policy areas, many perceive backlash as resurging in the 2010s and 2020s. Perversely, democratic reversions and gender equality rollbacks may actually indicate the women's rights era's success.

Thus, whether the women's rights era ends amid a global right turn has no easy answer. This book defines the women's rights era as five decades of significant and consequential global organizing for women's rights. Delimiting the women's rights era captures a period wherein unprecedented levels of women's organizing led to advocacy and to reform, and ultimately to progress – while acknowledging that progress was never consistent nor linear. Reversions are also neither uniform nor linear: despite 2025 falling amid an undeniable global right turn, the preceding chapters show that many countries remain steadfast in their upward trajectory. Women's organizing has continued, albeit in the more challenging and restricted circumstances created by accelerating de-democratization. In 2025 as in 1975, women form the backbone of pro-democracy movements, still demanding democracy where it remains absent and defending democracy where it has weakened.

As the stories below show, women – especially feminists – remain among the world's most committed democrats. Democracy may not consistently deliver gender equality, but it remains the best possible regime for realizing political and social equality, including for and among women. Consequently, women risk their physical safety in protest marches, demonstrations, and sit-ins. For many women, confronting opposition and bearing activism's costs are not new. Women's rights activists (regretfully) have always navigated enraged, intractable, and even violent opposition to their demands. The new and perhaps shocking climates of hostility in places like the United States are not necessarily new and shocking to women in places like Afghanistan. Especially in non-democratic and Global South contexts, women's rights gains have always been fragile and women have waged decades-long struggles for even modest advances. Persistence and courage are hallmarks of the women's rights era – and they are the keys to a feminist future.

Resistance as ever-present

Chapter 3 recounted how the third wave of democratization buoyed the women's rights era. The twinning of democracy with political equality generally and gender equality specifically meant that even autocracies felt pressure to pursue some reforms: they eschewed democracy, but they could adopt certain gender equality reforms to create a democratic veneer. Thus, Rwanda introduced gender quotas for women parliamentarians and Saudi Arabia removed restrictions on women driving. Though these changes stemmed from autocratic leaders' image management rather than principled commitments to women's rights, real-life women did benefit from these reforms. Saudi women have gained greater mobility and increased their workforce participation. Young girls in Rwanda grow up seeing women in parliament – the very same women MPs who then carry other women's rights laws forward.

That gender equality can progress even in non-democratic contexts is not new. Also not new is the fact that gender equality reforms *always* face resistance. This book has emphasized successes, linking women's advocacy to reform and emphasizing women's rights protagonists' wins. Achieving reform has always meant overcoming resistance, as most political elites are men and benefit from the patriarchal status quo. Autocracies may resist more, because they may ground their regimes on conservative ideologies and because they have fewer or no entry points for or reasons to respond to interest groups. As Chapter 3 shows, however, democracies have not run towards gender equality reforms with open arms.

Democracies are more 'naturally' allied with women's movements, given their premise of equality among citizens and their allowance of political pluralism and interest group lobbying. Yet democratic left governments are reactive, not proactive. Take the democratic or democratizing countries liberalizing abortion access since the 1994 Cairo conference (Chapter 7). Across cases, an organized feminist movement mobilized for years, if not decades, before the reform could pass. Even when left-wing parties came to power, feminists could only obtain legislative majorities by agreeing to more restrictive bills than they originally preferred. In general, feminists struggle to obtain their ideal reform, whether in the less transformative policy area of political rights or the more transformative one of reproductive rights; they often must accept loopholes or limitations to have the law pass. Further, across all policy areas, feminists must continue defending the laws, insisting on implementation and guarding against reversals. Democracies themselves are hardly eager gender equality champions. Women's rights advocates understand that victories are always partial and incomplete.

Further, women's rights advocates know that winning reforms and winning hearts and minds are not the same – and that the former can occur without the latter. In democracies and autocracies alike, elites might concede a gender equality reform because it looks good or detracts from other problems. Without principled commitments, political elites later neglect or subvert policy implementation. Opponents – usually men – might design the measure itself to be weak, as they did with countries' initial gender quota laws (Chapter 4), or they might allow reforms knowing that the resultant laws will be unwieldly and difficult to implement, as happens with measures to combat VAW (Chapter 8). Cecilia Josefsson analyses the tactics used by opponents she calls 'status quo defenders', and she concludes that gender equality laws' very weakness or unwieldiness constitutes a baked-in resistance to gender equality objectives.[10]

The book's conceptual schema for understanding why progress in some women's rights policy areas appears more straightforward than others accounts for this resistance (see Figure 1.1). The more the reform invokes myriad actors to consciously undo the gendered power structures of state and society, the more opportunities there are for some subsets of actors – whether citizens, bureaucrats, or elites – to simply refuse. And the more the reform requires extensive resources for monitoring and sanctioning noncompliance, the more impunity actors enjoy for refusing. Status quo defenders might preserve patriarchy consciously or unconsciously, because they are ignorant or indifferent, or because they are actively hostile to gender equality. Gender and politics scholars have analysed these myriad forms of resistance, cataloguing the differences between conscious and unconscious opposition to gender equality policies and their implementation. These different forms of opposition notwithstanding, the outcome remains the same: slow or halted progress on bridging the gap between adoption and implementation. The point is that, for women's rights advocates, neither non-democratic nor democratic regimes have been perfect allies and so operating within resistant or hostile contexts is not new. Dispiriting and even dangerous, yes. Different from what has transpired previously, not necessarily.

Women's rights amid democratic backsliding

If democracies have never automatically marched towards gender equality and countermovements have been ever present in all political regimes, what is new about how democratic backsliding threatens women's rights? The women's rights era offered a propitious landscape for global gender equality reform: the Mexico City, Copenhagen, Nairobi, and Beijing conferences gave women's transnational advocacy an enormous boost, but no UN-convened world conference on women has occurred since 1995. Despite the symbolic allure of marking the big anniversaries since Mexico City or Beijing, the global right turn has made calling a fifth world conference on women a risky proposition. With more right-wing governments at the table and more countermovements represented by activists and NGOs with UN consultative status, any resultant policy framework could express a weaker commitment to women's rights when compared to its predecessor documents. Protagonists have always faced opposition when authoring feminist blueprints, but UN Women's decision to not risk an updated but less progressive successor to the Beijing PfA reveals feminists' understanding that the roadblocks in 2025 are much stronger than in 1975 or 1995.[11]

Indeed, democratic backsliding has eroded the gravitational pull of gender equality as an internationally shared normative goal. No feminist blueprint ever spontaneously generated national-level lawmaking – women's activism was always needed to translate the international norm into a domestic reform – but feminist blueprints during the women's rights era constituted valuable discursive resources. After all, genderwashing would not work if appearing supportive of gender equality did not give governments some international bona fides. Even autocratic governments played along, using gender equality reforms to make themselves appear modern and democratic (even when they were not). A hallmark of the global right turn, however, is the explicit rejection of feminist blueprints and their underlying norm commitments.

Many contemporary autocrats gain and maintain power by outwardly rejecting what they perceive as a global, pluralist, and multicultural agenda. They derisively refer to this agenda as 'gender ideology' – the idea that, since gender identities, roles, and norms are socially constructed and therefore changeable, feminists would have people believe that there is no such thing as a 'man' or a 'woman'. Opposition to gender ideology helps autocrats to rally conservative voters and buoys countermovements. Now, when governments roll back protections not just for women but for LGBTQIA+ citizens and other minoritized groups, they do so not covertly but overtly, gleefully and often cruelly revelling in the reversals.

The examples extend beyond Turkey's now infamous withdrawal from the Istanbul Convention (Chapter 8). Russian President Vladimir Putin signed a law that decriminalizes domestic violence by reducing penalties for beatings that do not end with broken bones.[12] Tunisia and Georgia repealed their gender quota laws. Elected in 2022, South Korea's President Yoon Suk Yeol campaigned as an anti-feminist, removed the term 'gender equality' from new school textbooks, left the women's ministry leaderless and rudderless, and eliminated his predecessor's 30 per cent gender quota for ministerial posts.[13] Figures like Yoon Suk Yeol publicly embrace the rejection of egalitarian norms – and reap electoral rewards for doing so. US President Donald Trump similarly campaigned using astonishingly misogynistic language. This 'genderbashing' is the corollary to genderwashing. Without political elites needing to at least pretend to support gender equality, women's rights activists lose the lever of image management that previously helped them win reforms in autocracies and democracies alike.

Further, this loss of conformity pressure emboldens opponents who, in earlier moments, might have disliked gender equality reforms but remained silent. Jennifer Piscopo and Denise Walsh distinguish between ever present resistance and newly arrived backlash, suggesting that expanded coalitions of opponents indicate backlash.[14] With right-wing leaders offering permission to say the impolite parts aloud, moderates join extremists to create an enlarged, enraged, more powerful counterweight to feminist movements. At the international level, a growing circle of countries now assert that the family constitutes the foundational level of society. They further argue that there are two biological sexes – male and female – and that gender ideology undermines this (supposed) essential truth. Countries joining the anti-gender movement find themselves among strange bedfellows: they include Muslim-majority countries such as Turkey, Iran, and Iraq, former communist countries such as Russia, but also Belarus and Serbia, post-colonial autocracies such as Uganda and Zimbabwe, and once democratizing countries such as Catholic-majority El Salvador and Nicaragua. While these countries' leaders roll back women's and LGBTQIA+ rights at the national level, they obstruct feminist blueprint production at the international level. For example, this mix of countries prevented men's engagement in unpaid care from becoming an SDG 5 indicator.[15] In this way, countries leading the anti-gender ideology countermovement engage in what scholars call 'norm spoiling'. These obstructionist tactics include watering down or even deleting references to gender and sexuality from international frameworks and turning multilateral spaces against human rights and women's rights.[16]

Weakened international norms and emboldened opponents mean that international, transnational, and national feminist movements now fight uphill. Resistance to women's rights and gender equality is more explicit, more normalized, more intense, and better funded in 2025 than in 1975. The windows of opportunity created by democratization and by countries' quest for international approbation as democracies are fewer. Even the United Nations faces declining legitimacy and support. Its March 2025 'UN at 80' plan to improve operations included a proposed merger between UN Women and UNFPA. Women's rights activists and organizations have pushed back, fearing that a merger would dismantle the only UN agency with an explicit and unapologetic focus on women and girls.[17]

The landscape in 2025 thus appears bleak. Where women's rights could once be neglected, now the statutory mandates – and flagship agencies such as UN Women, which backed them – are facing removal. Repealing the on-paper reforms that encode women's rights has serious implications. When such reversals occur, advocates spend valuable energy and resources going on the defensive rather than on the offensive. Sometimes activists do successfully mitigate or halt the rollback, as when women mobilized to protect some forms of legal abortion in Poland and in certain US states (Chapter 7) and when women rallied to defeat the Gambia's effort to re-legalize female genital mutilation (Chapter 8). Yet these triumphs constitute only partial or temporary victories. Women are essentially fighting battles previously won, and in far more hostile conditions, and against more empowered opponents. Given these circumstances, it is no wonder that feminist scholars and activists feel less optimistic in 2025 than in 1975.

Old tactics in new times

So far, this chapter has used the terms 'resistance' and 'opposition' to describe those who are against gender equality reforms, meaning patriarchy's defenders. 'Resistance' and 'opposition' can also carry a more positive connotations, as marginalized groups fight oppression. Women activists in democracies and non-democracies alike have decades of experience resisting rollbacks to their rights and manifesting what some scholars call 'democratic resilience' or 'democratic self-defence'. As the examples of Poland and the Gambia show, women succeed when they combine their forces inside and outside the state, presenting a unified front that amplifies demands in both arenas. Women within the state can become squeaky wheels, jamming the gears of political processes that seek to remove their rights, while women outside the state mobilize, channelling and demonstrating popular discontent.

The women's rights era's recent years offer more and more stories of such resistance. In Iraq, women managed to slow down – though not ultimately halt – the reintroduction of gender-discriminatory clauses to the personal status law. Iraq has held regular parliamentary elections since 2005, though its democratization process remains incomplete, plagued by persistent corruption and electoral violence. Amid such democratic fragility, the 2021 elections brought to power a conservative governing coalition, dominated by hardline Shi'a groups.[18] Aligned with the anti-gender ideology campaign, these conservative parties introduced regressive amendments to the personal status code. The code was last revised in 1978, when the General Federation of Iraqi Women sought and won reforms such as setting the minimum marriage age at 15, prohibiting practices such as forced marriages and second marriages outside the legal system, and allowing maternal custody following divorce until children turn 15.[19]

Following the 2021 elections, conservative groups proposed an amendment circumventing these protections. The measure would allow couples signing a marriage contract to choose adherence to the personal status law or to an alternative code based on Islamic jurisprudence, with each sect's religious authorities determining the appropriate rules for its adherents.[20] For couples selecting the alternative code, women would be governed by religious laws, which offer fewer protections. For instance, certain religious groups permit child marriage for girls as young as nine. Other consequences of choosing the religious code include preventing pregnant women from giving birth in hospitals, which require civil marriage certificates for admission.[21]

Fortunately, Iraqi women had more voice in government in 2021 than in 1978. Iraq's 30 per cent gender quota, in place since 2005, yielded its best results in 2021, electing 95 women to comprise 29 per cent of the assembly. Fifteen Iraqi women MPs mobilized to protest the amendment, joining forces across parties. Legislators such as Noor al-Jilaihawi and Srwa Mohammed led a signature campaign, obtaining signatures from 124 women and men parliamentarians opposed to the reform.[22] Women politicians also joined protests across the country.[23] They did not manage to prevent the amendment's passage, but they extracted important moderations. The final version says that the alternative Islamic codes cannot contravene the personal status law's minimum marriage age of 18 (though judges may approve marriage for girls as young as 15). The final version also stipulates that a judge, not the husband, will resolve disputes between couples over whether the civil code or the religious code would apply.[24] With more women inside the state – precisely because of gains made earlier during the women's rights era – Iraqi women put up a fight against diminished legal status under personal status laws.

A similar process unfolded in Brazil, where right-wing anti-gender ideology forces have long mobilized. These forces won the presidency in 2019, electing right-wing populist Jair Bolsonaro (a Trump ally), who governed until 2023. Cognizant of the threat well before the Bolsonaro era, women legislators in the Chamber of Deputies devised procedures and strategies for blocking an ever-increasing number of anti-rights proposals from conservative legislators.[25] In 2016, progressive women deputies persuaded the Chamber leadership to form a legislative committee focused on women, naming this new committee the Women's Rights Defense Committee. Any bill touching upon women's rights would need to pass through this committee. Conservative actors responded, extending the policy powers of a different committee – the Family and Social Security Committee – to include bills concerning women and the unborn (among others). Conservative actors also attached the urgency label to anti-gender bills, allowing the proposals to skip committees' evaluation and proceed directly to the floor vote. In 2024, conservative actors introduced two urgent bills, one granting foetal rights from conception and another equating abortion with manslaughter and applying a 20-year prison sentence. Both proposals would remove the legal grounds for abortion in Brazil, which are rape, risk to the mother's life, and acephaly. Deprived of their ability to stall the bill in the Women's Rights Defense Committee, feminist legislators deployed other resistance tactics.

First, Women's Caucus members such as Sâmia Bomfim and women activists launched a public relations and social media campaign to rebrand the projects, focusing on their potentially dire consequences for underage women and rape victims. They renamed the proposals 'the child pregnancy bill' and 'the rape bill', using hashtags and slogans such as 'a child is not a mother'. Second, the legislators deployed various filibuster efforts to delay the floor votes. Third, they held public events in the Chamber, ensuring that their objections would receive near constant airing. Activist women participated in these public events – while also staging protests outside the Chamber and across at least thirteen Brazilian cities. The bills drew such negative attention that a polling firm launched one of the first-ever public surveys on abortion attitudes, finding that 65 per cent of Brazilians believe abortion should be allowed 'under the circumstances it is today, even more circumstances, or any circumstance'. Women's mobilization ultimately forced Chamber leaders to take the bills off the agenda. As Daniel Baldin Machado summarizes, '[w]omen's resilience played a role in denying the anti-abortion coalition their vote'.

Turkey provides another illustration of feminists forestalling reversions – for the moment. In 2024, the Constitutional Court responded to a petition brought by the women's movement and overturned the requirement that women adopt their husband's surname upon marriage. The parliament then proposed a measure reinstating this obligation. In response, the Equality for Women Platform (EŞİK) launched what became a months-long resistance campaign. Women leaders from opposition parties joined EŞİK in criticizing the initiative.[26] This outside–inside resistance led the parliament to finally abandon the proposal. Still, the frontlines shifted: the government proposed constitutional reforms that would introduce biologically based definitions of male and female, ban same-sex marriage, and reify the heterosexual family. Turkish women's groups and LGBTQIA+ groups mobilized in opposition, forcing the amendments to stall, but in May 2025 the Ministry of Family and Social Services issued a directive that bans public institutions from using concepts such as 'gender', 'LGBTIQ+', and 'comprehensive sexuality education'.[27]

Consequently, women may mobilize inside and outside the state to slow reversals down, but these results may not hold for long. Women's rights activists cannot rest: as seen with the never-safe character of abortion reform, victory for one side constitutes a loss for the other, provoking ongoing confrontations between feminists and conservatives. Yet the Iraqi, Brazilian, and Turkish examples share one feature: in these countries, women hold more political power and enjoy more day-to-day freedoms in the 2020s than they did in the 1970s. As Turkey's Berfu Şeker from the association Women for Women's Human Rights reflected, '[t]he government will continue its politics of polarization and hatred, nevertheless the solidarity of women and queers has already been established in the most unexpected places . . . Bad news for those who attack our rights; it is no longer possible to subordinate women, that era has long passed.'[28]

Şeker's statement captures how autocrats and anti-gender actors will attempt to undo gender equality, but the genie of women's rights will not be so easily stuffed back into the bottle. Women inside and outside the state provide critical 'no' votes and voices. In addition to obstructing attacks on their rights, they pursue another longstanding tactic: looking for places where advancement remains possible. While right-wing Argentine President Javier Milei blusters against abortion in Argentina, the lower chamber's Commission on Women and Diversity advanced an initiative that would add sexual harassment to the country's anti-VAW law.[29] While Mexican President Andrés Manuel López Obrador called feminists enemies of the state, women in the foreign ministry won a feminist foreign policy that formally includes women's rights and LGBTQIA+ rights in foreign policy priorities and funding.[30] True, these gains are modest. They do not undermine the chief executive's power and may be further instances of genderwashing, in which feminist gains in a less transformative policy area mask setbacks in sexual and reproductive rights and ongoing femicide epidemics. Nonetheless, feminist policymakers authored the reforms, operating in the space of the possible. Such policies keep women's rights inscribed within the state and gender equality alive in the public and political debate.

Women's mobilization against autocracy and for democracy

The Iraqi, Brazilian, and Turkish cases illuminate women's institutional resistance combined with mobilization and protest. Another longstanding tactic remains more squarely in the streets. Women have long led pro-democracy movements, and pro-democracy movements and women's movements often coevolve, as women advocate for democracy in the country and in the home. Movement participation and leadership constitute another way in which women activists have demanded democracy where it is absent or defended democracy where it is eroding.

Women seeking democratic transitions

Not all countries are experiencing democratic reversals. Some are still attempting to shed their authoritarian past. Like women participating in earlier democratic transitions, women joining recent pro-democracy movements are motivated by political goals and by gender equality. Take Sudan in 2019. Dictator Omar al-Bashir had installed strict public order and morality laws, which maintained political and social control – but also disproportionately affected women.[31] Taken together, the public order and morality laws required women's absolute adherence to restrictive Islamic dress codes, severely limiting their ability to work, travel, or simply exist in public space. Security forces zealously harassed women perceived as noncompliant.[32] Women's groups had sought the laws' repeal since the 1990s, but the broader revolution against Bashir's rule provided women with new opportunities to attain their objectives. After all, removing the dictator would also remove his laws. Sudanese women and women's NGOs quickly joined the protest activities. For instance, it was women from the Sudanese Women's Aid Organization that sent single mothers to the May 2019 sit-in at the army headquarters in the capital Khartoum.[33] Women protest leaders such as 22-year-old student Alaa Salah became international icons; videos of Salah leading chants went viral and she was reportedly shortlisted for the Nobel Peace Prize. The transitional government that replaced Bashir then repealed those sections of the criminal code that had regulated and controlled women's dress and behaviour.

In Sri Lanka in 2022, widespread protests over a plummeting economy forced the country's president, the iron-fisted autocrat Gotabaya Rajapaksa, to flee. His family had assumed power in the aftermath of Sri Lanka's civil war, imposing stability via authoritarian rule. Sri Lankan women have a long history of political activism, including as fighters during the war and as peace activists during the Rajapaksas' reign. As the 2022 uprising unfolded, wives and mothers continued their longtime tactic of camping outside government offices, demanding the return of family members disappeared by regime security forces. Other women led justice walks, marching silently and respecting curfews, while carrying placards with their demands.[34] Still other women participated in the broader protests, violating curfews and marching in the capital Colombo and other cities. Young women and women students joined the protest villages, including the villages GotaGoGama ('Gotta Go Village'), erected to occupy Colombo's business district, and HoruGoGama ('Go Home Thieves Village') in front of Sri Lanka's parliament.[35]

In addition to expressing anger over the failed peace process and government repression, Sri Lankan women raged against the economic crisis, which had magnified their care burdens by worsening their ability to feed and clothe their households. In the 2024 parliamentary elections that followed Rajapaksa's ouster, women candidates campaigned and won in record numbers.[36] One of these women, Harini Amarasuriya, secured more votes than the Rajapaksa men had received in each of their previous elections.[37] The new president appointed Amarasuriya prime minister, making her the first South Asian woman without a dynastic tie to attain this position.[38] The new government then made several promises related to women's economic opportunities, including recognizing the care economy, achieving pay parity, and encouraging gender-sensitive work environments.[39]

Not all pro-democracy movements succeed, however. Some, like Sri Lanka's, are young and their legacy is uncertain. Others, like Sudan's, decisively fail: the transitional military–civilian government could not hold, and the country descended into armed conflict between different groups. Elsewhere the democratic transition never even began. Such is the case of Belarus, where the 2020 protests against Alexander Lukashenko's rule did not result in his ouster. Yet the efforts catapulted women into leadership positions and brought women's concerns about militarism, state violence, and gender inequality to the fore. The Belarus protests began after Lukashenko's three male competitors in the 2020 presidential race were arrested or forced to flee. Three women emerged to take their place: Sviatlana Tsikhanouskaya, Maria Kalesnikava, and Veranika Tsapkala. None of the women initially intended to lead a pro-democracy movement. They formed a pact, campaigning for the presidency together and drawing crowds of supporters.[40] Their very presence – three women on stage – challenged Lukashenko's hyper-masculine security regime. Thousands of everyday women joined the protests. They made three demands: Lukashenko's removal, the abolishment of his security police, and gender equality.[41] Lukashenko's forces ultimately won, deploying repression, assaulting protestors, and forcing Tsikhanouskaya to flee. Still, Belarussian women established themselves as political leaders with agency. Even failed democratization attempts illuminate women's ongoing role in keeping democratic dreams alive.

Women leading democratic defence

Many polities have not taken democratic backsliding lightly. In Georgia in 2024, the capital Tbilisi erupted in protests after the prime minister suspended the country's bid for EU membership. Protestors – including woman president Salome Zurabishvili, women MPs, and women journalists – blocked the streets outside Georgia's parliament. In Serbia in 2024 and 2025, women students led rallies against the country's corrupt, patronage-ridden politics. The rallies would sometimes occur every day, for months at a time. Marching through the capital, Belgrade, women students carry protest banners that read 'women in front rows'.[42] Like their counterparts elsewhere, Serbian women want political reform and gender equality. Echoing the women activists from the Vienna Tribunal who linked political violence to violence against women, the women students held staged minutes of silence for men victims of the regime – and then tacked on additional minutes for women victims of domestic violence. These student-led rallies have attracted tens of thousands of people.[43]

Georgia's and Serbia's fate remain undecided, but women protestors decisively won the day in South Korea, extracting their revenge on the misogynistic Yoon Suk Yeol. The country erupted when, in December 2024, Yoon declared martial law and attempted to dissolve parliament. Young women in their teens, twenties, and thirties joined the demonstrations in record numbers, accounting for 35 per cent of the crowd, by comparison with men of the same age groups, who accounted for 10 per cent.[44] A 29-year school teacher told a journalist: 'So many women, including myself, have been waiting for a moment like this for a long time, because we were so sick and tired of all the hate towards us for the past two years.'[45] When rural farmers arrived in Seoul to join the anti-Yoon rallies but faced a police blockade, young women protestors placed themselves between the farmers and the police. The young women's use of their bodies dramatically illustrated the pro-democracy protestors' unity, forcing the security forces to yield.[46] After an intense four months of protest, the South Korean parliament impeached Yoon in early 2025, paving the way for elections. South Koreans refused Yoon's efforts to revert to undemocratic rule, with young women literally at the front of the barricades.

Feminist movements spur democracy's demand and defence

In Georgia, Serbia, and South Korea, movements to defend democracy attracted women participants who combined political demands with gender-based ones. As in Sudan, Sri Lanka, and Belarus, these pro-democracy movements enfolded women's movements. These examples are not exhaustive, but they illuminate how pro-democracy mobilization comes to encompass women's claims for safety, well-being, justice, and equality.

The reverse can also occur: women's mobilization for gender equality can come to encompass movements demanding or defending democracy. Feminists well understand the threat countermovements pose to their rights, not least because – as seen in the South Korean case – contemporary political leaders no longer hide their hostility towards women and feminists. As such, women's mobilization may precede pro-democracy mobilizations. Take US President Donald Trump's first election in 2016. US feminists organized the 2017 Women's March to coincide with inauguration day. Washington DC hosted the main march, with over 600 parallel marches taking place across the United States and abroad, with an estimated 3 million people participating.[47] The marchers' banners, signs, and slogans were explicitly feminist, defending those rights that Trump threatened, including reproductive rights. The Women's March then bolstered the United States' democratic defence. Scholars have tied the Women's March directly to the broader anti-Trump resistance that unfolded during his first term.[48] Districts in which more residents participated in the Women's March later became districts creating more 'indivisible groups' – anti-Trump groups not explicitly organized around gender equality claims.[49] These same districts also made more donations to the Democratic Party and raised turnout across the board in the 2018 midterm elections, when the Democrats defeated the Republicans.[50]

Similarly, in Argentina, #NiUnaMenos – founded to protest femicide – now mobilizes broad opposition to Javier Milei. Following his inauguration in December 2023, Milei wasted little time imposing economic austerity and attacking women's rights gains. By International Women's Day on 8 March 2024, Milei had eliminated funding for social insurance schemes and public university education, shuttered the women's ministry, and introduced legislation repealing legal abortion. The #NiUnaMenos leaders turned 8 March into an anti-Milei protest, recruiting participation from animal rights groups, LGBTQIA+ groups, trade unions, housing rights activists, and other progressive movements.[51] Similarly, in the June 2025 demonstrations marking #NiUnaMenos's 10th anniversary, the movement marked the occasion by organizing a multi-sectoral protest that would, as one activist explained, 'repudiate

Milei'.[52] Events included a rally outside the Argentine Congress followed by a day of strikes and marching. Joining #NiUnaMenos were doctors' unions and teachers' unions protesting budget cuts, LGBTQIA+ groups, and unemployed and laid-off workers, among others.

The 2022 Woman, Life, Freedom movement in Iran also illustrates how protests initially centring on women's rights turn into movements demanding democracy. In September 2022, 22-year-old Mahsa Amini died while in custody of Iran's morality police, who had detained Amini for allegedly not following the regime's mandatory hijab rule. Amini's Kurdish identity contributed to the public outrage: Kurds face systematic harassment and discrimination within Iran and Amini's death represented how Kurdish women are abused for their gender and their ethnicity. Protests ensued outside the hospital, but this activism did not emerge from a vacuum. As in all mobilizations discussed in this book, Iranian feminists – including Iranian Kurdish feminists – had long protested the Islamic Republic's treatment of women. Amini's death became a focusing event, an egregious yet still representative example of gender oppression that channelled women's anger. Those filling the streets in response to Amini's death chanted 'no to compulsory hijab', 'women's rights are human rights', and 'no to gender apartheid'.[53] Most centrally, however, they chanted a slogan coined by Kurdish women and previously deployed in other women's rights protests in various Muslim countries: 'woman, life, freedom'. As Iranian activist and scholar Rezvan Moghaddam explains, '[t]he freedom in the slogan denotes freedom from rigid religious orders, political and cultural repression, and social restrictions that hinder individual growth'.[54]

As the movement gained momentum, protestors began combining women's rights claims with pro-democracy ones. Chants came to include 'we want democracy, equality, and a secular system', 'this is the last word: our goal is to overthrow the regime', and 'poverty! corruption! shame on this tyranny' and 'death to the dictator'.[55] Rauf Rahimi and Sajjad Rezaei interviewed protestors, finding that their motivations extended beyond gender equality to encompass anger over economic stagnation, limited educational and workforce opportunities, and perceived government incompetence and corruption. Protestors included not only women's movement supporters but men and women representing students, diverse ethnic and religious groups, and rural as well as urban residents.[56] Perhaps frightened by the multisectoral and numerical scale of the protests, Iranian authorities acted harshly. Protestors and bystanders were detained, assaulted, and even killed. This repression demobilized the protests, but resistance did endure. In the years following the 2022 Woman, Life, Freedom protests, many Iranian women continued to quietly defy the headscarf ban, appearing hijab-less in public. In 2025, journalist Shabnam von Hein reported that the Iranian morality police had partially retreated, only intervening in the case of 'gross violations'.[57]

These examples illuminate the persistent and longstanding role that women play in envisioning and leading efforts to enact more democratic and more equitable futures. When the world's women convened in Mexico City in 1975, Global South feminists pointed out that attaining gender equality could not be separated from realizing profound, structural reforms to politics and economics, including ending the unjust hierarchies installed by decades of colonial and imperial rule. Women leading the ensuing decades' pro-democracy movements have echoed these arguments. Some countries have succeeded at their democratic transitions and others have failed; some never transitioned; and others now travel in the opposite direction. In all cases, demands for democracy and gender equality intertwine. Whether pro-democracy movements in the 2020s seek to dislodge long-time autocracies or to defend democracies against authoritarian-minded leaders, women activists lead movements that aspire to more equality, less violence, and more peace. Women, particularly feminists, remain committed democrats and, against many odds, they have not lost hope that better futures for themselves and their countries can be built.

Towards a feminist future?

The global women's rights movement has not quietly surrendered to 50 years of imperfect progress. Moreover, a central difference between 2025 and 1975 is, as Berfu Şeker wrote, that women now have tasted freedom. Women activists and women elites in diverse contexts are unanimous on this point: they will not go back. 'No going back', said Afghan women, holding protests in 2021 when the Taliban returned.[58] 'Not going back', read the signs held by Tunisian women in 2022, who rallied in protest against President Kais Saied's repeal of the gender quota law and other women's rights gains.[59] 'No going back', said US protestors denouncing Trump and marching in defence of abortion rights. 'We will not step back', insisted Kurdish woman leader Shahrazad al-Jassem following the 2024 fall of Syria's brutal dictatorship.[60] In her speech on 10 March 2025, at the 69th Commission of the Status of Women, UN Women Executive Director Sima Bahous said: 'We will not back down.'[61] One might think that these statements are mere posturing – after all, the Taliban did not listen. Yet with courage and conviction, the words are said.

There has been no fifth world conference on women, but the global women's movement continues. The international normative frameworks and policy toolkits have not disappeared, even as the current moment weakens their symbolic and persuasive power. The Beijing PfA, CEDAW, and all other feminist blueprints remain. They now serve a new generation of activists and leaders, as feminist organizing across borders persists.[62] From the young women leading UN Women's Generation Equality Forum, through the still large presence of feminists and feminist NGOs at international conferences, to the women protestors defying patriarchy and police to raise their voices, women's rights protagonists have not lost hope. Women political leaders similarly continue aspiring to new models, from Sri Lanka's Harini Amarasuriya to Iceland's Kristrún Frostadóttir of Iceland. The latter leads a coalition government where all political parties are headed by women. While other left-wing governments court right-wing voters and risk normalizing the very discourses that accelerate democratic backsliding, Frostadóttir aims to show that social spending can still deliver to citizens the quality of life they expect. She promises 'a new type of governance' – one led by women and enacting a progressive agenda.[63]

So, does the women's rights era end in 2025, amid a global right turn? Perhaps not, because perhaps 50 years remains too short a time to achieve the transformations feminists seek. At a UN Women Expert Group Meeting in February 2025, Bangladeshi scholar Naila Kabeer quipped: 'We've had four thousand years of patriarchy but not even fifty years of CEDAW.'[64] Her comment perfectly captures the glass half-full perspective this book urges: progress is not linear, but advocacy makes reform possible and reform does occur. Winning rights on paper constitutes the critical first step in a long journey towards equality and justice. Throughout the women's rights era, protagonists fought hard for better futures – they did not give up on their countries or their ideals, even with repressive forces arrayed or turned against them. For every woman protagonist whose name does and does not appear in these pages, their sacrifices and legacy are honoured by carrying the fight for women's rights into an uncertain future.

Acknowledgements

Thank you to the people who believed, from day one, that I had a book to write. This book would not have happened without Rose Sebastian's unwavering enthusiasm and support, which included a willingness to turn not one, but two summer vacations into writing retreats. Nor would it have happened without Nancy Cohen's inspiring example. Thank you to Derek Shearer, for introducing me to Louise Knight, my first editor at Polity. I am grateful that Louise supported this project, and I am grateful for the guidance and patience offered by her successor, Elise Heslinga. Thank you to Julia Zulver, who introduced me to Charli McMackin, the most amazing research assistant and without whom Chapters 5 and 6 would not look the way they do. Thank you, Charli! I am thankful also for additional research assistance provided by Kiran Sahota.

So many colleagues and friends supported this project from start to finish, more than I can list here. A special thank you, however, to those who cheered me on while I was writing: Amy Atchison, Phillip Ayoub, Tiffany Barnes, Elin Bjarnegård, Sarah Childs, Elizabeth Evans, Susan Franceschet, Malu Gatto, Jasmine Gideon, Amanda Gouws, Magda Hinojosa, Meryl Kenny, Malliga Och, Peter Siavelis, Kiran Stallone, Michelle Taylor-Robinson, Gwynn Thomas, Aili Tripp, Georgina Waylen, Christina Xydias, and Julia Zulver. Thank you to those who read chapters or passages and patiently answered my questions about countries or policies in your area of expertise. I had many generous readers, but I especially thank Elin Bjarnegård and Pär Zetterberg for the lively scholarly discussion about genderwashing that made Chapter 3 nuanced and, I hope, effective. Thank you to everyone who listened to me talk (or whine) about 'the Book', but particularly Amy, Christina, Malliga, Rose, and Brian.

Finally, thank you to all the women's rights activists. It is the greatest privilege of my career to travel the globe and to learn about you and from you. I am honoured by the sheer number of you who have met with me and shared your stories. I am humbled by your collective work to make the world a better place for women and girls. I hope that we never become so discouraged or cynical about all the work that remains to be done that we cease to value the work you did do. And a special thank you to Lois Wasserspring, who showed me the path and who will never be forgotten.

Notes

Notes to Chapter 1

1 UN Women, n.d. 'World conferences on women'. https://www.unwomen.org/en/how-we-work/intergovernmental-support/world-conferences-on-women.

2 Rebecca Turkington, 2023. '"Once and for all": The Fourth World Conference on Women and the institutionalization of women's human rights in American foreign policy'. *Gender & History* 35 (3): 846–861.

3 Turkington 2023.

4 Charlotte Bunch and Niamh O'Reilly, 1994. *Demanding Accountability: The Global Campaign and Vienna Tribunal for Women's Human Rights.* New Brunswick, NJ: Center for Women's Global Leadership, p. 5.

5 United Nations, 1993a. 'Vienna Declaration and Programme of Action', paragraph 18. https://www.ohchr.org/en/instruments-mechanisms/instruments/vienna-declaration-and-programme-action.

6 Martha Alter Chen, 1995. 'Engendering world conferences: The international women's movement and the United Nations'. *Third World Quarterly* 16 (3): 477–494, at p. 478.

7 United Nations, 1975. *Report of the World Conference of the International Women's Year, Mexico City, 1975*. New York: United Nations. Document E/CONF.66/34. https://docs.un.org/en/E/CONF.66/34.

8 This paragraph draws from Summer Forester, Kaitlin Kelly Thompson, Amber Lusvardi, and S. Laurel Weldon, 2022. 'New dimensions of global feminist influence: Tracking feminist mobilization worldwide, 1975–2015'. *International Studies Quarterly* 66: sqab093.

9 Pamela Paxton, Melanie Hughes, and Jennifer Green, 2006. 'The international women's movement and women's political representation, 1893–2003'. *American Sociological Review* 71 (6): 898–920, at p. 915.

10 Varieties of Democracy Institute (V-Dem), 2024. 'Democracy report 2024: Democracy winning and losing at the ballot'. Gothenburg: University of Gothenburg. https://v-dem.net/documents/43/v-dem_dr2024_lowres.pdf.

11 Martha Finnemore and Michelle Jurkovich, 2020. 'The politics of aspiration'. *International Studies Quarterly* 64 (4): 759–769; Mala Htun and S. Laurel Weldon, 2018. *The Logics of Gender Justice: State Action on Women's Rights around the World.* New York: Cambridge University Press.

12 Karen Beckwith, 2010. 'Introduction: Comparative politics and the logics of a comparative politics of gender'. *Perspectives on Politics* 8 (1): 159–168, at p. 160.

13 Maxine Molyneux, 1985. 'Mobilization without emancipation? Women's interests, the state, and revolution in Nicaragua'. *Feminist Studies* 11 (2): 227–254, at p. 231.

14 Karen Celis and Sarah Childs, 2012. 'The substantive representation of women: What to do with conservative claims?' *Political Studies* 60 (1): 213–255.

15 National Museum of African American History and Culture, n.d. 'Women in the Modern Civil Rights Movement'. Washington, DC. https://nmaahc.si.edu/sites/default/files/images/black_women_civil_rights_movement_5.pdf.
16 Manal Al-Sharif, 2017a. 'I can't wait to drive again in Saudi Arabia'. *New York Times*, 27 September, https://www.nytimes.com/2017/09/27/opinion/saudi-arabia-women-driving-.html.
17 Leta Hong Fincher, 2018. *Betraying Big Brother: The Feminist Awakening in China.* London: Verso, 59–72.
18 Mathias Braschler and Monika Fischer, 2023. 'The women forced out of Iran: "Every act of resistance is a spark of hope"'. *Guardian*, 18 March. https://www.theguardian.com/society/2023/mar/18/women-forced-out-of-iran-acts-of-resistance-hope.
19 IPAS, 2024. '3 reasons abortion access is crucial for mothers'. 10 May. https://www.ipas.org/news/3-reasons-abortion-access-is-crucial-for-mothers.
20 Laura Harrison and Sarah B. Rowley, 2011. 'Babies by the bundle: Gender, backlash, and the Quiverfull Movement'. *Feminist Formations* 23 (1): 47–69, at p. 47.
21 Julie Suk, 2020. *We the Women: The Unstoppable Mothers of the Equal Rights Amendment.* New York: Skyhorse Publishing, p. 151.
22 Maud Anne Bracke, 2023. 'Contesting "Global Sisterhood": The global women's health movement, the United Nations, and different meanings of reproductive rights'. *Gender & History* 35: 811–829; Lisa Levenstein, 2020. *They Didn't See Us Coming: The Hidden History of Feminism in the Nineties.* New York: Basic Books.
23 Bracke 2023; Hannah Harris Green, 2018. 'The world's most common contraception has a dark past'. BBC, 11 September. https://www.bbc.co.uk/future/article/20180906-why-female-sterilisation-is-so-popular-in-india.
24 Nitza Berkovitch, 1999. 'The emergence and transformation of the international women's movement'. In *Constructing World Cultures: International Non-Governmental Organizations since 1875*, ed. by John Boli and George M. Thomas. Stanford: Stanford University Press, 100–126, at p. 101.
25 Bracke 2023.
26 United Nations, 1995. *Beijing Platform for Action.* New York: United Nations, paragraph 115. https://www.un.org/womenwatch/daw/beijing/pdf/BDPfA%20E.pdf.
27 Mary Hawkesworth, 2012. *Political Worlds of Women.* Boulder, CO: Westview Press.
28 Audre Lorde, 1984. 'The master's tools will never dismantle the master's house'. In her *Sister Outsider: Essays and Speeches.* Trumansburg, NY: Crossing Press, 110–114.
29 Tània Verge and Montserrat Pineda-Lorenzo, 2025. 'Lessons from Catalonia: Advancing sexual and reproductive rights through feminist policymaking and governance'. *Sexual and Reproductive Health Matters* 33 (1): 2529072.
30 Tània Verge, 2024. 'Feministizing policymaking in practice: How gender and politics scholarship inspires government policy, and vice versa'. *Politics & Gender* 20 (4): 1015–1021.
31 IPSOS, 2023. 'Global views on abortion'. Institut Public de Sondage d'Opinion Secteur (IPSOS), 22 August. https://www.ipsos.com/en-uk/global-views-abortion-2023.
32 Natali Francine Cinelli Moreira and Kelly Komatsu Agopyan, 2021. 'The desire to change everything: *La potencia feminista* and the Tribune of the World Conference of International Women's Year'. *Feminist Perspectives* (blog), King's College London, 28 May. https://www.kcl.ac.uk/the-desire-to-change-everything.

33 Htun and Weldon 2018.
34 Htun and Weldon 2018.

Notes to Chapter 2

1 Account drawn from Karmen Tornius, 2023. 'Pan-African gender governance: The politics of aspiration at the African Union'. *Review of International Studies* 49 (4): 741–762.
2 Gita Sen, 2019. 'Gender equality and women's empowerment: Feminist mobilization for the SDGs'. *Global Policy* 10 (S1): 28–38.
3 Archivo Nacional de Chile, n.d. 'El movimiento feminista en la dictadura militar (1973–1990)'. https://www.archivonacional.gob.cl/galeria/el-movimiento-feminista-en-la-dictadura-militar-1973-1990.
4 Amrita Basu, ed. 1995. *The Challenge of Local Feminisms*. Boulder, CO: Westview Press, p. 9.
5 Margaret E. Keck and Kathryn Sikkink. 1998. *Activists beyond Borders: Advocacy Networks in Local Politics*. Ithaca, NY: Cornell University Press.
6 Valentine Moghadam, 2023. 'Transnational feminism and global governance'. In *Handbook of Feminist Governance*, ed. by Marian Sawer, Lee Ann Banaszak, Jacqui True, and Johanna Kantola. Cheltenham: Edwin Elgar, 274–285.
7 Julie Ballington and Sonia Palmieri, 2023. 'Tools of the trade: feminist governance in the field'. In *Handbook of Feminist Governance*, ed. by Marian Sawer, Lee Ann Banaszak, Jacqui True, and Johanna Kantola. Cheltenham: Edwin Elgar, 189–201, at p. 191.
8 Association of Southeast Asian Nations (ASEAN). 2021. 'ASEAN Declaration on the gender-responsive implementation of the ASEAN community Vision 2025 and Sustainable Development Goals'. https://asean.org/wp-content/uploads/2021/01/ASEAN-Declaration-on-the-Gender-Responsive-Implementation-of-the-ASEAN-Community-Vision-2025-and-Sustainable-Development-Goals.pdf.
9 Amanda Edgell, 2017. 'Foreign aid, democracy, and gender quota laws'. *Democratization* 24 (6): 1103–1141.
10 Silke Roth, 2007. 'Sisterhood and solidarity? Women's organizations in the expanded European Union'. *Social Politics* 14 (4): 460–487.
11 Berkovitch 1999, p. 7.
12 Katherine M. Marino, 2019. *Feminism for the Americas: The Making of an International Human Rights Movement*. Chapel Hill: University of North Carolina Press.
13 Emma Schubert, 2020. 'The struggles for women's suffrage in Lebanon'. *Meridians* 19 (1): 202–208.
14 Sumita Mukherjee, 2016. 'The All-Asian Women's Conference 1931: Indian women and their leadership of a pan-Asian feminist organisation'. *Women's History Review* 26 (3): 363–381. See esp. the abstract at https://www.tandfonline.com/doi/full/10.1080/09612025.2016.1163924#abstract.
15 Mona Siegel, 2020. *Peace on Our Terms: The Global Battle for Women's Rights after the First World War*. New York: Columbia University Press.
16 Mukherjee 2016.
17 Siegel 2020.
18 Marino 2019, p. 198.

19 Some historical sources conflict on whether certain women were delegates or scientific advisors. This book follows Marino's classification.

20 Katherine Marino, 2022. 'From women's rights to human rights: The influence of Pan-American feminism on the United Nations'. In *Women and the UN: A New History of Women's International Human Rights*, ed. by Rebecca Adami and Dan Plesch. New York: Routledge, 1–16, at p. 1.

21 Marino 2019, p. 208.

22 United Nations, 1948. *United Nations Charter*. New York: United Nations. https://www.un.org/en/about-us/un-charter/full-text.

23 UN Women, 2019. *A Short History on the Commission on the Status of Women*. New York: United Nations. https://www.unwomen.org/sites/default/files/Headquarters/Attachments/Sections/Library/Publications/2019/A-short-history-of-the-CSW-en.pdf.

24 Marino 2019, pp. 223–224.

25 Jocelyn Olcott, 2017. *International Women's Year: The Greatest Consciousness-Raising Event in History*. Durham, NC: Duke University Press, p. 57.

26 Olcott 2017, p. 69.

27 Olcott 2017, p. 72.

28 Olcott 2017, p. 72.

29 Olcott 2017, p. 72.

30 Chen 1995, p. 478.

31 Olcott 2017, pp. 79–83.

32 Olcott 2017, p. 5.

33 United Nations 1975.

34 United Nations 1975, pp. 110–113.

35 Olcott 2017, p. 189.

36 Olcott 2017.

37 Olcott 2017, p. 239.

38 See United Nations General Assembly Resolution 32/142 of 1977, at https://docs.un.org/en/A/RES/32/142.

39 Ellen Chesler, 2022. 'Who wrote CEDAW?' In *Women and the UN: A New History of Women's International Human Rights*, ed. by Rebecca Adami and Dan Plesch. New York: Routledge, 104–124; Lisa Baldez, 2014. *Defying Convention: US Resistance to the UN Treaty on Women's Rights*. New York: Cambridge University Press.

40 Chen 1995.

41 United Nations, 1980. *Report of the World Conference of the United Nations Decade for Women: Equality, Development and Peace*, paragraphs 47–52. New York: United Nations. Document A/CONF.94/35. https://docs.un.org/en/A/CONF.94/35.

42 United Nations, 1985. *Report of the World Conference to Review and Appraise the Achievements of the United Nations Decade for Women: Equality, Development, and Peace*, paragraph 10. New York: United Nations. https://www.un.org/womenwatch/confer/nfls/Nairobi1985report.txt.

43 Sarah De Jong, 2017. *Complicit Sisters: Gender and Women's Issues across North–South Divides*. New York: Oxford University Press, p. 17.

44 Bina Agarwal, 1996. 'From Mexico 1975 to Beijing 1995'. *Indiana Journal of Gender Studies* 3 (1): 87–92.

45 United Nations 1985, paragraph 11.

46 United Nations 1985, paragraphs 26 and 68.
47 Levenstein 2020, p. 12.
48 Forester et al. 2022.
49 Sonia E. Álvarez, 1999. 'Advocating feminism: The Latin American feminist NGO "boom"'. *International Feminist Journal of Politics* 1(2): 181–209.
50 UN Fund for Population Activities (UNFPA), 1994. *Programme of Action Adopted at the International Conference on Population and Development, Cairo, 5–13 September 1994*. New York: UNFPA. https://www.unfpa.org/sites/default/files/event-pdf/PoA_en.pdf.
51 Levenstein 2020, pp. 102–104.
52 Levenstein 2020, p. 109; Chen 1995, p. 484.
53 Chen 1995, pp. 484–485.
54 Bunch and Reilly 1994, p. 103.
55 United Nations 1993a.
56 Turkington 2023.
57 Hillary Clinton, 1995. 'Remarks for the United Nations Fourth World Conference on Women'. 5 September. https://www.un.org/esa/gopher-data/conf/fwcw/conf/gov/950905175653.txt.
58 Joan Dunlop, Rachel Kyte, and Mia MacDonald. 1996. 'Women redrawing the map: The world after the Beijing and Cairo Conferences'. *SAIS Review* 16 (1): 153–165, at p. 157.
59 United Nations 1995, paragraph 1.
60 United Nations 1995, paragraph 2.
61 United Nations 1995, paragraphs 189, 293, and 297.
62 Department of the Prime Minister and Cabinet (Australia). 2024. 'Beijing+30 gender equality report'. 18 July, https://ministers.pmc.gov.au/gallagher/2024/beijing-30-gender-equality-report.
63 Government of Samoa, 2024. 'Samoa national report'. Asia Pacific Portal for Gender Inequality, https://www.asiapacificgender.org/sites/default/files/2024-06/American%20Samoa%27s%20National%20Review%20for%20Implementation%20of%20the%20Beijing%20Platform%20for%20Action%20%282024%29.pdf.
64 Republic of Mozambique, 2024. 'Beijing+30'. UN Economic Commission for Africa https://www.uneca.org/eca-events/sites/default/files/resources/documents/gender-poverty-social-policy/beijing-30/mozambique_narrative_report.pdf.
65 Carol Cohn, Helen Kinsella, and Sheri Gibbings. 2004. 'Women, peace, and security: Resolution 1325'. *International Feminist Journal of Politics* 6 (1): 130–140, at p. 131.
66 Cornelia Weiss, 2022. 'Creating UNSCR 1325: Women who served as initiators, drafters, and strategists'. In *Women and the UN: A New History of Women's International Human Rights*, ed. by Rebecca Adami and Dan Plesch. New York: Routledge, 139–160, at p. 144.
67 Soumita Basu, 2016. 'The Global South writes 1325 (too)'. *International Political Science Review* 37 (3): 362–374, at p. 365.
68 Weiss 2022, p. 144.
69 Weiss 2022, p. 140.
70 Weiss 2022, pp. 140–141.
71 United Nations, 2000. 'Windhoek Declaration'. https://www.un.org/womenwatch/osagi/wps/windhoek_declaration.pdf.

72 Weiss 2022, p. 145.
73 Weiss 2022, pp. 146–147.
74 United Nations Security Council, 2000. 'Resolution 1325'. S/RES/1325. https://documents.un.org/doc/undoc/gen/n00/720/18/pdf/n0072018.pdf.
75 Victoria Scheyer and Marina Kumskova. 2023. 'Feminist peace and security governance and the UN Security Council'. In *Handbook of Feminist Governance*, ed. by Marian Sawer, Lee Ann Banaszak, Jacqui True, and Johanna Kantola. Cheltenham: Edwin Elgar, 238–249.
76 Scheyer and Kumskova 2023, p. 245.
77 Basu 2016, pp. 366–367.
78 Heidi Hudson, 2017. 'The power of mixed messages: Women, peace, and security language in national action plans from Africa.' *Africa Spectrum* 3: 3–29.
79 Camille Boutron, 2018. 'The international gender nomenclature of peace politics and women's participation in the Colombia peace process'. *Journal of Peacebuilding & Development* 13 (2): 116–121.
80 Sara Rose Taylor, 2020. 'UN Women's feminist engagement with governance by indicators in the Millennium and Sustainable development goals'. *Global Social Policy* 20 (3): 352–366.
81 Andrea den Boer and Kristen Haack, 2023. 'UN Women: A case of feminist global governance'. In *Handbook of Feminist Governance.* In *Handbook of Feminist Governance*, ed. by Marian Sawer, Lee Ann Banaszak, Jacqui True, and Johanna Kantola. Cheltenham: Edwin Elgar, 286–298.
82 Den Boer and Haack 2023.
83 Den Boer and Haack 2023.
84 Taylor 2020.
85 Sen 2019; Taylor 2020.
86 Sen 2019.
87 Sen 2019, p. 34.
88 Taylor 2020.
89 Elise Dietrichson and Fatima Sator, 2022. 'The Latin American women: How they shaped the UN charter and why Southern agency is forgotten'. In *Women and the UN: A New History of Women's International Human Rights*, ed. by Rebecca Adami and Dan Plesch. New York: Routledge, 17–38, at pp. 30–31.
90 Levenstein 2020, p. 117.
91 Taylor 2020, p. 357.

Notes to Chapter 3

1 BBC, 2008. 'Saudi women make video protest'. BBC News, 11 March, http://news.bbc.co.uk/1/hi/world/middle_east/7159077.stm.
2 BBC 2008.
3 BBC 2008.
4 Manal Al-Sharif, 2017b. *Daring to Drive.* New York: Simon & Schuster.
5 Inmaculada Macias-Alonso, HaRyung Kim, and Alessandra L. González. 2023. 'Self-driven women: Gendered mobility, employment, and the lift of the driving ban in Saudi Arabia'. *Gender, Place, and Culture* 30 (11): 1574–1593.
6 Macias-Alonso et al. 2023, p. 1587.

7 Matt McGarry, 2019. 'The journey to nowhere: Little hope for Saudi women since driving ban was lifted'. ABC News, 25 June. https://abcnews.go.com/International/journey-hope-saudi-women-driving-ban-lifted/story?id=63667888.

8 Associated Press, 2018. 'Saudi Arabia tortured female right-to-drive activists, says Amnesty'. *Guardian*, 20 November. https://www.theguardian.com/world/2018/nov/21/saudi-arabia-tortured-female-right-to-drive-activists-says-amnesty#maincontent.

9 Elin Bjarnegård and Pär Zetterberg, 2022. 'How autocrats weaponize women's rights'. *Journal of Democracy* 33 (2): 60–75.

10 IPU, 2020. 'Women in parliament, 1945–2018'. Inter-Parliamentary Union. https://data.ipu.org/dataset/percentage-of-women-in-parliament-between-1945-2018.

11 Nanako Tamaru and Marie O'Reilly, 2018. 'How women influence constitution-making after conflict and unrest' (research report). Inclusive Security. https://www.inclusivesecurity.org/wp-content/uploads/2018/02/How-Women-Influence-Constitution-Making.pdf.

12 IPU 2020.

13 UN Women, 2018. 'Revisiting Rwanda five years after record-breaking parliamentary elections'. 13 August. https://www.unwomen.org/en/news/stories/2018/8/feature-rwanda-women-in-parliament.

14 IPU, 2025c. 'Ranking as of 1 July 2025'. Inter-Parliamentary Union. https://data.ipu.org/women-ranking/?date_year=2025&date_month=07.

15 Jennie Burnet, 2012. 'Women's Empowerment and Cultural Change in Rwanda'. In *The Impact of Gender Quotas*, ed. by Susan Franceschet, Mona Lena Krook, and Jennifer M. Piscopo. New York: Oxford University Press, 190–207 at p. 193.

16 Burnet 2012.

17 Bjarnegård and Zetterberg 2022.

18 Reporters without Borders, 2024. 'Rwanda: RSF sounds the alarm on President Kagame's horrific press freedom record as election looms'. RSF, 10 July. https://rsf.org/en/rwanda-rsf-sounds-alarm-president-kagame-s-horrific-press-freedom-record-election-looms.

19 Lisa Baldez, 2010. 'The gender lacuna in comparative politics'. *Perspectives on Politics* 8 (1): 199–205.

20 Sheila Bunwaree, 2025. *Advancing Women in Politics in the Republic of Mauritius*, p. 27. Mauritius: Gender Links. https://www.genderlinks.org.za/uploads/files/Mauritius-Research-Women-in-Politics.pdf.

21 Aili Mari Tripp, 2016. 'Women's movements and constitution making after civil unrest and conflict in Africa: The cases of Kenya and Somalia'. *Politics & Gender* 12 (1): 78–106; Bunwaree, 2025.

22 Meredith Heagney, 2013. 'Justice Ruth Bader Ginsburg offers critique of *Roe v. Wade* during law school visit'. University of Chicago, 15 May. https://www.law.uchicago.edu/news/justice-ruth-bader-ginsburg-offers-critique-roe-v-wade-during-law-school-visit.

23 Melody Ellis Valdini, 2019. *The Inclusion Calculation: Why Men Appropriate Women's Representation.* New York: Oxford University Press.

24 Merike Blofield, Christina Ewig, and Jennifer M. Piscopo. 2017. 'The reactive left: Gender equality and the Latin American Pink Tide'. *Social Politics* 24 (4): 345–369.

25 Stéphanie Rousseau and Christina Ewig. 2017. 'Latin America's left-turn and the political empowerment of Indigenous women'. *Social Politics* 24 (4): 425–451.

26 Martin Chulov and Nadia al-Faour. 2017. '"This is a huge step for us": jubilation as Saudi women allowed to drive'. *Guardian*, 27 September. https://www.theguardian.com/world/2017/sep/27/huge-step-jubilation-saudi-arabian-women-allowed-to-drive.
27 Sharon Wolchik, 1992. 'Women and work in communist and post-communist Central and Eastern Europe'. In *Women's Work and Women's Lives: The Continuing Struggle Worldwide*, ed. by Hilda Kahne and Janet Z. Giele. Boulder, CO: Westview Press, 119–139.
28 Kristen Ghodsee, 2010. 'Revisiting the United Nations decade for women: Brief reflections on feminism, capitalism, and Cold War politics in the early years of the international women's movement'. *Women's Studies International Forum* 33: 3–12.
29 United Nations 1985, p. 9, paragraph 22.
30 Wolchik 1992.
31 Wolchik 1992.
32 France24, 2022. 'It's a man's world: no more women leaders in China's Communist Party'. France24 (news TV network), 24 October. https://www.france24.com/en/live-news/20221024-it-s-a-man-s-world-no-more-women-leaders-in-china-s-communist-party.
33 Wolchik 1992.
34 Tamaru and O'Reilly 2018.
35 Marius Mehrl, 2022. 'Female combatants and rebel group behaviour: Evidence form Nepal'. *Conflict Management and Peace Science* 403 (3): 268–280; Council on Foreign Relations, 2017. 'Women's participation in peace processes: Nepal'. CFR Interactives, 2 November. https://www.cfr.org/womens-participation-in-peace-processes/explore-the-data.
36 Alma Beltrán y Puga, 2022. 'The loving embrace: Women's legal mobilization in favor of a feminist constitution in Colombia in 1991'. *Women's History Review* 32 (3): 334–357.
37 Tamaru and O'Reilly 2018.
38 All the discussion of Nepal's constitutional process in this chapter comes from Tamaru and O'Reilly 2018, pp. 12–13.
39 Tripp 2016.
40 The Kenya narrative draws on Tripp 2016 and Tamaru and O'Reilly 2018.
41 Tamaru and O'Reilly 2018, p. 21.
42 The Tunisian narrative draws on Tamaru and O'Reilly 2018 and Rangita de Silva de Alwis, Anware Mnasri, and Estee Ward, 2017. 'Women and the making of the Tunisian constitution'. *Berkeley Journal of International Law* 35 (1): 90–149.
43 Government of Tunisia, 2024. 'Constitution of Tunisia', Article 21. https://www.constituteproject.org/constitution/Tunisia_2014.
44 Kamau Maichuhle, 2022. 'How equality push gained momentum in Kibaki's reign'. *Daily Nation*, 26 April. https://nation.africa/kenya/news/gender/how-equality-push-gained-momentum-in-kibaki-s-reign-3794716.
45 BBC, 2011. 'Kenya's cabinet rejects quota for female MPs'. BBC News, 19 August. https://www.bbc.co.uk/news/world-africa-14590598.

Notes to Chapter 4

1 IPU, n.d. '50 years of history at a glance'. Inter-Parliamentary Union. http://archive.ipu.org/wmn-e/history.htm.

2 IPU, 2025b. 'Women in parliament, 1995–2025'. Inter-Parliamentary Union. https://www.ipu.org/resources/publications/reports/2025-03/women-in-parliament-1995-2025.
3 Bjarnegård and Zetterberg 2022.
4 United Nations, 1979. *Convention on the Elimination of All Forms of Discrimination against Women*. New York: United Nations. https://www.ohchr.org/en/instruments-mechanisms/instruments/convention-elimination-all-forms-discrimination-against-women.
5 United Nations 1979.
6 United Nations 1995, paragraph 190a.
7 The Costa Rica narrative draws from: Michelle Saint-Germain and Martha I. Morgan, 1991. 'Equality: Costa Rican women demand "the real thing".' *Women & Politics* 11 (3): 23–75.
8 Saint-Germain and Morgan 1991, p. 39.
9 Melanie M. Hughes, Pamela Paxton, Amanda Clayton, and Pär Zetterberg, 2017. 'Quota adoption and reform over time (QAROT), 1947–2015'. Ann Arbor, MI: Inter-University Consortium for Political and Social Research (distributor). https://doi.org/10.3886/E100918V1.
10 Melanie M. Hughes, Pamela Paxton, Amanda Clayton, and Pär Zetterberg. 2019. 'Global gender quota adoption, implementation, and reform'. *Comparative Politics* 51 (2): 219–238.
11 Hughes et al. 2019, pp. 227–229.
12 IPU, 2018. 'Women in parliament: 1945–2018'. Inter-Parliamentary Union. https://data.ipu.org/dataset/percentage-of-women-in-parliament-between-1945-2018.
13 Lisa Baldez, 2004. 'Elected bodies: The gender quota law for legislative candidates in Mexico'. *Legislative Studies Quarterly* 29 (2): 231–258.
14 Petra Meier, 2012. 'From laggard to leader: Explaining the Belgian gender quotas and parity clause'. *West European Politics* 35 (2): 396–379.
15 Malu C. Gatto, 2025. *Resistance to Gender Quotas in Latin America*. New York: Oxford University Press.
16 Hughes et al. 2019.
17 Research interview conducted by the author with a senator from Mexico (15 May 2015, Mexico City).
18 The China narrative draws on Xinhui Jiang and Yunyun Zhou, 2025. 'When socialist legacy meets international norms: Gender quota adoption and institutional change in China'. *Journal of Contemporary China* 34 (151): 161–180.
19 Jiang and Zhou 2025, p. 161.
20 The Morocco narrative draws from: James Sater, 2012. 'Reserved seats, patriarchy, and patronage in Morocco'. In *The Impact of Gender Quotas*, ed. by Susan Franceschet, Mona Lena Krook, and Jennifer M. Piscopo. New York: Oxford University Press, 75–86; Delana Sobhani, 2021. 'Gender quotas and women's political representation: Lessons from Morocco'. Georgetown Institute for Women, Peace, and Security, 21 July. https://giwps.georgetown.edu/2021/07/21/gender-quotas-and-womens-political-representation-lessons-from-morocco.
21 Malu Gatto, Teresa Sacchet, Victor Tadeu de Oliveira, and Kristin Wylie provided information on Brazil.

22 Ki-Young Shin and Soo Hyun Kwon, 2023. '"Above all, it will boil down to money problems": The impact of gender-targeted public financing on political parties and women candidates in South Korea'. *International Political Science Review* 44 (1): 91–106.
23 Magnus Ohman, 2018. 'Gender-targeted public funding for political parties'. International Institute for Democracy and Electoral Assistance (IDEA). https://www.idea.int/sites/default/files/publications/gender-targeted-public-funding-for-political-parties.pdf. See esp. p. 50.
24 Danielle Kurtzleben, 2018a. 'If a parent's day job is running for Congress, can the campaign pay for child care?' NPR, 22 April. https://www.npr.org/2018/04/22/604339101/if-a-parents-day-job-is-running-for-congress-can-the-campaign-pay-for-child-care.
25 Danielle Kurtzleben, 2018b. 'FEC says that candidates can use campaign funds for childcare'. NPR, 10 May. https://www.npr.org/2018/05/10/610099506/fec-says-that-candidates-can-use-campaign-funds-for-child-care.
26 Sonia Palmieri and Lenita Freidenvall, 2024. 'Critical culture: The role of institutional norms in gender sensitizing parliaments'. In *Suffrage and Its Legacy in the Nordics and Beyond*, ed. by Josefina Erikson and Lenita Freidenvall. Cham: Palgrave, 221–245, at p. 223.
27 Stella Creasy, 2021. 'Here's why my baby was banned from parliament – and why we must all fight this'. *Guardian*, 25 November. https://www.theguardian.com/commentisfree/2021/nov/25/baby-banned-parliament-women-politics-stella-creasy.
28 Creasy 2021.
29 Palmieri and Freidenvall 2024, p. 233.
30 Christina Julios, 2022. 'Despite #MeToo, tackling sexual harassment of women in parliament remains a challenge'. *LSE British Politics and Policy* (blog), 6 April. https://blogs.lse.ac.uk/politicsandpolicy/metoo-parliament.
31 Juliana Restrepo Sanín, 2022. 'Criminalizing violence against women in politics: Innovation, diffusion, and transformation'. *Politics & Gender* 18 (1): 1–32.
32 Details on Canada, Australia, New Zealand, and the United Kingdom come from Marian Sawer, 2024. 'Her rights at work: Women in parliament'. In *Suffrage and Its Legacy in the Nordics and Beyond*, ed. by Josefina Erikson and Lenita Freidenvall. Cham: Palgrave, 181–198.
33 IPU, 2025a. 'Women's caucus'. Inter-Parliamentary Union. https://data.ipu.org/specialized-bodies/womens-caucus.
34 I am grateful to Jyldyz Abdyldaeva for information on the Central Asian cases.
35 Niki Johnson and Cecilia Josefsson, 2016. 'A new way of doing politics? Cross-party women's caucuses as critical actors in Uganda and Uruguay'. *Parliamentary Affairs* 69: 845–859.
36 Johnson and Josefsson 2016, p. 853.
37 USAID, 2023. 'Women's political participation and leadership final report: Kyrgyz Republic Assessment'. USAID and NORC, January. www.norc.org.
38 USAID 2023, p. 16.
39 USAID 2023, p. 17.
40 Own research, expanding from USAID 2023, p. 16.
41 Johnson and Josefsson 2016, p. 849.
42 Johnson and Josefsson 2016, p. 849.
43 United Nations 1995, paragraph 79.

44 United Nations, 1997. *Report of the Economic and Social Council for 1997*. New York: United Nations. Document A/52/3/Rev.1. https://digitallibrary.un.org/record/271316?ln=en&v=pdf.
45 Kelsi Caywood and Gary L. Darmstadt, 2024. 'Gender mainstreaming at 25 years: Toward an inclusive, collaborative, and structured research agenda'. *Journal of Global Health* 1 (4): 04011.
46 The Fiji narrative is based on Kerryn Baker and Sonia Palmieri, 2024. 'The power of norms: Gender equality reforms in the parliaments of Fiji and Samoa'. *Politics and Governance* 12: 8091.
47 Petra Ahrens and Silvia Erzeel, eds. 2024. *Beyond Numbers: Stories of Gender Equality in and through Parliaments*. Geneva: International Institute for Democracy and Electoral Assistance (IDEA), 10 October. https://www.idea.int/sites/default/files/2024-10/stories-of-gender-equality-in-parliaments.pdf. See esp. p. 18.
48 Italy and Chile examples from Ahrens and Erzeel 2024.
49 Jennifer M. Piscopo, Nancy L. Cohen, and Natalia Vega Varela. 2024. 'Roadmap for an equitable future: Placing a gender lens on American public policy'. Gender Equity Policy Institute and Royal Holloway, May. https://thegepi.org/GEPI-RHUL-Roadmap-for-an-equitable-future.pdf.
50 OECD, 2023. 'Gender budgeting in OECD Countries 2023'. Paris, OECD, July. https://www.oecd.org/content/dam/oecd/en/publications/reports/2023/07/gender-budgeting-in-oecd-countries-2023_d04134bb/647d546b-en.pdf.
51 Jennifer M. Piscopo, 2011. 'Do women represent women? Gender and policy in Argentina and Mexico'. PhD dissertation, University of California, San Diego.
52 The timeline here is drawn from p. 40 of UNDP, 2013. 'Parliaments and gender equality'. Panama, UNDP, April. https://www.undp.org/sites/g/files/zskgke326/files/publications/parliaments-and-gender-equality--gender-mainstreaming-in-legislatures.pdf.
53 Hawkesworth 2012, pp. 223–224.
54 United Nations 1995, paragraph 201.
55 S. Laurel Weldon, 2002. 'Beyond bodies: Institutional sources of representation for women in democratic policymaking'. *Journal of Politics* 64 (4): 1153–1174.
56 Moki Edwin Kindzeka, 2022. 'Cameroon women rally to demand more political representation'. Voice of America, 8 March. https://www.voanews.com/a/6475289.html.
57 Melissa Cheman, 2025. 'Nigeria: hundreds of Nigerian women protest in push for more female MPs'. AllAfrica.com, 26 September. https://allafrica.com/stories/202509250498.html.

Notes to Chapter 5

1 Ashoka.org, n.d. 'Casimira Rodríguez'. Ashoka: Innovators for the Public. https://www.ashoka.org/en-gb/fellow/casimira-rodr%C3%ADguez#accordion.
2 Ashoka.org, n.d.
3 Zoe Beaty, 2022. 'For one woman, defending the rights of garment workers is the fight of her life'. *British Vogue*, 8 March. https://www.vogue.co.uk/fashion/article/kalpona-akter-garment-workers-living-wages.
4 ActionAid.org. 2019. '80% of garment workers in Bangladesh have experienced or witnessed sexual violence and harassment at work'. ActionAid, 10 June. https://actionaid.

org/news/2019/80-garment-workers-bangladesh-have-experienced-or-witnessed-sexual-violence-and.

5 Sarah Stillman, 2013. 'Death traps: The Bangladesh garment factory disaster'. *New Yorker*, 1 May. https://www.newyorker.com/news/news-desk/death-traps-the-bangladesh-garment-factory-disaster; Amnesty International, 2024. 'The Rana Plaza collapse and Tazreen Fashions fire'. 4 June. https://www.amnesty.org/en/latest/campaigns/2024/06/the-rana-plaza-collapse-and-tazreen-fashions-fire-an-interview-with-taqbir-huda.

6 HR Dive, 2025. 'Salary history bans'. HR Dive, 30 April. https://www.hrdive.com/news/salary-history-ban-states-list/516662.

7 Stacy Cowley, 2016. 'Illegal in Massachusetts: Asking your salary in a job interview'. *New York Times*, 2 August. https://www.nytimes.com/2016/08/03/business/dealbook/wage-gap-massachusetts-law-salary-history.html.

8 Fawcett Society, 2021. 'The Fawcett Society calls on employers to stop asking salary history'. Fawcett Society, 18 November. https://www.fawcettsociety.org.uk/news/fawcett-society-calls-on-employers-to-stop-asking-salary-history.

9 International Labour Organization (ILO), n.d. 'Gender equality'. Geneva, ILO. https://libguides.ilo.org/gender-equality-en/standards.

10 International Labour Organization (ILO), 2023. 'Women and men in the informal economy: A statistical update', p. 15. Geneva, ILO. https://www.ilo.org/sites/default/files/wcmsp5/groups/public/%40ed_protect/%40protrav/%40travail/documents/publication/wcms_869188.pdf.

11 ILO 2023, p. 50.

12 Bina Agarwal, 1997. '"Bargaining" and gender relations: Within and beyond the household'. *Feminist Economics* 3 (1): 1–51.

13 Agarwal 1997, p. 11.

14 United Nations 1995, paragraph 51.

15 United Nations 1995, paragraph 162.

16 United Nations 1975, paragraph 16.

17 World Economic Forum, 2024. 'Global gender gap 2024: Insight report'. Geneva, World Economic Forum. https://www3.weforum.org/docs/WEF_GGGR_2024.pdf.

18 United Nations, 1991. *The World's Women: 1970–1990*, p. 58. New York: United Nations. https://unstats.un.org/unsd/demographic-social/products/worldswomen/documents/ww1990.pdf.

19 World Bank Gender Group, n.d. 'Sub-Saharan Africa'. https://genderdata.worldbank.org/en/regions/sub-saharan-africa.

20 United Nations 1991, p. 59.

21 World Bank Gender Group n.d.

22 World Economic Forum 2024.

23 World Bank Group, n.d. 'Europe & Central Asia'. World Bank Gender Data Portal. https://genderdata.worldbank.org/en/regions/europe-central-asia; World Bank Group, n.d. 'Latin America & Caribbean'. World Bank Gender Data Portal. https://genderdata.worldbank.org/en/regions/latin-america-caribbean.

24 The World Bank and UNICEF, 2009. *Abolishing School Fees in Africa: Lessons from Ethiopia, Ghana, Kenya, Malawi, and Mozambique.* Washington, DC: World Bank. https://www.right-to-education.org/sites/right-to-education.org/files/resource-attachments/UNICEF_WB_Abolishing_School_Fees_in_Africa_2009.pdf.

25 Equality Now, 2020. 'Court case filed against Tanzania to overturn ban on pregnant girls attending school', 19 November. https://equalitynow.org/press_release/tanzania_african_court_pregnant_schoolgirls_nov2020.
26 Human Rights Watch, 2025b. 'Tanzania: Protect right to education in pregnancy, parenthood', 23 January. https://www.hrw.org/news/2025/01/23/tanzania-protect-right-education-pregnancy-parenthood.
27 Human Rights Watch, 2021. 'Africa: Rights progress for pregnant students', 29 September, https://www.hrw.org/news/2021/09/29/africa-rights-progress-pregnant-students.
28 Government of Zimbabwe, 2020. 'Education amendment'. https://www.veritaszim.net/sites/veritas_d/files/EDUCATION%20AMENDMENT%20ACT,%202019%20[%20Act%2015-2019]_0.pdf.
29 Farai Shawn Matiashe, 2020. 'Zimbabwe makes it illegal for schools to expel pregnant girls'. Reuters, 25 August. https://www.reuters.com/article/world/zimbabwe-makes-it-illegal-for-schools-to-expel-pregnant-girls-idUSKBN25L1UT.
30 UNESCO, 2020. *A New Generation: 25 Years of Efforts for Gender Equality in Education*. Paris: UNESCO. https://gem-report-2020.unesco.org/gender-report/laws-and-policies-promoting-gender-equality-in-education-are-inadequately-implemented.
31 Alanna Vagianos, 2019. '14-Year-old Kenyan girl dies by suicide after teacher allegedly period-shamed her'. *Huffington Post*, 13 September. https://www.huffingtonpost.co.uk/entry/14-year-old-kenyan-girl-dies-by-suicide-after-teacher-allegedly-period-shamed-her_n_5d7bb47be4b03b5fc88285e7.
32 Kirsty Strickland, 2020. 'Ending period poverty has made Scotland a better place to global applause'. *Scotsman*, 29 November, https://www.scotsman.com/news/opinion/columnists/ending-period-poverty-has-made-scotland-a-better-place-to-global-applause-kirsty-strickland-3050486.
33 Strickland 2020.
34 Tània Verge, 2021. 'Gender equality policy and universities: Feminist strategic alliances to re-gender the curriculum'. *Journal of Women, Politics, and Policy* 42 (3): 191–206.
35 Olena Mykhalchenko and Isabel Santagostino Recavarren, 2021. 'In 38 countries, women can still be fired for being pregnant'. World Bank Blogs, 13 May. https://blogs.worldbank.org/en/developmenttalk/38-countries-women-can-still-be-fired-being-pregnant.
36 Mykalchenko and Santagostino Recavarren 2021.
37 United Nations 1975, pp. 23–24.
38 United Nations 1995, paragraph 29.
39 United Nations 1995, paragraph 165.
40 Maddy Savage, 2024. 'Sweden: Where it's taboo for dads to skip parental leave'. BBC, 1 February. https://www.bbc.co.uk/worklife/article/20240130-sweden-where-its-taboo-for-dads-to-skip-parental-leave.
41 Jeremy Shiffman, Marina Skrabalo, and Jelena Subotic, 2002. 'Reproductive rights and the state in Serbia and Croatia'. *Social Science and Medicine* 54 (4): 625–642; Ivana Dobrotić, 2018. 'Ambivalent character of leave policies development in Croatia: Between pronatalist and gender equality agenda'. *Revista del Ministerio de Empleo y Seguridad Social* 136: 107–126. https://ora.ox.ac.uk/objects/uuid:c27b4477-999f-47e3-825a-cd2fa8ce80db/files/s5t34sj96p.
42 Siegel 2020, pp. 216–225.

43 World Alliance for Breastfeeding Action, n.d. 'ILO / Maternity Protection (MP) campaign'. https://waba.org.my/whatwedo/womenandwork/ilompcampaign.htm.
44 Keonhi Son, 2022. "Do international treaties have an impact only on ratifying States? The influence of the ILO Maternity Protection Conventions in 160 countries between 1883 and 2018'. *International Labour Review* 162 (2): 245–269.
45 IndustriALL, 2016. 'World day for decent work: Women mobilize for maternity protection', 10 October. https://www.industriall-union.org/world-day-for-decent-work-women-mobilize-for-maternity-protection.
46 IndustriALL 2016.
47 IndustriALL, 2018. 'Victory as the Philippines passes expanded maternity leave law', 2 October, https://www.industriall-union.org/victory-in-the-philippines-as-expanded-maternity-leave-law-passed.
48 Industrial Relations and Labour Law, 2024. 'Indonesia: Law on the maternal and child welfare in the first thousand days of life adopted'. IndustriALL (newsletter), November. https://industrialrelationsnews.ioe-emp.org/industrial-relations-and-labour-law-september-2024/news-1/article/indonesia-law-on-the-maternal-and-child-welfare-in-the-first-thousand-days-of-life-adopted.
49 Florence Bonnet, Françoise Carré, Martha Alter Chen, and Joan Vanek, 2021. 'Home-based workers in the world: A statistical profile'. WIEGO. https://www.wiego.org/wp-content/uploads/2021/02/WIEGO_Statistical_Brief_N27_HBW_Global.pdf.
50 Marlese von Broembsen, 2020. 'Inside India's "T-shirt factory of the world"'. *WIEGO Blog*, 21 April. https://www.wiego.org/blog/worlds-most-vulnerable-garment-workers-arent-factories-and-global-brands-need-step-protect.
51 Bhatt, Ela, 2006. *We Are Poor but So Many: The Story of Self-Employed Women in India*. Oxford: Oxford University Press, 17–18.
52 Webster, Edward, 2011. 'Organizing in the informal economy: Ela Bhatt and the Self-Employed Women's Association of India'. *LABOUR, Capital and Society* 44 (1): 99–125.
53 WIEGO, 2019. *Celebrating Marty Chen*. Manchester: WIEGO. https://www.wiego.org/wp-content/uploads/2019/09/Celebrating-Marty-Chen.pdf.
54 Sinha, Shalini, 2016. 'Remembering a postcard from Geneva and reaffirming a campaign'. WIEGO blog, 17 June, https://www.wiego.org/blog/commemorating-20-years-landmark-convention-homeworkers.
55 WIEGO, n.d. 'Our history'. https://www.wiego.org/history.
56 Zehra Khan and Krithika Dinesh, 2022. 'The journey from "factories in homes" to legal recognition and rights for home-based workers in Pakistan'. WIEGO. https://www.wiego.org/wp-content/uploads/2023/02/wiego-organizing-law-brief-No-13.pdf.
57 Khan and Dinesh 2022.
58 The Bolivia narrative relies on two sources: Pablo Castaño, 2018a. 'Laws, legitimacy, and ongoing struggle: Lessons from Bolivian policies on domestic workers' rights'. WIEGO. https://www.wiego.org/wp-content/uploads/2019/09/Castano_Tierno-Bolovian-Policies-Domestic-Workers-Rights-WIEGO-PB17.pdf; and Pablo Castaño, 2018b. 'The mobilization of Bolivian domestic workers'. WIEGO. https://www.wiego.org/wp-content/uploads/2019/09/Castano_Mobilization_Bolivian_Domestic_Workers_WIEGO_OB10.pdf.

59 Castaño, 2018b, p. 5
60 IOL, 2003. 'A new deal for domestic workers'. IOL (news agency), 24 May. https://iol.co.za/business-report/companies/2003-05-24-a-new-deal-for-domestic-workers.
61 IOL, 2003.
62 Alan Cowell, 2023. 'Myrtle Witbooi, who fought for domestic workers' rights, dies at 75'. *New York Times*, 25 January. https://www.nytimes.com/2023/01/25/world/africa/myrtle-witbooi-dead.html.
63 For the history of C189, I have drawn on Celia Mather, 2013. *'Yes, We Did It!' How the World's Domestic Workers Won Their International Rights and Recognition*. Manchester: WIEGO. https://www.wiego.org/wp-content/uploads/2019/09/Mather_Yes%20we%20did%20it!_2013.pdf.
64 International Domestic Workers Federation, n.d. 'Our history' (web page). https://idwfed.org/about-us.
65 International Labour Organization (ILO), 2011. 'C189: Domestic Workers Convention, 2011 (No. 189)'. Geneva, ILO. https://normlex.ilo.org/dyn/nrmlx_en/f?p=NORMLEXPUB:12100:0::NO::P12100_INSTRUMENT_ID%2CP12100_LANG_CODE:2551460%2Cen
66 International Labour Organization (ILO), 2013. 'Snapshot: ILO in action: Domestic workers'. Geneva, ILO. https://www.ilo.org/sites/default/files/wcmsp5/groups/public/%40ed_protect/%40protrav/%40travail/documents/publication/wcms_214499.pdf.
67 Mather 2013, p. 70.
68 Mather 2013. p. 84.
69 Mather 2013, p. 70.

Notes to Chapter 6

1 Joseph E. Gagnon, Steven B. Kamin, and John Kearns, 2023. 'The impact of the COVID-19 pandemic on global GDP Growth'. *Journal of Japanese and International Economies* 68: 101258.
2 Calculations based on 'time use' from the OECD Data Explorer (DSD_TIME_USE@F_TIME_USE) at https://data-explorer.oecd.org/vis.
3 UN Women, 2020. *Whose Time to Care? Unpaid Care and Domestic Work during COVID-19*. New York: UN Women. https://data.unwomen.org/sites/default/files/inline-files/Whose-time-to-care-brief_0.pdf.
4 Musawah, 2020. *Survey Findings on the Impacts of the COVID-19 Pandemic on Women Living under Discriminatory Muslim Family Laws*. Kuala Lumpur: Musawah. https://www.musawah.org/wp-content/uploads/2021/01/Musawah-Survey-Findings-on-Impacts-of-COVID-19-brief-1.pdf.
5 Alex R. Piguero, Wesley G. Jennings, Erin Jemison, Catherine Kaukinen, and Felicia Marie Knaul, 2021. 'Domestic violence during the COVID-19 pandemic: Evidence from a systematic review and meta-analysis'. *Journal of Criminal Justice* 74: 101806.
6 Gender and Public Health Emergencies, 2025. 'Gender and COVID-19 Project'. https://genderandcovid-19.org/project-page. Since 2021, Jennifer Piscopo has joined the Gender and COVID-19 Project's steering group – the group that organized the conference and contributed to the manifesto.
7 At the time, this code governed West Germany; communist East Germany had a different family code.

8 Levenstein 2020, pp. 102–103.
9 United Nations 1979, Article 16.
10 Htun and Weldon 2018, p. 121.
11 Htun and Weldon 2018, p. 121.
12 Htun and Weldon, 2018, p. 122.
13 Musawah, 2019. *Comparative Legal Review.* Kuala Lumpur: Musawah, https://www.musawah.org/wp-content/uploads/2019/12/Comparative-Legal-Review-Impact-Muslim-Family-Laws-on-Women-Commonwealth-Asia-Africa.pdf.
14 Rachel Rinaldo, 2013. *Mobilizing Piety: Islam and Feminism in Indonesia.* New York: Cambridge University Press, 108–109.
15 Rinaldo, 2013, p. 143.
16 Rinaldo, 2013, pp. 98–99.
17 Rinaldo 2013, pp. 109 and 143.
18 Rinaldo 2013, pp. 143–145.
19 Africa Union, 2003. *Protocol to the African Charter on Human and Peoples' Rights on the Rights of Women in Africa.* https://au.int/en/treaties/protocol-african-charter-human-and-peoples-rights-rights-women-africa.
20 African Union 2003, Article II.
21 Htun and Weldon 2018, p. 122.
22 The Moroccan account derives from three sources: Center for Public Impact, 2016. 'Reforming Moroccan family law: The Moudawana' (web page), 2 May. https://centreforpublicimpact.org/public-impact-fundamentals/reforming-moroccan-family-law-the-moudawana; Alex Frye, 2011. 'Moroccan feminist groups campaign to reform Moudawana, 1992–2004'. Global Nonviolent Action Database, 15 May. https://nvdatabase.swarthmore.edu/content/moroccan-feminist-groups-campaign-reform-moudawana-personal-status-codeislamic-family-law-19; and Leila Hanafi, 2012. 'Moudawana and women's rights in Morocco: Balancing national and international law'. *ILSA Journal of International & Comparative Law* 18 (2): 515–529.
23 Frye 2011.
24 Hanafi 2012, p. 15.
25 Natalie Triche, 2025. 'What Morocco's family law reform process shows about governance in the Kingdom'. Carnegie Endowment, 28 July. https://carnegieendowment.org/posts/2025/07/morocco-family-law-moudawana-reform-governance?lang=en.
26 Freedom House, 2010. 'Women's rights in the Middle East and North Africa 2010 – Jordan', 3 March. https://www.refworld.org/reference/countryrep/freehou/2010/en/72322.
27 Edouard Al-Dahdah, Cristina Corduneanu-Huci, Gael Raballand, Ernest Sergenti, and Myriam Ababsa, 2016. *Rules on Paper, Rules in Practice: Enforcing Laws and Policies in the Middle East and North Africa.* Washington, DC: World Bank Group, p. 94.
28 Musawah, n.d. 'Global repository of Muslim family laws: Jordan' (web page). https://campaignforjustice.musawah.org/repository/jordan; *Jordan Times*, 2019. 'Parliament ends dispute by rejecting raising marriage age to 16'. *Jordan Times*, 9 April. https://jordantimes.com/news/local/parliament-ends-dispute-rejecting-raising-marriage-age-16#:~:text=The%202010%20temporary%20PSL%20allowed,related%20to%20marriage%20and%20divorce.

29 Equality Now et al., 2017. Letter to the secretary of the Human Rights Committee, 6 January. UN Human Rights Committee Archives, Geneva, Switzerland.
30 Global Campaign for Equal Nationality Rights, n.d. 'The problem'. https://www.equalnationalityrights.org/the-problem.
31 Kay C. Lee, 1995. 'Confucian ethics, judges, and women: Divorce under the revised Korean Family Law'. *Pacific Rim Law and Policy Journal* 4 (2): 479–503, at p. 480.
32 Lee 1995.
33 Mary Hallward-Driemeier and Ousman Gajigo, 2013. 'Strengthening economic rights and women's occupational choice: The impact of reforming Ethiopia's family law'. World Bank Policy Research Working Paper 6695.
34 Soledad Prillaman Artiz kindly fact-checked this paragraph for me.
35 Minali Grover and Ajay Sharma, 2025. 'Women's inheritance rights reforms and impact on women's empowerment: Evidence from India'. *Review of Economics of the Household*, published online 15 January. https://link.springer.com/article/10.1007/s11150-025-09784-3.
36 Louise Toupin, 2018. *The History of Wages for Housework*. London: Pluto.
37 Pluto Press, n.d. '*The History of Wages for Housework*, by Louise Toupin'. Pluto Press (blog). https://www.plutobooks.com/blog/wages-housework-campaign-history.
38 Pluto Press n.d.
39 Toupin 2018, pp. 146–147.
40 Emily Callaci, 2022. 'Care work in a wageless world'. *The Boston Review*, 2 March. https://www.bostonreview.net/articles/selma-james-care-work; Toupin 2018, pp. 146–147.
41 Toupin 2018, p. 146.
42 Callaci 2022.
43 Yvonne Mahelona, Tamera Heine, Khara Jabola-Carolus, and Amanda Shaw. 2020. 'The story and sisterhood behind the world's first feminist economic recovery plan for COVID-19'. In *The Value of Hawai'i*, ed. by Noelani Goodyear-Ka'opua, Craig Howes, Jonathan Kay Kamakawiwo'ole Osorio, and Aiko Yamashiro. Honolulu: University of Hawai'i Press, pp. 223–226.
44 Hawai'i State Commission on the Status of Women, 2020. 'Building bridges not walking on backs: A feminist economic recovery plan for COVID-19'. April. https://humanservices.hawaii.gov/wp-content/uploads/2020/04/4.13.20-Final-Cover-D2-Feminist-Economic-Recovery-D1.pdf.
45 Feminists Deliver, 2020. '"This economic labour hurts the arch of our backs": A feminist economic recovery plan from COVID-19'. July. https://feministsdeliver.com/wp-content/uploads/2020/07/FINAL-Report-cover-Feminists-Deliver-Feminists-Recovery-Plan-merged-compressed.pdf.
46 Corinna Dengler, 2024. 'Rereading the Wages for Housework campaign: Feminist degrowth reflections on social reproduction, commons, and a care income'. *Hypatia* 39 (3): 538–557.
47 Dengler 2024.
48 Laura Pautassi, Pilar Arcidiácono and Mona Straschnoy, 2014. 'Conditioning care: Universal assignation for social protection by child in Argentina'. *Íconos: Revista de Ciencias Sociales* 50: 61–75.

49 EuroCarers.Org, n.d. 'Ireland' (web page). https://eurocarers.org/country-profiles/ireland.
50 This is according to the European bank Wise (see https://wise.com/gb/blog/cost-of-living-in-ireland).
51 OECD, 2019. *Enabling Women's Economic Empowerment: New Approaches to Unpaid Care Work in Developing Countries.* Paris: OECD.
52 Soledad Salvador, 2019. 'El sistema nacional integrado de cuidados en Uruguay: Una oportunidad para el empoderamiento económico de las mujeres'. ONU Mujeres. https://lac.unwomen.org/sites/default/files/Field%20Office%20Americas/Documentos/Publicaciones/2019/10/SNIC%20DIGITAL%20BAJA.pdf.
53 OECD 2019.
54 United Nations 1980, paragraph 95.
55 United Nations 1985, paragraph 120.
56 Republic of Bolivia, 2009. 'Constitution of 2009'. https://pdba.georgetown.edu/Constitutions/Bolivia/bolivia09.html.
57 Interview conducted by the author with a former Colombian legislator in April 2025.
58 Action Aid Bangladesh, 2025. 'Counting the invisible: Why recognising women's unpaid work is a game-changer for Bangladesh', 5 June. https://actionaidbd.org/post/media-coverage/counting-invisible-why-recognising-womens-unpaid-work-game-changer.
59 Action Aid Bangladesh 2025.
60 Manusher Jonmo Foundation, n.d. 'Campaign & advocacy' (web page). https://www.manusherjonno.org/what_we_do/campaign-advocacy.
61 Action Aid Bangladesh 2025.
62 Nilima Jahan, 2025. 'Women's unpaid work to finally get recognized'. *Daily Star*, 3 June. https://www.thedailystar.net/business/bangladesh-budget-2025-26/news/womens-unpaid-work-finally-get-recognised-3909471.
63 Dengler 2024.
64 Manuela Zechner, 2022. 'Childcare commons: Of feminist subversions of community and commune in Barcelona'. *Ephemera: Theory and Politics in Organization* 22 (2): 19–49.
65 UN Women, 2021. *Beyond COVID-19: A Feminist Plan for Sustainability and Social Justice.* New York: UN Women. https://www.unwomen.org/en/digital-library/publications/2021/09/beyond-covid-19-a-feminist-plan-for-sustainability-and-social-justice.
66 UN Women 2021, p. 12.
67 United Nations, 2024. *Transforming Care Systems in the Context of the Sustainable Development Goals and Our Common Agenda.* New York: United Nations. https://unsdg.un.org/sites/default/files/2024-07/FINAL_UN%20System%20Care%20Policy%20Paper_24June2024.pdf.
68 United Nations 2024, p. 3.
69 Rosario Aguirre, Karina Batthyány, Natalia Genta, and Valentina Perrotta, 2014. 'Los cuidados en la agenda de investigación y en las políticas públicas en Uruguay'. *Íconos* 50: 43–60.
70 Rosario Aguirre Cuns, 2014. 'La política de cuidados en Uruguay: ¿Un avance para la igualdad de género? *Revista Estudios Feminista* 22 (3): 795–813.
71 Aguirre et al. 2014.
72 Ana Laura Cafaro Mango, 2019. 'El sistema nacional integrado de Cuidados en Uruguay: ¿Accesso equitativo para la ciudadanía en tanto derecho universal?' *CUHSO: Cultural-Hombre-Sociedad* 10 (2): 295–314.

73 Real Reform for Early Childhood Development (ECD) in South Africa, n.d. Website. https://www.ecdreform.org.za.
74 Real Reform . . . in South Africa n.d.
75 Ilifa Labantwana, 2025. 'Budget 2025: The first step towards a children's budget'. 13 March, https://ilifalabantwana.co.za/budget-2025-the-first-step-towards-a-childrens-budget.
76 Ilifa Labantwana 2025.
77 Department of Finance Canada, 2020. *Supporting Canadians and Fighting Covid-19: Fall Economic Statement*, p. 76. Department of Finance Canada. https://www.budget.canada.ca/fes-eea/2020/report-rapport/FES-EEA-eng.pdf.
78 Government of Canada, 2021. *A Recovery Plan for Jobs, Growth, and Resilience: Budget 2021*, p. 19. Government of Canada, April 19. https://www.budget.canada.ca/2021/home-accueil-en.html.
79 Selma James, 1975. 'Wageless of the world'. In *All Work and No Pay*, ed. by Wendy Edmond and Suzie Fleming, 25–34. Bristol: Falling Wall Press.

Notes to Chapter 7

1 This paragraph relies on two articles: Harriet Sherwood, 2018. '"Remember Savita': Father's plea for voters to end Ireland's abortion ban'. *Guardian*, 23 May. https://www.theguardian.com/world/2018/may/23/ireland-abortion-referendum-savita-father-galway; and Jon Henley, 2018. 'What you need to know: The Irish abortion referendum explained'. *Guardian*, 25 May. https://www.theguardian.com/world/2018/may/25/irish-abortion-referendum-explained-what-you-need-to-know.
2 Government of Ireland, 1983. 'Eighth Amendment of the Constitution Act, 1983'. Irish Statute Book. https://www.irishstatutebook.ie/eli/1983/ca/8/enacted/en/print.html.
3 Henry McDonald, 2016. 'Ireland compensates woman forced to travel to Britain for an abortion'. *Guardian*, 30 November. https://www.theguardian.com/world/2016/nov/30/ireland-compensates-abortion-amanda-mellet-britain.
4 Henley 2018.
5 Karen Hand, 2023. 'Together, they say yes'. New Economics Foundation, 13 February. https://neweconomics.org/2023/02/together-they-say-yes.
6 BBC, 2018. 'Irish abortion referendum: Ireland overturns abortion ban'. BBC News, 26 May. https://www.bbc.co.uk/news/world-europe-44256152.
7 Henley 2018.
8 Central Statistics Office, 2016. 'Census of Population 2016 Profile 8 Irish Travellers, Ethnicity, and Religion'. https://www.cso.ie/en/releasesandpublications/ep/p-cp8iter/p8iter/p8rrc.
9 BBC, 2018. 'Irish abortion referendum: The people travelling #HomeToVote'. BBC News, 26 May. https://www.bbc.co.uk/news/world-europe-44223949.
10 BBC 2018.
11 This paragraph draws on the following article: Véronica Pérez-Betancur, Jennifer M. Piscopo, and Cecilia Rocha-Carpuic, 2025. 'Adoption and implementation as a two-stage process: Feminist strategies and conservative resistance in the quest for legislative abortion reform'. *Perspectives on Politics*, 1–21. doi:10.1017/S1537592725102284.
12 Samantha Schmidt, 2022. 'How green became the color of abortion rights'. *Washington Post*, 3 July. https://www.washingtonpost.com/world/interactive/2022/abortion-green-roe-wade-argentina.

13 Katy Mayall, Laurene Ajayi, and Caitlin Gruer, 2025. 'Global progress in abortion law reform: A comparative legal analysis since the International Conference on Population and Development (1994–2023)'. *Reproductive Health Matters* 33 (1). https://doi.org/10.1080/26410397.2025.2499324.
14 Pérez-Betancur et al. 2025.
15 Pérez-Betancur et al. 2025.
16 National Abortion Federation, 2024. 'NAF 2024 Violence & Disruption Report'. https://nationalabortionfederation.org/safety-security/2024-naf-violence-disruption/#:~:text=The%20National%20Abortion%20Federation's%202023,abortion%20care%20in%20many%20regions.
17 Joshua D. Kertzer, Dara Kay Cohen, Dorothy Manevich, and Thomas Zeitzof, 2024. '"If abortions aren't safe, neither are you": Public support for violent tactics in US abortion politics'. Working paper, Harvard Kennedy School. https://jkertzer.sites.fas.harvard.edu/Research_files/Abortion-KCMZ.pdf.
18 Amnesty International, 2023. 'An unstoppable movement: A global call to recognize and protect those who defend the right to abortion', 24 November. https://www./amnesty./org/en/documents/pol40/7420/2023/en.
19 Meg Tirrell, 2024. 'The origins of Trump's false claim that Democrats want to allow "execution" of babies after birth'. CNN, 12 September. https://edition.cnn.com/2024/09/12/health/trump-abortion-after-birth; Matt Lavietes, 2024. 'Trump repeats false claims that children are undergoing transgender surgery during the school day'. NBC News, 9 September. https://www.nbcnews.com/nbc-out/out-politics-and-policy/trump-false-claims-schools-transgender-surgeries-rcna170217.
20 Amy J. Higer, 1999. 'International women's activism and the 1994 Cairo Population Conference'. In *Gender Politics and Global Governance*, ed. by Mary K. Meyer and Elisabeth Prugl. New York: Rowman and Littlefield, 131–150.
21 World Health Organization, 2014. 'Eliminating forced, coercive, and otherwise involuntary sterilization: An interagency statement'. WHO. https://www.unaids.org/sites/default/files/media_asset/201405_sterilization_en.pdf.
22 United Nations 1975, p. 28.
23 United Nations 1975, p. 81.
24 United Nations 1975, p. 58.
25 United Nations 1985, paragraph 156.
26 United Nations 1985, paragraph 157.
27 C. Allison McIntosh and Jason L. Finkle, 1995. 'The Cairo Conference on Population and Development: A new paradigm?' *Population and Development Review* 21 (2): 223–260.
28 Higer 1999, p. 131.
29 Higer 1999.
30 Higer 1999.
31 This paragraph draws from Higer 1999.
32 UNFPA 1994, paragraph 7.24.
33 Susan A. Cohen and Cory L. Richards, 1994. 'The Cairo consensus: Population, development, and women'. *Family Planning Perspectives* 26 (6): 272–277.
34 McIntosh and Finkle 1995, p. 224.
35 United Nations 1995, paragraph 94.

36 United Nations 1995, paragraph 95.
37 United Nations 1995, paragraph 106k.
38 Dunlop et al. 1996; Levenstein 2020.
39 UN Committee on Economic, Social, and Cultural Rights. 2016. 'General Comment No. 22'. United Nations Digital Library, https://digitallibrary.un.org/record/832961?ln=en&v=pdf.
40 African Union 2003.
41 Economic Commission on Latin America and the Caribbean, 2013. 'Montevideo Consensus on Population and Development'. Santiago. https://repositorio.cepal.org/server/api/core/bitstreams/7b0a9e22-002a-49ec-966e-796a24d468ca/content, at p. 13.
42 UNFPA, n.d. 'About us'. https://www.unfpa.org/about-us#transformative-results.
43 UNFPA n.d.
44 UNFPA, 2023. *Performance Measurement Framework: 2023 Results Report*. New York: UNFPA. https://www.unfpa.org/sites/default/files/resource-pdf/UNFPA%20Supplies%20Performance%20Measurement%20Report%202023_WEB.pdf.
45 UNFPA 2023, p. 9.
46 UNFPA, 2022. *SWEDD: Annual Report 2022*. New York: UNFPA. https://wcaro.unfpa.org/sites/default/files/pub-pdf/en-swedd-annual_report_2022.pdf.
47 UNFPA 2023, pp. 105–108.
48 UNFPA 2023, p. 108.
49 UK Health Security Agency. 2021. 'Understanding disparities in reproductive health'. 9 July, https://ukhsa.blog.gov.uk/2021/07/09/understanding-disparities-in-reproductive-health.
50 The Argentine narrative derives from Jennifer M. Piscopo, 2014. 'Female leadership and sexual health policy in Argentina'. *Latin American Research Review* 49 (1): 104–127.
51 UNESCO, 2023. 'On the journey towards comprehensive sexuality education with 50 new country profiles'. *World Education Blog*, 15 February. https://world-education-blog.org/2023/02/15/on-the-journey-towards-comprehensive-sexuality-education-with-50-new-country-profiles.
52 Mayall et al. 2025.
53 Mayall et al. 2025.
54 Pérez-Betancur et al. 2025.
55 Pérez-Betancur et al. 2025.
56 This paragraph draws on Pérez-Betancur et al. 2025.
57 Quoted in Pérez-Betancur et al. 2025, p. 6.
58 Quoted in Pérez-Betancur et al. 2025, p. 6.
59 The Guyana narrative is based on Fredrick E. Nunes and Yvette M. Delph, 1995. 'Making abortion law reform happen in Guyana: A success story'. *Reproductive Health Matters* 3 (6): 12–23.
60 Barbara Klugman and Sanjani Jane Varkey, 2001. 'From policy development to policy implementation: The South African Choice on Termination of Pregnancy Act'. In *Advocating for Abortion Access: Eleven Country Studies*, ed. by Barbara Klugman and Sanjani Jane Varkey. Johannesburg: University of the Witwatersrand, 251–282.

61 African National Congress, 1984. 'The Women's Charter for Effective Equality'. 27 February. https://www.anc1912.org.za/policy-documents-1994-the-womens-charter-for-effective-equality.
62 Sally Guttmacher, Farzana Kapadla, Jim Te Water Naude, and Helen de Pinho, 1998. 'Abortion reform in South Africa: A case study of the 1996 Choice on Termination of Pregnancy Act'. *International Perspectives on Sexual and Reproductive Health* 24 (4): 191–194, at p. 193.
63 Klugman and Varkey 2001.
64 Klugman and Varkey 2001.
65 Klugman and Varkey 2001.
66 Kaiser Family Foundation, 2025. 'Abortion in the United States dashboard', 2 September. https://www.kff.org/womens-health-policy/abortion-in-the-u-s-dashboard/#legal.
67 These counts are based on results published in Kaiser Family Foundation, 2024. 'Related state constitutional amendment measures in the 2024 election', 6 November. https://www.kff.org/womens-health-policy/ballot-tracker-status-of-abortion-related-state-constitutional-amendment-measures.
68 As a result of repeated legal reforms in the 1990s, abortion on the grounds of economic or social need was first permitted, then prohibited, then permitted again, and finally prohibited once more.
69 Pawe Szelegieniec, 2018. 'Behind the "Black Protests": The struggle for abortion rights in Poland'. *Monthly Review* 70 (1). https://monthlyreview.org/articles/behind-the-black-protests.
70 Carmen Cecilia Martínez and Milagro Valverde, 2025. 'The UN Human Rights Committee decides: Girls have a right to be girls and not mothers'. *Human Rights in Context* (blog), 8 July. https://www.humanrightsincontext.be/post/the-un-human-rights-committee-decides-girls-have-a-right-to-be-girls-and-not-mothers.
71 This paragraph is based on Tiago Rogero, 2024. 'International court rules against El Salvador in key abortion case'. *Guardian*, 20 December. https://www.theguardian.com/world/2024/dec/20/el-salvador-abortion-death-ruling.

Notes to Chapter 8

1 CBS, 1999. 'Bride shot before wedding'. CBS News, 28 September. https://www.cbsnews.com/news/bride-shot-before-wedding.
2 Maria Alvarez, 1999. 'Murdered bride laid out in wedding dress'. *New York Post*, 1 October, https://nypost.com/1999/10/01/murdered-bride-laid-out-in-wedding-dress.
3 Brides' March, n.d. 'Brides' March'. https://bridesmarch.com.
4 CNN, 2011. 'Turkey women protest', CNN International, 24 July. Archived news report.
5 Liangyu Fu and Meredith Kahn, n.d. 'Bloody brides against domestic violence'. University of Michigan Library, Online Exhibits. https://apps.lib.umich.edu/online-exhibits/exhibits/show/aboveground/domestic-violence/bloody-brides.
6 BBC, 2017a. 'Lebanon rape law: Wedding dresses hang in Beirut sea front protest'. BBC News, 22 April. https://www.bbc.co.uk/news/world-middle-east-39680838.
7 BBC, 2017b. 'Lebanon rape law: Parliament abolishes marriage loophole'. BBC News, 17 August. https://www.bbc.co.uk/news/world-middle-east-40947448.

8 For India, see videos of the marches shared by the non-profit anti-VAW group Blank Noise (https://www.blanknoise.org/home).
9 Natalie Clarkson, 2023. 'Life in leggings: Dismantling gender-based violence'. Virgin, 27 November. 'https://www.virgin.com/virgin-unite/latest/life-in-leggings-dismantling-gender-based-violence.
10 Lora Strum, 2017. 'Twitter chat: What #MeToo says about sexual abuse in society'. PBS News, 25 October. https://www.pbs.org/newshour/nation/twitter-chat-what-metoo-says-about-sexual-abuse-in-society.
11 Samuel Getachew, 2019. '#MeTooEthiopia: Empowering citizens to demand change'. *Reporter*, 20 July. https://www.thereporterethiopia.com/8343.
12 Colectivo LASTESIS, 2019. 'A rapist in your path'. Letras Chile. https://letraschile.com/colectivo-lastesis/a-rapist-in-your-path.
13 GeoChicas, n.d. 'Un violador en tu camino'. UMAP. https://umap.openstreetmap.fr/es/map/un-violador-en-tu-camino-20192021-actualizado-2905_394247#2/14.1/-27.6.
14 Shamani Joshi, 2019. '"The rapist is you": Women sang the Bengali version of the Chilean feminist anthem to oppose the CAA'. Vice, 20 January. https://www.vice.com/en/article/the-rapist-is-you-women-sang-the-bengali-version-of-the-chilean-feminist-anthem-to-oppose-the-caa.
15 France24, 2019. 'Tunisian women perform Chilean song against rape'. France 24 (news TV network), 14 December. https://www.france24.com/en/20191214-tunisian-women-perform-chilean-song-against-rape.
16 DW, 2019. 'Turkey's women lawmakers stage "rapist is you" protest'. Deutsche Welle, 15 December, https://www.dw.com/en/turkeys-women-lawmakers-stage-las-tesis-rapist-is-you-protest/a-51684425.
17 Jamillah Bowman Williams and Elizabeth Tippett, 2022. 'Five years on, here's what #MeToo has changed'. Politico, 14 Obtober. https://www.politico.com/newsletters/women-rule/2022/10/14/five-years-on-heres-what-metoo-has-changed-00061853.
18 Angela Giuffrida, 2024. '"We need a cultural revolution": Femicide victim's family seeks change in Italy'. *Guardian*, 26 November. https://www.theguardian.com/world/2024/nov/26/we-need-a-cultural-revolution-femicide-victims-family-seek-change-in-italy.
19 Wanted in Rome, 2023. 'Italy clamps down on violence against women', 23 November. https://www.wantedinrome.com/news/italy-violence-against-women-giulia-cecchetin.html.
20 Gopal Sharma, 2017. 'Nepal court demands quick compensation for acid attack victims'. Reuters, 19 June. https://www.reuters.com/article/world/nepal-court-demands-quick-compensation-for-acid-attack-victims-idUSKBN19A108.
21 Meenakshi Ganguly, 2020. 'Victory for acid attack campaigners in Nepal'. Human Rights Watch, 1 October. https://www.hrw.org/news/2020/10/01/victory-acid-attack-campaigners-nepal.
22 Almaz Kumenov, 2024. 'Kazakhstan toughens domestic violence laws'. Eurasianet, 17 April. https://eurasianet.org/kazakhstan-toughens-domestic-violence-laws.
23 Mala Htun and Laurel Weldon, 2019. 'Critical dialogue: No shortcut to change'. *Perspectives on Politics* 17 (3): 820–825.
24 Ionel Zamfir, 2025. 'Violence against women in the EU'. European Parliamentary Research Service, Document PE 772.921. https://www.europarl.europa.eu/RegData/etudes/BRIE/2025/772921/EPRS_BRI(2025)772921_EN.pdf

25 International Criminal Court, 1998. 'Rome Statute of the International Criminal Court'. https://treaties.un.org/pages/ViewDetails.aspx?src=TREATY&mtdsg_no=XVIII-10&chapter=18&clang=_en.

26 Eva Selene Hernández Gress, Martin Flegl, Aleksandra Krstikj, and Christina Boyes. 2023. 'Femicide in Mexico: Statistical evidence of an increasing trend'. *PloS One* 18 (12): e0281234.

27 Vera Baird, 2022. 'The distressing truth is that if you are raped in Britain today, your chances of seeing justice are slim'. Victims Commissioner, 22 June. https://victimscommissioner.org.uk/news/the-distressing-truth-is-that-if-you-are-raped-in-britain-today-your-chances-of-seeing-justice-are-slim/#:~:text=Yet%20the%20number%20of%20completed,2021%20resulted%20in%20a%20charge.

28 United Nations 1975, p. 13.

29 United Nations 1975, p. 78.

30 United Nations 1979.

31 UN Committee on the Elimination of Discrimination against Women (CEDAW), 1992. 'General Recommendation No. 19'. https://www.refworld.org/legal/resolution/cedaw/1992/en/96542.

32 United Nations, 1993b. 'Declaration on the Elimination of Violence against Women'. General Assembly Resolution 48/104. https://www.ohchr.org/en/instruments-mechanisms/instruments/declaration-elimination-violence-against-women.

33 United Nations, 1993b, Article 4.

34 United Nations 1995, paragraph 118.

35 Conny Roggeband, 2016. 'Ending violence against women in Latin America: Feminist norm setting in a multilevel context'. *Politics & Gender* 12: 143–167, at p. 156.

36 Roggeband 2016.

37 Roggeband 2016, p. 156.

38 The sources for this summary are Caroline Bettinger-López, 2018. 'Violence against women: Normative developments in the Inter-American Human Rights System'. In *The Legal Protection of Women from Violence*, ed. by Rashida Manjoo and Jackie Jones. New York: Routledge, 166–198; and Lorena P. Sosa, 2017. 'Inter-American case law on femicide: Obscuring Intersections?' *Netherlands Quarterly of Human Rights* 35 (2): 85–103.

39 Paragraph 451 in Inter-American Court of Human Rights (IACHR), 2009. *González et al. ('Cotton Field') v. Mexico*. IACHR Series C No 205. https://www.corteidh.or.cr/docs/casos/articulos/seriec_205_ing.pdf.

40 IACHR 2009, paragraph 450.

41 Bettinger-López 2018.

42 Bettinger-López 2018; Jaqueline Sáenz Andujo, 2013. 'The Cotton Field case in Mexico: Setting legal precedents for fighting gender-based violence'. ELLA Policy Brief. https://assets.publishing.service.gov.uk/media/57a08a0be5274a31e00003c2/130810_GOV_GenVio_BRIEF2.pdf.

43 Cecilia Gebruers, 2023. 'From structural discrimination to intersectionality in the inter-American system of human rights: Unravelling categorial framings'. *Age of Human Rights Journal*, June. https://revistaselectronicas.ujaen.es/index.php/TAHRJ/article/view/7629/7711#citations.

44 Maame Efua Addadzi-Koom, 2020. 'Of the women's rights jurisprudence of the ECOWAS Court: The role of the Maputo Protocol and the Due Diligence Standard'. *Feminist Legal Studies* 28: 155–178.
45 African Union 2003.
46 African Union 2003, Article 5.
47 African Union 2003, Article 6.
48 African Union 2003, Article 13.
49 African Union 2003, Article 4.
50 Equality Now, n.d. 'Women's rights and international law'. https://equalitynow.org/promoting_african_womens_rights.
51 This summary comes from Addadzi-Koom 2020, passim.
52 This summary is based on the following sources: Nataliia Karpova, 2021. 'European law and protection of women against violence: history and promotion of the Istanbul Convention'. *Supremația Dreptului* 2021 (2): 160–172; and Ronagh J. A. McQuigg, 2017. *The Istanbul Convention, Domestic Violence, and Human Rights*. New York: Routledge.
53 McQuigg 2017, p. 46.
54 McQuigg 2017, p. 50.
55 Gizem Guney, 2020. 'The Istanbul Convention: A genuine confirmation of the structural nature of domestic violence against women within a human rights law framework?' In *Preventing Sexual Violence*, ed. by Stephanie Kewley and Charlotte Barlow. Bristol: Bristol University Press, 131–148.
56 Dubravka Šimonović, 2014. 'Global and regional standards of violence against women: The evolution and synergy of the CEDAW and Istanbul Conventions'. *Human Rights Quarterly* 36 (3): 590–606.
57 Elife Çiğdem Artan, 2023. 'Law No. 6248 in practice after withdrawing from the Istanbul Convention'. Istanbul Policy Center, Sanaci University. https://ipc.sabanciuniv.edu/Content/Images/CKeditorImages/20230427-12045242.pdf.
58 Sofia Globe, 2023. 'Bulgaria's Parliament approves amendments to Protection against Domestic Violence Act', 21 July. https://sofiaglobe.com/2023/07/21/bulgarias-parliament-approves-amendments-to-protection-against-domestic-violence-act.
59 RFL/RL Bulgaria Service, 2023. 'Following public outrage, Bulgaria makes changes in domestic violence legislation'. Radio Free Europe and Radio Liberty, 7 August. https://www.rferl.org/a/bulgaria-domestic-violence-changes-laws/32537737.html.
60 European Court of Justice, 2024. Document 62021CJO621. https://eur-lex.europa.eu/legal-content/EN/TXT/?uri=celex:62021CJ0621.
61 Gesa Kübek and Jonas Bornemann, 2024. 'International law as a trailblazer for a gender-sensitive refugee system in the EU: The Court of Justice's ruling in case C-621/21, women who are victims of domestic violence'. *European Law Blog*, 29 January. https://www.europeanlawblog.eu/pub/0a98cmvt/release/1. This interpretation is not solely motivated by the Istanbul Convention, but the Istanbul Convention is cited as foundational to it.
62 Coalition of Women MPs from Arab Countries to Combat Violence against Women, 2022. 'The Arab League launches the Arab Declaration to Combat Violence against Women and Girls', 15 December. Regional Portal Archive (originally available at https://cvaw-arabcoalition.org/ar/3799-2).

63 Coalition of Women MPs from Arab Countries to Combat Violence against Women, 2017a. 'Founding members'. Regional Portal Archive (originally available at https://cvaw-arabcoalition.org/ar/category/founding-members).
64 Coalition of Women MPs from Arab Countries to Combat Violence against Women, 2017b. 'Founding Statement'. Regional Portal Archive (originally available at: https://cvaw-arabcoalition.org/ar/category/founding-statement).
65 Coalition of Women MPs . . . 2022.
66 GREVIO, 2023. *United Kingdom Response to GREVIO's Questionnaire on the Legislative and Other Measures Giving Effect to the Provisions of the Council of Europe Convention on Preventing and Combating Violence against Women: June 2023*. Council of Europe, 3 July. https://rm.coe.int/state-report-uk-baseline-evaluation/1680abd6d3.
67 Hannah Rought-Brooks, 2023. 'The family court and domestic abuse: Any change?' Garden Court Chambers, 20 December. https://gardencourtchambers.co.uk/the-family-court-and-domestic-abuse-any-change.
68 Ronagh J. A. McQuigg, 2021. 'Northern Ireland's new offence of domestic abuse'. *Statute Law Review* 44 (1): 1–19.
69 Karpova 2021; Helle Jacobsen, 2020. 'Denmark's rape law is now consent-based'. *Newsweek*, 17 December, https://www.newsweek.com/denmarks-rape-law-now-consent-based-it-took-movement-opinion-1555529; Finnish Government, 2022. 'Revised legislation on sexual offences enters into force at the beginning of next year'. 21 December. https://valtioneuvosto.fi/en/-//1410853/revised-legislation-on-sexual-offences-enters-into-force-at-the-beginning-of-next-year.
70 I thank Elin Bjarnegård for this point.
71 Peace Medie, 2020. *Global Norms and Local Action: The Campaigns to End Violence against Women in Africa*. New York: Oxford University Press, p. 31.
72 Freida M'Cormack, 2018. 'Prospects for accessing justice for sexual violence in Liberia's hybrid system'. *Stability: International Journal of Security and Development* 7 (1): 1–16.
73 Lara Kalwinski, 2007. 'Challenges of implementing the Rape Amendment Act in post-conflict Liberia'. *Agenda* 74: 142–149.
74 Kalwinski, 2007, p. 145.
75 National Council of Chiefs and Elders of Liberia (NACCEL), 2023. 'Joint statement of support by the international community on the Ban on Female Genital Mutilation/Cutting (FGM/C) in Liberia'. 20 February. https://liberia.un.org/en/220039-joint-statement-support-international-community-ban-female-genital-mutilationcutting-fgmc.
76 WomenVoices Newspaper, 2025. 'Stakeholders review anti-FGM bill', 14 March. https://www.womenvoicesnewspaper.org/stakeholders-review-anti-fgm-bill.
77 WomenVoices Newspaper 2025.
78 Gabrielle Emanuel, 2024. 'A victory for opponents of female genital mutilation in the Gambia'. NPR, 16 July. https://www.npr.org/2024/07/16/nx-s1-5040481/female-genital-mutilation-gambia.
79 Emanuel, 2024.
80 Mala Htun and Francesca R. Jensenius, 2022. 'Expressive power of anti-violence legislation: Changes in social norms of violence against women in Mexico'. *World Politics* 74 (1): 1–36.
81 Stéphanie Rousseau, Debora Lopreite, and Eduardo Dargent Bocanegra, 2025. 'From aspirational laws to the implementation of legislation against gender-based violence:

bottom-up pressure in Peru and Argentina'. *European Journal of Politics and Gender* 18 (12): 1–23. https://doi.org/10.1332/25151088Y2025D00000080.

82 Saskia Brechenmacher and Francesca Nyakora, 2024. 'Kenyan women are pushing for action on femicide: They have a road map'. Carnegie Endowment, 12 February. https://carnegieendowment.org/emissary/2024/02/kenyan-women-are-pushing-for-action-on-femicide-they-have-a-road-map?lang=en.

83 Allan Olingo and Kamau Maichuhie. 2025. 'Kenya's empty promises on protecting women'. *Foreign Policy*, 31 January. https://foreignpolicy.com/2025/01/31/kenya-femicide-misogyny-violence-government-failure-protecting-women.

Notes to Chapter 9

1 UN Women, 2025b. *Women's Rights in Review: 30 Years after Beijing*. New York: UN Women, p. 8. https://www.unwomen.org/en/digital-library/publications/2025/03/womens-rights-in-review-30-years-after-beijing.

2 UN Women 2025b, p. 8.

3 UN Women, 2025a. *Progress on the Sustainable Development Goals: The Gender Snapshot 2025*. New York: UN Women. https://www.unwomen.org/en/digital-library/publications/2025/09/progress-on-the-sustainable-development-goals-the-gender-snapshot-2025.

4 World Economic Forum 2024.

5 UN Women 2025b, p. 8.

6 Freedom House, 2024. 'The mounting damage of flawed elections and armed conflict'. https://freedomhouse.org/report/freedom-world/2024/mounting-damage-flawed-elections-and-armed-conflict.

7 V-Dem 2024.

8 Anna Funder, 2025. 'Trump's Orwellian erasure of women'. *Time*, 10 May. https://time.com/7284644/trumps-erasure-of-women.

9 Jennifer M. Piscopo and Denise Walsh, 2020. 'Backlash and the future of feminism: Introduction'. *Signs: Journal of Women and Culture in Society* 45 (2): 265–278.

10 Cecilia Josefsson, 2025. *Defending the Status Quo: On Adaptive Resistance to Electoral Gender Quotas*. New York: Oxford University Press.

11 Joanne Sandler and Anne Marie Goetz, 2020. 'Can the United Nations deliver a feminist future?' *Gender and Development* 28 (2): 239–263.

12 Shaun Walker, 2017. 'Putin approves legal change that decriminalizes some domestic violence'. *Guardian*, 7 February. https://www.theguardian.com/world/2017/feb/07/putin-approves-change-to-law-decriminalising-domestic-violence.

13 Hawon Jung, 2024. 'Young women are leading the "Light Stick Revolution" to oust South Korea's antifeminist president'. *Nation*, 27 December. https://www.thenation.com/article/world/south-korea-feminist-movement-light-stick-revolution-yoon-suk-yeol.

14 Piscopo and Walsh 2020.

15 Anne Marie Goetz, 2020. 'The new competition in multilateral norm-setting: transnational feminists and the illiberal backlash'. *Daedalus* 149 (1): 160–179.

16 Constanza Tabbush, 2025. 'Understanding backlash against gender equality: Evidence, trends and policy responses'. UN Women. https://www.unwomen.org/en/digital-library/publications/2025/09/understanding-backlash-against-gender-equality-evidence-trends-and-policy-responses.

17 Isabel Choat, 2026. 'Will UN plans to transform the way it works "throw equality under the bus"?' *Guardian*, 8 March. https://www.theguardian.com/global-development/2026/mar/08/un-plans-merge-women-unfpa-equality-reform
18 Rend Al-Rahim, 2024. 'Amendment to personal status law: A blow to Iraqi women and society'. Wilson Center, 22 August. https://www.wilsoncenter.org/blog-post/amendment-personal-status-law-blow-iraqi-women-society.
19 Noga Efrati, 2005. 'Negotiating rights in Iraq: Women and the personal status law'. *Middle East Journal* 59 (4): 577–595.
20 Sarah Sanbar, 2024. 'Iraq's amended personal status law could make 9-year-olds brides'. Human Rights Watch, 19 September. https://www.hrw.org/news/2024/09/19/iraqs-amended-personal-status-law-could-make-9-year-olds-brides.
21 Sanbar 2024.
22 Sanbar 2024; Rudaw, 2024. 'Women MPs organize to block Iraqi personal status amendment'. Rudaw Media Network, 1 September. https://www.rudaw.net/english/categories/iraq/81934; Ahmed Mohammed, 2024. 'Female politicians rally against proposed amendments to Iraq's personal status law'. Channel 8, September 18. https://channel8.com/english/21407.
23 Rudaw 2024; Mohammed 2024.
24 Human Rights Watch, 2025a. 'Iraq: Personal status law amendment sets back women's rights', 10 March. https://www.hrw.org/news/2025/03/10/iraq-personal-status-law-amendment-sets-back-womens-rights.
25 The Brazil narrative is based on my interview with Daniel Baldin Machado, who also provided me with evidence.
26 MedyaNews, 2024. 'Turkey's judicial reform package restricts women's rights to choose surname'. MedyaNews, 16 June. https://medyanews.net/turkeys-judicial-reform-package-restricts-womens-right-to-choose-surname.
27 Esra Akgemci, 2026. 'Turkey's "Year of the Family" as a bridge between authoritarian populism and anti-gender politics: Whose family? Whose future?' *European Journal of Politics and Gender*. https://bristoluniversitypressdigital.com/view/journals/ejpg/aop/article-10.1332-25151088Y2025D000000127/article-10.1332-25151088Y2025D000000127.xml.
28 Berfu Şeker, 2024. 'Women powerfully keep on struggling for their rights on the 8th of March'. Heinrich Böll Stiftung, 7 March. https://tr.boell.org/en/2024/03/07/women-powerfully-keep-struggling-their-rights-8th-march.
29 Mariana Carbajal, 2024. 'Diputados dictamina el acoso sexual laboral'. *Página/12*, 6 November. https://www.pagina12.com.ar/780561-diputados-dictamina-el-acoso-sexual-laboral.
30 Martha Delgado, 2020. 'Mexico's feminist foreign policy'. *Transatlantic Policy Quarterly* 19 (1): 35–39. https://martha.org.mx/una-politica-con-causa/wp-content/uploads/2020/06/Mexico%E2%80%99s-Feminist-Foreign-Policy-1.pdf.
31 The source of the material in this paragraph is Liv Tønnessen, 2020. 'Sudanese women's revolution for freedom, dignity, and justice continues'. Chr. Michelsen Institute, *CMI Sudan Blog*. https://www.cmi.no/publications/7355-sudanese-womens-revolution-for-freedom-dignity-and-justice-continues.
32 Sarrah O. Nugdulla, 2020. 'The revolution continues: Sudanese women's activism'. In *Gender, Protests, and Political Change in Africa*, ed. by Awino Okech. New York: Springer, 107–130.

33 Hamza Mohamed, 2019. 'Sudan's female protesters leading the pro-democracy movement'. Aljazeera, 22 April. https://www.aljazeera.com/news/2019/4/23/sudans-female-protesters-leading-the-pro-democracy-movement.
34 Manimekalai, 2024. 'Every history of oppression is always a history of resistance'. Rosa Luxemburg Stiftung, 8 March. https://www.rosalux.de/en/news/id/51738/every-history-of-oppression-is-always-a-history-of-resistance.
35 Samal Vimukthi Hemachandra and Sujit Siasundaram, 2024. 'Historical vistas on Sri Lanka's 2022 people's uprising'. *History Workshop Journal* 97: 3–42; Nihal Perera, 2024. 'Aragalaya: Struggle for space and the spaces of the struggle'. *Polity*, 22 October. https://polity.lk/aragalaya-struggle-for-space-and-the-spaces-of-the-struggle-nihal-perera.
36 Muhib Mashal and Pamodi Waravita, 2025. 'When a strongman failed, women are now fueling a democratic revival'. *New York Times*, 4 February. https://www.nytimes.com/2025/02/04/world/asia/sri-lanka-politics-women.html.
37 Mashal and Waravita 2025.
38 Mashal and Waravita 2025.
39 Mashal and Waravita 2025.
40 Yasmeen Serhan, 2020. 'When women lead protest movements'. *Atlantic*, 12 September.
41 Tomas Bajelis, 2022. 'Rage against the regime: A case study of women protestors in the 2020 pro-democracy Belarusian protests'. *Yale Review of International Studies*, 29 January. https://yris.yira.org/winter-issue/rage-against-the-regime-a-case-study-of-women-protesters-in-the-2020-pro-democracy-belarusian-protests.
42 Voice of America, 2025. 'Female students lead protests against corruption in Serbia'. Voice of America, 8 March. https://www.voanews.com/a/female-students-lead-protests-against-corruption-in-serbia/8003766.html.
43 Voice of America 2025.
44 Jung 2024.
45 Jung 2024.
46 Jung 2024.
47 Jonathan Pinckney, 2025. 'Turning protest into power: How the women's march worked'. *Social Forces*, 21 June. https://doi.org/10.1093/sf/soaf083; Magdalena Larreboure and Felipe González, 2021. 'The impact of the women's march on the US house elections', working paper. https://fagonza4.github.io/womenmarch.pdf.
48 Pinckney 2025; Larreboure and Gonzalez 2021.
49 Pinckney 2025.
50 Pinckney 2025; Larreboure and Gonzalez 2021.
51 Dolores Curia, 2024. '8M: A la motosierra, resistencia'. *Página/12*, 9 March. https://www.pagina12.com.ar/719255-8-m-a-la-motosierra-resistencia.
52 UTI-CI, 2025. 'Argentina: Massive united march against Milei'. Unidad Internacional de Trabajadoras y Trabajadores – Cuarta Internacional (UTI-CI), 9 June. https://uit-ci.org/index.php/2025/06/09/argentina-massive-united-march-against-milei/?lang=en.
53 Rezvan Moghaddam, 2024. 'The roots of the revolutionary women's movement in 2022 in Iran'. *Journal of Middle East Women's Studies* 20 (1): 132–140.
54 Moghaddam 2025, p. 137.
55 Moghaddam 2025, p. 137.
56 Rauf Rahimi and Sajjad Rezaei, 2025. 'The 2022 Iran protests: The view from the streets'. *Middle East Policy*, 21 May. https://doi.org/10.1111/mepo.12809.

57 Shabnam von Hein, 2025. 'Why Iran "cannot turn back time" on public hijab rule'. Deutsche Welle, 21 June, https://www.dw.com/en/why-iran-cannot-turn-back-time-on-public-hijab-rule/a-72616469.

58 Al Jazeera, 2021. '"No going back": Afghan women protest exclusion from interim government'. Al Jazeera, 10 September. https://liberties.aljazeera.com/en/afghan-women-protest-exclusion-form-interim-government.

59 Kenza Ben Azouz, 2022. 'President Saied derides the economic and social rights of Tunisian women'. Human Rights Watch, 1 September. https://www.hrw.org/news/2022/09/01/president-saied-derides-economic-and-social-rights-tunisian-women.

60 Natasha Walter, 2025. '"Woman, life, freedom": The Syrian feminists who forged a new world in a land of war'. *Guardian*, 9 February. https://www.theguardian.com/world/2025/feb/09/woman-life-freedom-the-syrian-feminists-who-forged-a-new-world-in-a-land-of-war.

61 Sima Bahous, 2025. 'Speech: We will not back down'. UN Women, 10 March. https://www.unwomen.org/en/news-stories/speech/2025/03/speech-we-will-not-back-down-a-turning-point-to-push-forward-for-rights-equality-and-empowerment-for-all-women-and-girls.

62 Sandler and Goetz 2020.

63 Miranda Bryant, 2025. '"A welfare state with a budget on the right side of zero": Iceland's youngest-ever prime minister has a plan for a new kind of governance'. *Guardian*, 12 January. https://www.theguardian.com/world/2025/jan/12/a-welfare-state-with-a-budget-on-the-right-side-of-zero-icelands-youngest-ever-prime-minister-has-a-plan-for-a-new-kind-of-governance.

64 Used with permission.

Index

abortion, 6, 9, 10, 12, 17, 21, 22, 24–25, 27, 28, 30, 52, 73, 76, 78, 129, 166–69, 170, 171–73, 174–75, 176, 179, 188, 215, 217, 219, 223, 225, 226, 231, 234, 259 n.68
  access to, 181–85
  reform, 181–87
activism, 3, 15, 31, 32, 48, 77, 92, 125, 135, 149, 154, 198, 204, 207, 218, 220, 228, 232
Addadzi-Koom, Maame Efua, 201
advocacy networks, transnational, 9, 35, 36, 38, 39, 41, 50
Afghanistan, 7, 216–17, 218, 233
African National Congress (ANC), 184
African Women's Development and Communication Network (FEMNET), 32
African Union (AU), 3, 32, 37, 38, 57, 176, 195, *see also* Maputo Protocol
Agarwal, Bina, 49, 118, 153
Agopyan, Kelly Komatsu, 25
Ahmed, Ebtisam Hejres, 206
Ajayi, Laurenne, 168
Akter, Kalpona, 110–11
Alfonsín, Raúl, 180
Alkhutabi, Intisar, 206
All-China Women's Federation (ACWF), 96–97
Alqawasmi, Sahar, 206
Alsalem, Reem, 198, 210
Álvarez, Sonia, 50
Amarasuriya, Harini, 228, 234
Amini, Mahsa, 232
Amsterdam, the Netherlands, 137
Andorra, 90
apartheid, 47, 135–36, 139, 176, 184
Arab Spring, 34, 66, 98
Argentina, 74–75, 93, 95, 124, 138, 157, 158–59, 167–68, 169, 180, 182, 207, 212, 214, 226, 231–32
Arias, Óscar, 93
armed conflict, 2, 3, 5, 34, 54, 55, 80, 191, 193, 198, 201, 209, 215, 229
Armenia, 204
Ashipala-Musavyi, Selma Ndeyapo, 56
Association of Southeast Nations (ASEAN), 37–38, 57
asylum, 201, 205–206
Australia, 40, 42, 43, 45, 48, 54, 62, 101, 102, 106, 116, 123, 146, 159, 190
Austria, 57, 157
autocrats, 62, 63, 66, 67, 68, 70, 72, 75, 76–77, 79, 90, 91, 218, 219, 221, 222, 226, 228, 233
Azcúnaga de Meléndez, Milagro, 198–99

Babangida, Maryam, 32
Babikir, Amira Elsir-Omer, 206
Bachelet, Michelle, 167, 182
backlash, 150, 204, 207, 211, 217, 222
backsliding, democratic, 7, 31, 215–16, 220–23, 229, 234
Baghdad, Iraq, 40
Bahamas, the, 190
Bahous, Sima, 162, 234
Bahrain, 138, 206
Baldez, Lisa, 70
Ballington, Julie, 37

Baltimore, US, 40
Bangladesh, 56, 110, 120, 160, 234, 248 n.4
Barbados, 190
Barcelona, Spain, 161
al-Bashir, Omar, 227–28
Beatriz case (El Salvador), 186–87
Beckwith, Karen, 12
Beijing, China, 1, 5, 25, 32, 33, 54, 55, 96–97, 136, 146, 176, 180, 189, 191, 196, 214, 215, 220
Beijing Platform for Action (PfA), 2, 5, 6, 22, 35, 37, 39, 43, 50, 52–53, 56, 58, 59, 92, 98, 105, 108, 113, 119, 150, 175, 195, 197, 198, 234
Beirut, Lebanon, 40, 189
Belarus, 222, 229, 230
Belém do Pará Convention (1994), 195, 199–200, 201–202, 204, 205, 207
Belgium, 57, 93, 94, 106
Belgrade, Serbia, 230
Benin, 124, 168
Berer, Marge, 174
Berkovitch, Nitza, 21
Berlin Wall, fall of, 78
Bernardino, Minerva, 41, 42, 44
Bhatt, Ela, 132–33
Bill of Rights, US
bin Salman, Mohammed, crown prince of Saudi Arabia, 61–62, 76
birth rates, 128, 172
Bjarnegård, Elin, 62, 236
Black women, 15, 20, 135, 155
Blofield, Merike, 75
Bocanegra, Eduardo Dargent, 212
Bogotá, Colombia, 57, 82
Bolivia, 75, 76, 88, 90, 102–103, 108, 110, 120, 135, 138, 139, 159, 160, 207
Bolsonaro, Jair, 224
Bondfield, Margaret, 129–30
Bomfim, Sâmia, 225
Bosnia and Herzegovina, 57, 100
Bouvier, Jeanne, 129–30
branches of government, 67–68, 95, 162
Brazil, 5, 38, 41, 43, 80, 99, 136, 138, 199, 207, 214, 224, 225, 226, 227
breastfeeding, 101, 124, 130
Briggs-Mensah, Moisa, 210
Brown, Willamette, 155
Bucharest, Romania, 45
Buddhism, 153
Bulgaria, 204–205
Bunch, Charlotte, 52, 59
Bunwaree, Sheila, 71
Burkina Faso, 178
Burnet, Jennie, 63
Busan, South Korea, 190

Caesar, Ruth, 209–10
Cairo, Egypt, 2, 6, 40, 50–51, 168, 173–76, 177, 179, 180, 181, 219
Cambodia, 131, 178
Cameroon, 109
Canada, 40, 56, 66, 69, 80, 102, 106, 108, 116, 120, 123, 143, 154, 156, 159, 164
Cape Town, South Africa, 136
care work, 13, 26, 79, 121, 134, 141, 143, 155
  cost of, 159–60
  economy of, 161–64
  new agenda for, 164–65
Caribbean, 53, 120, 123, 134, 136–37, 176, 183, 190, 199
Caribbean Confederation of Domestic Workers (CONLACTRAHO), 136
Casablanca, Morocco, 150
Castaño, Pablo, 135
Catalonia, 24
Catholic Church, 135, 167, 180, 222
Caywood, Kelsi, 105
Cecchettin, Giulia, 193–94
Celis, Karen, 14
Center for Women's Global Leadership (CWGL), 52

Central Asia, 103, 116, 123, 126
Chad, 178
Chen, Martha, 133
Chen, Muhua, 96, 97
Chesoni, Atsango, 84
childbearing, 127, 170, 172, 173, 192
childcare, 100, 102, 112, 128, 133, 142, 156, 160, 161, 164
Childs, Sarah, 14
Chile, 34, 40, 80, 82, 99, 106, 158, 161, 162, 163, 167, 168, 169, 182, 190, 207, 214
China, 1, 16, 41, 54, 79, 96, 97, 98, 141
China Women's Research Society (CWRS), 97
Chinese Communist Party (CCP), 96
CIA (Central Intelligence Agency), 17
citizenship, 12, 15, 42, 43, 69, 80, 82
Ciudad Juárez, Mexico, 199, 200
Civil Rights movement, US, 15
class, 14, 20, 77, 111, 120, 135
Clinton, Bill, 1
Clinton, Hillary, 1, 10, 32, 41, 52, 53, 214
Cochabamba, Bolivia, 110, 135, 139
Cohen, Nancy, 106
Cold War, 44, 78
Colombia, 21, 45, 57, 58, 80, 82, 88, 160, 163, 170, 181, 182
colonialism, 21, 22, 42, 47, 78, 80, 117, 155, 156
communism, 45, 53, 65, 70, 76, 77–80, 81, 117, 186, 222, *see also* Chinese Communist Party (CCP)
complementarity, 85
Confucianism, 152
Congo, Democratic Republic of, 124
consent, affirmative, 209
conservatism, 5, 6, 11, 16, 17, 19, 24, 27, 57, 75, 150, 151, 169, 173, 181, 185, 186, 211, 218, 221, 223, 224, 225, 226
constitutions, 5, 6, 12, 23, 24, 31, 33, 69–70, 73, 77, 80, 82–86, 87, 207
contraception, 21–22, 24, 168, 173, 176, 177–81, 217, *see also* family planning
Convention on the Elimination of All Forms of Discrimination against Women (CEDAW), 33, 35, 36, 37, 39, 48, 58, 92, 93, 98, 146, 171, 196–97, 198, 199, 203, 206, 234
Coomaraswamy, Radhika, 198
Copenhagen, Denmark, 2, 33, 48, 49, 50, 78, 92, 108, 146, 159, 171, 220
Copenhagen Declaration, 48–49
Costa Rica, 88, 90, 93, 94–95, 103, 136, 159, 207
Cotton Field judgment, 199–200, 202
coverture, 145–46
COVID-19 pandemic, 15, 139, 141–43, 155, 161–62, 164
Council of Europe, 181, 202–203, 205
Creasy, Stella, 101
Croatia, 78, 100, 129, 194, 198
Cruz, María del Carmen, 135, 138
Cuba, 58, 79
customary law, 85, 143–44, 145, 146, 148
Cyprus, 194
Czech Republic, 78, 157, 204

Damascus, Syria, 40
Danuwar, Sonu, 138
Darmstadt, Gary, 105
Dashti, Rola, 206
decision-making, 65, 103, 108
Declaration on the Elimination of Violence against Women (DEVAW), 197–98, 199
decolonization, 34, 46, 156
democratization, 5, 34, 65, 69, 70, 80, 88, 90, 94, 218–19, 222, 223
Dengler, Corinna, 156
Denmark, 128, 141, 208, 211
dictatorship, 13, 14, 34, 51, 52, 65, 80, 94, 161, 234

Dietrichson, Elise, 59
Diop, Bineta, 32
disability, 6, 17, 95, 121, 132, 135, 141, 159, 160, 201, 208
discrimination, gender, 26, 84, 120, 125, 126, 153, 193, 204, 213
divine right of kings, 69
divorce, 40, 41, 77, 87, 142, 153, 145, 149–50, 151, 152, 164, 214, 224
Djibouti, 206
Dobbs v Jackson, 181, 185–86
driving ban, Saudi Arabia, 61–62, 64, 77
domestic work, 11, 14, 21, 46, 110, 111, 115, 120, 121–22, 131, 134–38, 139, 154, 157
Dominican Republic, 41, 189, 190
Dublin, Ireland, 158, 167
Durrant, Patricia, 56
Dyfan, Isha, 55, 56

Al Eadat, Na'ayem, 206
early childhood development (ECD), 163–64
Echevarría, Luis, 45
Economic and Social Commission (ECOSOC), 43, 44–45, 48
Ecuador, 88, 187
education, 3, 9, 13, 17, 26, 27, 29, 40–41, 46, 47, 53, 54, 78–79, 84, 98, 112–13, 119, 121, 141, 160, 168, 171, 173, 176, 177, 178, 179, 180–81, 188, 209, 214, 215, 226, 231, 232
  as a right, 122–26
Egypt, 32, 40, 194, 206
Eighth Amendment (Ireland), 166–67
El Salvador, 70, 181, 186, 187, 198, 207, 222
Elnewishi, Magda, 206
empowerment, economic, 112, 113–14, 116, 118, 119, 120, 128, 139–40
Encuentros Feministas, 3, 4
Enlightenment, the, 68–69, 144
environment, 3, 47, 54, 114, 125, 155, 156, 162
Equal Rights Amendment (ERA), proposed (US), 20, 69
Ertürk, Yakin, 198
Ethiopia, 100, 123, 152, 168, 190
European Court of Human Rights (ECHR), 205
European Union (EU), 3, 38–39, 57, 195, 204, 205, 229
  European Court of Justice (ECJ), 205
Ewig, Christina, 75

Faludi, Susan, 217
family law, 13, 26, 30, 41, 142, 143, 145, 146–48, 215
  discriminatory, 149–53, 164
family planning, 21, 172, 173, 177–81, *see also* contraception
Federal Election Commission (FEC), US, 100
Federici, Silvia, 161, 162
femicide, 74, 194, 195, 199, 200, 212, 227, 231
feminism, 3, 5, 7, 8, 13, 14, 15, 16–18, 22, 25, 28, 30, 31, 33, 34, 35, 36, 37, 38, 40, 47, 51, 54, 55, 57, 58, 64, 72, 78, 79, 85, 87, 91, 92, 96, 108, 113, 114, 116, 117, 118, 125, 127, 131, 134,138, 139, 145, 147–48, 151, 153, 154, 159, 161, 162, 167, 177, 178, 180, 181–82, 185, 186, 191, 192, 193, 194, 195, 196, 197, 198, 199, 201, 202, 203, 205, 206, 207–208, 209, 210, 217, 218, 219, 220–21, 222, 225, 226–27, 230, 231, 232
  blueprints on reproductive rights, 170–76
  activists, 23, 52–53, 86, 142, 144, 164
  future of choice and autonomy, 187–88, 233–35
  intersectional, 155–56

feminism (*cont.*)
Latin American, 42–43, 44, 45, 50, 93, 109, 169, 190
perspectives on women, money, and work, 119–22
quest for women's safety and integrity, 211–13
scholars, 128–29, 143, 159, 163, 165, 223
FENATRAHOB (National Federation of Paid Workers in the Home), 135, 136
Fernández, Alberto, 168
Fiji, 106
Finland, 125–26, 157, 159, 208, 211
First World War, 40
Flowers, Mary, 20
France, 54, 93, 129, 157, 187, 194
Freeland, Chrystia, 164
Freidenvall, Lenita 101
Frostadóttir, Kristrún, 234

Galway, Ireland, 166
Gambia, the, 210, 211–12, 223
garment factories, 110–11, 112, 131
Garrón de Doryan, Victoria, 93
Gatto, Malu, 95
gay rights, 46, 175, 185
GDP, 160
gender equality, 1, 4, 5, 6, 7, 8, 10, 12, 13, 17, 22, 24–25, 26, 27, 28, 33, 35, 37, 39, 45, 46, 49, 51, 53, 58, 59–60, 62, 63, 64, 67, 71, 72, 75, 86, 91, 93, 104, 105, 106–108, 123, 126, 127, 177, 181, 184, 204, 208, 214–15, 216–17, 218–21, 222, 223, 226, 227, 229, 230–31, 232, 233
opponents of, 18–20
women's interest in, 13–16
working wages and, 116–19
gender interests, 14, 15, 16, 19
gender justice, 13, 16, 21
gender quota laws, 7, 24, 26–28, 63, 75, 76, 83, 85, 86, 88, 89, 90, 92, 99, 104, 109, 127, 169, 218, 219, 221, 224, 233
adoption of, 93–96
in non-democracies, 96–98
gender blindness, 71, 117, 118
'genderwashing', 62, 64, 76, 86–87, 90, 95, 107, 221, 227, 236
Generation Equality forums, 2, 234
Geneva, Switzerland, 133, 137
genital mutilation, female, 32, 51, 52, 144, 174, 177, 192, 201, 210, 211–12, 223
Georgia, 159, 221, 229–30
Germany, 5, 40, 47, 111–12, 120, 145, 154, 157, 252 n.7
Ghana, 48, 170
Ghodsee, Kristen, 78
Ginsburg, Ruth Bader, 73
girls, 3, 54, 55, 74, 110, 123–24, 125, 138, 142, 144, 151, 177, 178, 179, 187, 191, 192, 194, 195, 196, 199, 200, 206, 210, 212, 213, 218, 222, 224
Global North, 7, 19, 21, 38, 49, 51, 59, 102, 108, 111, 119, 123, 128, 130, 143, 145, 172, 214
Global South, 5, 7, 9, 17, 21, 22, 34, 35, 36, 38, 43, 46, 49, 51, 59, 102, 111, 116, 119, 123, 125, 130, 131, 132, 134, 138, 144, 145, 146, 165, 172, 174, 209, 214, 218, 233
González, Alessandra L., 61
Green, Jennifer, 4
'green wave', 168
Grover, Minali, 153
Gruer, Caitlin, 168
Guatemala, 21, 56, 187, 207
Guelle, Aicha Dabar, 206
Gujarat, India, 132
Guyana, 183–84, 190

Halappanavar, Savita, 166
Hanafi, Leila, 151

Hand, Karen, 167
Haridas, Shobaa, 111
Harrison, Laura, 19
Harvard University, 133, 139
Hassan II, king of Morocco, 149, 150
Havana, Cuba, 58
Hawai'i, 125, 143, 155–56
Hawkesworth, Mary, 22
health, 3, 22, 24, 47, 53, 78, 107, 124, 130, 131, 134, 141, 162, 167, 168, 171, 173–76, 182, 185, 186, 187, 188
  sexual, 177–81, 214
healthcare, 10, 12, 21, 27, 40, 69, 77, 121, 142, 143, 168, 169, 184, 196
Heaney, Victoria, 125
hierarchies, gender, 14, 17, 18, 20, 23, 24, 116, 193
Hinduism, 152–53
HIV/AIDS, 168, 175
homeworking, 131–34, 139
Hong Kong, 136
Hontiveros, Risa, 131
household work, 120, 135, 160
  wages for, 153–56
Htun, Mala, 26, 146, 147, 194, 212
Hudson, Heidi, 57
Hughes, Melanie, 4
human rights, 1–3, 5, 12, 13, 33, 34, 35, 41, 42, 43, 44, 45, 50–54, 59, 64, 65, 68, 84, 146, 148, 175, 176, 182, 187, 192, 195, 196, 197, 199, 205, 209, 211, 212, 214, 222, 232
Hungary, 24, 70, 78, 204
al-Huwaider, Wajeha, 61

Iceland, 80, 204, 234
Iiyambo, Aina, 56
implementation, 24, 25–28, 30, 39, 43, 47, 54, 55, 72, 86, 89, 90, 105, 106, 108, 125, 165, 195, 197, 199, 211, 212, 214, 219, 220
India, 21, 38, 40, 43, 44, 48, 49, 51, 94, 118, 132, 136, 141, 152–53, 189, 190
Indigenous peoples, 9, 12, 69, 75–76, 87, 95, 102, 110, 135, 139, 156, 172, 200, 208
Indonesia, 131, 137, 139, 147
infanticide, female, 192
inheritance, 40, 53, 63, 77, 83, 119, 142, 149, 151–52, 153, 164
Inter-Allied Women's Conference (IAWC), 40
Inter-American Court of Human Rights (IACHR), 187–88, 199–200, 202
Inter-Parliamentary Union, 98, 103
International Domestic Workers' Network (IDWN), 137–38, 139
International Monetary Fund (IMF), 37, 38, 113
International Women's Day, 48
International Women's Year (IWY), 2, 33
intersectionality, 18, 20, 21, 22, 121, 122, 156, 198, 200, 208, 212
Ipas, 17
Iran, 16, 45, 46, 168, 222, 232–33
Iraq, 206, 222, 223–24, 226, 227
Ireland, 48, 80, 145, 158, 166–67, 168, 169
Islam, 142, 147, 149, 152, 173, 207, 210, 222, 224, 227, 232
  Shi'a, 223
Islamism, 85, 147, 150
Istanbul, Turkey, 189
Istanbul Convention (2012), 195, 202–206, 208, 211, 221
Italy, 106, 141, 154, 157, 193, 194
Ivory Coast, 178

Jainism, 153
Jamaica, 46, 56, 136, 138, 190
James, Selma, 165
Japan, 71–72, 73, 129
al-Jassem, Shahrazad, 234
Jehlen, Pat, 111

Jerusalem, 40
Jhabvala, Renana, 133
Jiagge, Annie, 48
Jiang, Xinhui, 97
al-Jilaihawi, Noor, 224
Jong, Sarah de, 49
Jordan, 151, 152, 194, 198, 206
Josefsson, Cecilia, 219
Julios, Christina, 102

Kabeer, Naila, 234
Kagame, Paul, 63–64, 70, 72, 75
Kalesnikava, Maria, 229
Karachi, Pakistan, 134
Karpinsky, Rose Mary, 93
Kazakhstan, 78, 103, 194
Kazunga, Mary, 52
Keck, Margaret, 35, 36
Kedgley, Susan Jane, 46
Kennedy, John F., 15
Kentucky Health Justice Network, 9–10, 12
Kenya, 47–48, 57, 83–85, 86–87, 123, 125, 136, 138, 212
Kenya's Federation of Women Lawyers (FIDA), 84
Khartoum, Sudan, 228
Kibaki, Mwai, 86
Kimb, HaRyung, 61
Kirchner, Néstor, 180
Kurds, 232, 234
Kuwait, 67, 207
Kyrgyzstan, 103, 104

La Paz, Bolivia, 135
Laos, 79
labour, division of, 11, 14, 29, 30, 79, 140
Lahore, Pakistan, 40
Latin America, 2, 3, 4, 26, 40, 42, 50, 53, 59, 65, 75, 80, 81, 88, 93, 94, 102, 104, 109, 123, 126, 135, 136, 137, 158, 160, 163, 167, 168, 169, 176, 181, 190, 194, 198–200, 202, 208, 209, 212
Le Blanc, Ida, 138
League of Arab States, 206
Ledón, Amalia de Castillo, 42, 43, 44
Lennon, Monica, 125
lesbians, 6, 16, 155, 176
Levenstein, Lisa, 50
LGBTQIA+ people, 6, 18, 66, 95, 191, 204, 221, 222, 226, 227, 231, 232
Liberia, 57, 80, 181, 198, 209–10
literacy, 115, 122, 123, 126, 150
Lithuania, 204
lobbying, 3, 4, 7, 9, 36, 38, 44, 46, 59, 74, 83, 84, 86, 102, 104, 129, 130, 131, 132, 137, 153, 159, 160, 169, 174, 175, 176, 184, 185, 201, 203, 205, 206, 208, 210, 219
London, UK, 55, 111, 167
López Obrador, Andrés Manuel, 227
Lopreite, Debora, 212
Lorde, Audre, 23, 57
Lü, Feng, 96
Lukashenko, Alexander, 229
Lutz, Bertha, 41–43
Luveni, Jiko, 106

Macarthur, Mary, 129–30
Macedonia, 80
Machado, Daniel Baldin, 225
Macias-Alonso, Inmaculada, 61
mainstreaming, gender, 5, 37, 39, 51, 56, 57, 59, 91, 105–108, 109, 137
Malawi, 123
Mali, 100, 178, 202
Malta, 194
Manjoo, Rashida, 198
Maputo Protocol, 32, 33, 37, 59, 148, 176, 195, 200–202, 204, 205, 206
Marcos, Ferdinand, 51
marriage, 40, 41, 42, 71, 85, 142, 146, 164, 170, 172, 194, 214

child, 25, 124, 134, 143, 144, 145, 190, 191, 192, 196, 201, 224
forced, 25, 143, 149, 177, 192, 196, 201, 224
marital age, 149, 151, 197, 224
same-sex (marriage equality), 66, 67–68, 226
Marsit, Hasnaa, 206
maternal mortality, 4, 173, 177–78
maternity leave, 4, 40, 77, 112, 127–30, 131, 134, 140
Mauritania, 124, 178
Mauritius, 71–72, 73
Mayall, Katy, 168
Medie, Peace, 209
Mehta, Hansa, 44
Mellet, Amanda, 166
Méndez, Luz, 56
Menem, Carlos, 74–75, 180
menstruation, 124–25
#MeToo movement, 102, 190, 193
Mexico, 5, 42, 43, 45, 80, 90, 95, 103, 107, 141, 159, 163, 182, 195, 199–200, 207, 212
Mexico City, Mexico, 2, 4–5, 25, 33, 36, 38, 45–49, 50, 53, 78, 80–81, 92, 108, 121, 127, 146, 171, 172, 173, 196, 214, 220, 233
Mexico City Declaration, 47–48
Middle East, 11, 19, 26, 40, 51, 80, 190, 207
Middle East and North Africa (MENA), 127, 142–43, 146
migrants, 6, 9, 120–21, 134, 138, 167, 189
Milei, Javier, 226, 231–32
Mink, Patsy, 125
Misihairabwi-Mushonga, Priscilla, 124
Moghadam, Valentine, 35, 232
Moghaddam, Rezvan, 232
Mohamed, Faiza Jama, 56
Mohammed, Srwa, 224
Mohammed VI, king of Morocco, 98, 150
Moisa, Mariana, 187
Moldova, 100
Molyneux, Maxine, 13–14
Montevideo, Uruguay, 42
Montevideo Consensus, 176
Morales, Evo, 75–76, 87, 108
Moreira, Natali Francine Cinelli, 25
Moroccan Women's Democratic Association (ADFM), 149–50
Morocco, 24, 67, 97–98, 149–51, 152, 194, 206
motherhood, 6, 126, 127, 184, 187
Moudawana reform (Morocco), 149–51
Mozambique, 54
Mubarak, Suzanne, 32
Mudaliar, Arcot Ramaswami, 43
Mulo, Evaline, 138, 139
Mustafa, Wafa' Bani, 206
Myanmar, 76

NAACP (National Association for the Advancement of Colored People), 42
Nairobi, Kenya, 2, 4, 33, 49, 50, 51, 78, 92, 108, 146, 159, 171, 173, 190, 220
Nairobi Forward-Looking Strategies for the Advancement of Women (FLS), 49–50, 54
Namibia, 55–56
Naranjo, Carmen, 93
natalism, 129, 158
National Action Plans (NAPs), 57
NATO (North Atlantic Treaty Organization), 37
Nandi-Ndaitwah, Netumbo, 55
neoliberalism, 49
Nepal, 57, 80, 81, 82–83, 85, 87, 138, 168, 194
Netherlands, the, 157, 159
New York, US, 55, 155, 189
New Zealand, 101, 102, 116, 146, 168

NGOs, 1, 3, 4, 9, 17, 32, 35, 39, 42, 46–47, 48, 49, 50–51, 53, 55, 56, 58, 103, 130, 135, 142, 177–78, 179, 188, 194, 203, 205, 210, 216, 220, 228, 234
Nicaragua, 13, 15, 19, 90, 138, 181, 186–87, 207, 222
Niger, 100, 178
Nigeria, 25, 32, 47, 57, 109, 124, 202
North Korea, 79
Northern Ireland, 48, 66, 143, 208
Norway, 40, 157, 190

O'Rielly, Niamh, 52
Obergefell v Hodges, 66–67
Odio, Elizabeth, 93
Ogot, Jane, 84
Olcott, Jocelyn, 46, 47
Organization for Economic Cooperation and Development (OECD), 3, 37, 107, 133, 141
Organization for Security and Cooperation in Europe (OSCE), 37
Organization of African Unity (OAU), 32
Organization of American States (OAS), 3, 37, 163, 195, 198, 199

Pacific Islands Forum, 57
Pakistan, 134, 175
Palestine, 194, 206
Palmieri, Sonia, 37, 101
Papua New Guinea, 100
Paris, France, 2
Paris Peace Conference (1919), 40, 41
patriarchy, 8, 11–12, 13, 15, 16, 18, 19, 20, 22, 49, 61, 62, 71, 76, 78, 79, 87, 111, 117, 147–48, 149, 171, 172, 184, 190, 191, 192–93, 195, 204, 215, 218, 220, 223, 234
  encoded by legal systems, 144–46
Paxton, Pamela, 4
peacekeepers, UN, 55, 56, 57
Penón, Margarita, 93
period poverty, 85, 125
personal status laws, 142, 148, 149, 151, 152, 170, 223–24
Peru, 21, 47, 136, 137
Philippines, the, 48, 80, 131, 138, 143
Picado, Sonia, 93
Pinochet, Augusto, 34
Pinto de Vidal, Isabel, 41, 42
Piscopo, Jennifer, 75, 106, 221
Planned Parenthood v Casey, 9
pluralism, political, 68, 219
Poland, 25, 78, 181, 186, 187, 204, 223
policymaking, 2, 3, 5, 9, 22, 26, 29, 35–39, 67, 70, 74, 88, 89, 91, 105, 107, 108, 109, 135, 143, 159, 163, 164, 179, 188, 193, 208, 212, 215
political equality, 4, 68, 91, 103, 216, 218
polygamy, 32, 147–48, 149, 151
population control, 51, 172, 177
Portugal, 103, 194, 207
poverty, 3, 51, 53, 85, 113, 117, 119, 123, 125, 158, 164, 172, 232
Prado, Mimi, 93, 95
pregnancy, 24, 124, 126–27, 131, 166–67, 170, 171, 172, 184–85, 187, 194
prostitution, 46, 52, 194, 196
protectionist legislation, 10–11
protests, 8, 16, 82, 83, 166, 169, 186, 188, 189, 191, 193, 194, 205, 212, 224, 225, 228, 229, 232–33
Putin, Vladimir, 221

Quiverfull movement, 19
Quran, 147

Rabat, Morocco, 150
Rabbaa, Naima, 206
race, 13, 14, 17, 20, 42, 122, 229
Rahimi, Rauf, 232
Rajapaksa, Gotabaya, 228

rape, 2, 22, 51, 52, 55, 152, 167, 182, 184, 186, 187, 193, 195, 196, 201, 208, 210, 214, 225
marital, 7, 143, 145, 151, 194, 209, 212
'reactive left', 75
reproductive rights, 2, 4, 5, 10, 12, 17, 18, 21, 22, 26, 27, 28, 30, 36, 51, 53, 85, 166–88, 214, 219
Rezaei, Sajjad, 232
Ricart, Gladys, 189, 193
Rinaldo, Rachel, 147
Rio de Janeiro, Brazil, 50, 51, 58, 174
Riyadh, Saudi Arabia, 61
Rodríguez, Casimira, 110, 111, 120, 131, 135, 139
Roe v Wade, 181, 185
Romania, 44, 100
Rome Statute, 194
Roosevelt, Eleanor, 44
Rousseau, Stéphanie, 212
Rowley, Sarah, 19
Russia, 40, 54, 221, 222, 229
Rwanda, 63–64, 70, 71–72, 73, 75, 76, 80, 86, 87, 90, 218

Sadik, Nafis, 175
Sahel Women's Empowerment and Demographic Dividend (SWEDD), 178
Saied, Kais, 233
St Lucia, 187, 190
Salah, Alaa, 228
salary history bans, 110–11, 115, 139
Samba, Absa, 211
San Francisco, US, 41, 42
Sandinistas, 13, 14
Santa Cruz, Bolivia, 135
Sator, Fatima, 59
Saudi Arabia, 16, 61–63, 64, 67, 72, 76, 77, 86, 87, 218
Scandinavia, 112, 128, 130, 161
Scotland, 21, 66, 125, 166
Second World War, 34, 41, 65, 186
Şeker, Berfu, 226, 233
Self-Employed Women's Association (SEWA), Gujarat, 132–34, 137
Senegal, 32, 80
Seoul, South Korea, 190, 230
Serbia, 222, 229–30
sex trafficking, 2, 115
sexism, 7, 16, 46, 47, 49, 90, 94, 96, 98
sexual harassment, 49, 99, 100–101, 102, 112, 125, 126, 193, 195, 197, 201, 214, 227
sexually transmitted diseases, 168, 175, 178
Shafie, Asfar Sonia, 16
Shahani, Leticia Ramos, 48
al-Sharif, Manal, 16, 61–62
Sharma, Ajay, 153
Shirey, Gretchen, 100
Siegel, Mona, 129, 130
Sierra Leone, 24, 55, 56, 124
Sikhism, 153
Sikkink, Kathryn, 35, 36
Šimonović, Dubravka, 198, 206
Singapore, 138, 157
Singhateh, Mama Fatima, 210
Sipilä, Helvi, 45, 47
Sirleaf, Ellen Johnson, 210
Slovakia, 204
socioeconomic status, 17, 77, 111, 120, 122
Solidarity for African Women's Rights (SOAWR) Coalition, 201–202
Solomon Islands, 100
Somoza, Anastasio, 13, 14
Son, Keonhi, 130
South Africa, 21, 38, 135–36, 138, 139, 141, 155, 163–64, 176, 184–85, 198, 212
South African Domestic and Allied Workers Union (SADSAWU), 136
South African Domestic Workers Union (SADWU), 136
South Korea, 99, 152, 190, 221, 230, 231

South Sudan, 124, 198
Southeast Asia, 116, 120, 131, 146, 209
Soviet Union, 34, 41, 78, 79, 81, 104, 204
Soweto, South Africa, 155
Spain, 106, 126, 138, 162, 168, 194, 214
Sri Lanka, 198, 228, 229, 230, 234
sterilization, forced, 21, 22, 36, 52, 172
Street, Jessie, 42, 43
sub-Saharan Africa, 4, 116, 122–23, 124, 127, 146, 195
Sudan, 206, 227–28, 229, 230
suffrage movements, 6
Supreme Court, US, 9–10, 66, 73, 169, 181, 185
Suyati, 139
Sweden, 40, 120, 129, 141, 157, 161, 208, 211
Switzerland, 154, 204

Tajikistan, 103
Taka, Tanaka, 129
Taliban, 7, 216, 233, 234
Tanzania, 103, 124, 136
Taylor, Sara Rose, 59
Tbilisi, Georgia, 229
Tehran, Iran, 40
Teriba, Yetunde, 32
Thailand, 48, 131, 138, 168
Tirupur, India, 132
Title IX (US), 125
Togo, 100, 168
Tokyo, Japan, 190
torture, 51, 62, 76, 81
Toupin, Louise, 154–55
trade unions, 127, 129, 132, 133, 134, 184, 231
Trinidad and Tobago, 136, 137, 138, 190
Tripp, Aili, 83
Trudeau, Justin, 164
Trump, Donald, 216, 221, 224, 231, 234
Tsapkala, Veranika, 229
Tsikhanouskaya, Sviatlana, 229
Tunisia, 66, 80, 82, 85, 150, 191, 194, 206, 221, 233
Turkey, 40, 181, 189, 191, 198, 204, 211, 221, 222, 225, 226, 227
Turkmenistan, 103, 181

Uganda, 57, 104, 222
Ukraine, 57, 80
unemployment, 136, 164, 232
United Arab Emirates (UAE), 90
United Kingdom, 5, 40, 41, 54, 66, 101–102, 123, 126, 141, 157, 167,179, 187–88, 204, 208, 214
United Nations (UN), 1, 2, 3, 19, 25, 28, 33, 35, 36–37, 39, 42, 43, 46, 48, 53, 54, 58–60, 78, 80, 122, 123, 172, 177, 129, 193, 215, 222
  Charter, 35, 41, 42, 59
  Children's Fund (UNICEF), 178
  Commission on the Status of Women (CSW), 39, 43, 44, 45, 48, 50, 54, 55
  Conference on International Organization, 41
  Decade for Women, 2, 45–50, 108, 171–73, 174
  Development Fund for Women (UNIFEM), 48, 56, 58, 133, 177
  Development Programme (UNDP), 48, 58
  General Assembly, 44–45, 48, 54, 177, 197
  High Commission for Human Rights (UNHCR), 39, 198
  International Labour Organization (ILO), 113, 116, 129–31, 133, 136–38, 139
  Population Fund (UNFPA), 177–79, 211, 222
  Secretary-General (UN), 56, 58
  Security Council (UNSC), 33, 54, 54, 55–57

Security Council Resolution 1325 on Women, Peace, and Security (UNSCR 1325), 33, 35, 37, 54, 57, 58, 59, 81, 209
Special Rapporteur on Violence against Women, 198, 203, 206, 210
Sustainable Development Goals (SDGs), 33, 36, 58–59, 177, 215, 222
women involved in founding, 41–43
United States, 1, 9, 40, 41, 48, 54, 66, 68, 69, 100, 111, 116, 123, 125, 126, 129, 130, 143, 155, 170, 181, 185, 187, 190, 214, 215, 217, 218, 231
Universal Declaration of Human Rights (UDHR), 43–44
universities, 52, 77, 78, 122, 123, 124, 125–26, 141, 163, 193, 216, 217, 231
Uruguay, 41, 42, 94, 103–104, 138, 158, 163, 167, 168, 169, 182
Uzbekistan, 78, 103

Valdini, Melody Ellis, 74–75
Van Luijken, Anneke, 137
Vancouver, Canada, 190
Vatican, the, 19, 173, 176, 180
Vega Varela, Natalia, 106
Venezuela, 138, 163, 207
Verge, Tània, 24
Verveer, Melanne, 1, 10
Vienna, Austria, 1, 50, 51, 191, 193, 196
Vienna Declaration, 1–2, 52, 53, 59, 197–98, 230Vietnam, 79, 138
violence against women (VAW), 51, 52, 53–54, 189–213
achievements in anti-VAW reform, 207–11
international normative framework for, 196–198
naming and acting on, 19–96
regional frameworks for combating, 198–207
von Hein, Shabnam, 233

wages, 11, 15, 79, 110, 111, 112, 114, 115, 116–19, 121, 126, 128, 131, 132, 134, 142, 158, 162
for housework, 153–56, 157, 159, 161, 165
Wales, 66, 94
Walsh, Denise, 221
war, *see* armed conflict
Washington, DC, 40, 41, 66, 129, 231
March on, 15
Weinstein, Harvey, 190, 195
Weldon, Laurel, 26, 108, 146, 147, 194
welfare, 4, 38, 55, 155, 196, 201
Windhoek Declaration, 55, 56
WINGOs (Women's International NGOs), 4, 9, 33, 35, 44, 50, 52, 83, 132
Witbooi, Myrtle, 136, 137, 138, 139
Women in Informal Employment: Globalizing and Organizing (WIEGO), 132, 133, 137
Women in Law and Development in Africa (WiLDAF), 32
Women's Bench, the, 103–104
women's caucuses, 51, 52, 84, 91, 103, 104, 108, 109, 174, 225
Women's Global Network for Reproductive Rights, 22
Women's International Democratic Federation (WIDF), 44
Women's Nationality Treaty, 41–42, 43
Women's March (2017), 231
women's policy agencies (WPAs), 107–108
World Bank, 3, 37, 113, 122, 123, 126, 133
World Conference on Women, 1–2, 32, 33, 35, 36, 48, 50, 53, 54, 96, 214, 220, 234
World Economic Forum, 122, 215
World Health Organisation (WHO), 178

Yemen, 57
Yoon, Suk Yeol, 221, 230
Yugoslavia, 78–79

Zambia, 52, 181
Zetterberg, Pär, 62
Zhou, Yunyun, 97
Zimbabwe, 124, 222
Zouein, Gilberte, 206
Zuma, Nkosazana, 176, 185
Zurabishvili, Salome, 229